US NATIONAL MISSILE DEFENSE STRATEGY

US NATIONAL MISSILE DEFENSE STRATEGY

(POLICY DOCUMENTS)

M.P. Srivastava
Ph.D., D.Litt., F.R.A.S. (London)

GYAN PUBLISHING HOUSE
New Delhi–110 002

US NATIONAL MISSILE DEFENSE STRATEGY
(International Studies)

Rs. 590

ISBN: 81-212-0782-7

Published in 2002 in India by
Gyan Publishing House
5, Ansari Road, Daryaganj
New Delhi–110 002

Phones: 3282060, 3261060, Fax: 3285914

E-mail: gyanbook@vsnl.com

visit our web site At http:\\www.gyanbooks.com

Lasertypesetting by: VARSHA GRAPHICS, DELHI
Printed at: Mehra Offset Press, Delhi

Contents

Preface

This work, having deep bearing on the scientific temper and policy matter of the United States of America and Allied Partners, could trace its origin, in a serious way, with the dawn of dissolution of the Soviet Union and the emergence of the Chinese nuclear proliferation. It was felt at the global level that a new but serious phase of threat from deadly terrorism and the nuclear weapons would endanger the smooth equilibrium of power in Middle East, Asia, Europe and elsewhere. Hence the need for new researches arose to checkmate this dangerous style which should not disturb the proper balance of power.

The Defence-based theme consisting of thirty-three chapters deal exhaustively with several phases of ballistic missiles, revolutionary technology, defense flight tests, nuclear strategies, and the allied scientific programmes. Undoubtedly the USA, at present a most powerful nation in our globe, is undertaking such programmes to meet the most dangerous challenges, of course with the cooperation of other powers. It is indeed a process based on consistent and meticulous scientific researches involving billions of dollars on them. Obviously the success of this scientific programme is based on several centres of research manned by the most competent scientific brains who have been engaged in this arduous and difficult task.

M.P. Srivastava

Introduction

President George W. Bush and his Administration has embarked upon the National Missile Defense program to protect the United States and the Allies from any possible nuclear attack from the rival Nuclear Powers particularly from the 'Rogue' states, who are engaged in blackmail of nuclear weapons and have developed long-range missile attack capabilities in proxy strategies directly threatening the security of the United States and the U.S. Allies.

The NMD has created a turbulence in the international security, in perspective, and has engaged the policy analysts, both in government and organisational think tanks, worldwide, and a great need is felt and the search is on for the core analysis of the exact nature and extent of the policy pronouncements. Bush Administration, the congressional debates and the U.S. Defense Secretary Donald Rumsfeld architectural mosaic of the NMD: and its global installations.

The U.S. National Missile Defense is a highly ambitious and expensive "Star War" peace offensive, which has been designed as a long time defense strategy of the United States.

It is significant that simultaneously with the unloading of the policy status of the U.S. NMD, the policy analysts of think tanks on international security worldwide have downloaded the contents of historic significance. Russian-Chinese treaty of strategic cooperation in diterrence, and thus the world nuclear powers have been divided into two nuclear coups—thus heralding the new era of 'Peace Offensive' from the two rival coups which has made again the think tanks analysts busy in assessing the cooperative capabilities of muscle show on themes of Mutual Assured Destruction, Nuclear Winter and keen surveillance on the issue of nuclear proliferation and blackmail by 'Rogue' states.

Besides the missile development programme of North Korea and its proliferation to Pakistan, the turbulence in Afghanistan and the Persian Gulf is volcanic eruption of 'fundamentalist' forces, engaged in 'terror' and 'violence', have created a greater sense of insecurity for the United States and India, which has led to the Indian strategic betrothel with the United States. India's unconditional support to the U.S. National Missile Defense program has led India to join the galaxy of nuclear powers and with U.S. support India can confidently boast of on embarking new initiatives in international security.

So the strategic turbulence, created by Afghanistan and Persian Gulf, and the turbulent strategies of Osama Bin Laden and Saddam Hussein have led to the creation the desk of new Asstt Secretary of State for Afghanistan and Persian Gulf headed by Zamel Khalilzad in the White House.

Hardly less turbulent are the elite credentials of Professor Srivastava who holds a D.Litt on 'International Rivalry in the Persian Gulf Region' and the author of the first ever book. 'Soviet Intervention in Afghanistan', soon after Soviet occupation of Afghanistan (Feb. 1980), who had predicted that 'Detente' is dead and the incident will engage the nuclear powers in long term strategy.

This is purely a compilation of U.S. policy documents, deliberately unedited, so as to feed an unedited fact sheets of U.S. policy on NMD for the use of policy analysts worldwide.

The U.S. Missile Defense Strategy and search for global partnership embraces the concept of strategic statesmanship and appears to be an adventurous leap forward in upholding the U.S. unipolar stronghold in the dilapidated strategic infrastructure of the lukewarm multipolar plurality.

A rare combination of top-seded generic inheritence of both civil and military intelligence, the U.S. President George W. Bush, along with Dick Cheney and Rumsfeld, has confidently lambasted on the need of a Defense Missile Strategy in the pandemonium of Chines nuclear proliferation and the volcanic eruption of Islamic terrorism culminating in the community of interests of both Russia and the U.S.

While the world is sitting at the epicentre of volcanic eruption, the Think Tanks have yet to respond. India has emerged as the closest partner and supporter of U.S. policies, after a long isolation of the non-aligned utopaion attempt of self-styled isolation of bankrupt annonimity.

The cover of "National Missile" Defense appears to be highly glamourised in the offensive strategic modular deterrante in the New Millenium. It is an umbrella of U.S. strategic cover-ledership over all ill-fated recalcitrant manouvering thus souring place and protection over arrogant and rogue rationalism with the volatility of susceptible eruption globally.

The ever increasing threat-perceptions from China and the proxy-perceptions from North Korea, Pakistan and Iraq have created a sense of incredibility in strategic balance in structural pattern of relationships that the U.S. is forced to develop a Missile Shield Cover Defense Program to ensure its own survival in strategic leadership. India promises significant strategic co-partnership with U.S. in this major "Peace Offensive" in the new millennium.

After the dissolution of the Soviet Union and the emerging outlets of China nuclear proliferation, proxy perception from North Korea and Pakistan, the threat of terrorist culture in Afghanistan as center and overlapping patterns of fundamentalism, the disturbing war patterns in Chechnya, Iraqi occupation of Kuwait, threat biological and chemical weapons, bomb blast in Kenyan U.S. embassy have necessitated the need of missile shield cover for strategic defense to protect U.S. and Allied Partners interest and security in Asia.

Dr. Srivastava, a distinguished scholar, having specialised in conflict analysis and threat perception, has attempted to examine the new developing patterns of conflict culture which have necessitated the U.S. Missile Defense Strategy and search for global partnership to ensure an electronic defense shield and India's role in U.S. partnershiop in the ever-increasing patterns of conflict culutre in the new millennium

President George W. Bush and his Administration has embarked upon new envigorated Missile Defense Strategy with a view to re-establish an undiscipated and unquestionable strategic leadership and a glorified arbiter in harbouring peace by combing symogues sporadic and diversified revolutionary threats by infusing deterrence in cross-cultural outbursts in Asia. Dick Cheney and Rumsfeld, who are the architect and staunch advocates of Missile Defense, have commenced an era of 'strategic statesmanship' in 'qualified dignity' in providing 'peace and stability' in the new millennium against the persuasive attempts of reconciliation in the last decade.

Prof. M.P. Srivastava
President
World 2000
New Delhi

1

National Missile Defense: Issues for Congress

Summary

Many in Congress and outside the government have shown strong interest in deploying a ballistic missile defense to protect the United States from attack. The ABM Treaty prohibits nationwide defense but permits the United States to deploy up to 100 interceptors for long-range ballistic missiles at a single site. Many supporters of National Missile Defense (NMD) argue that the United States must amend or abrogate this treaty so that it can pursue a more robust defense.

The United States has pursued the development and deployment of defenses against long-range ballistic missiles since the early 1950s. It deployed a treaty-compliant site in North Dakota in the mid-1970s, but shut it down after only a few months of operation. President Reagan launched a research and development effort into more extensive defenses in the early 1980s, but these plans were scaled back several times during the Reagan and Bush Administrations.

The Clinton Administration initially focused NMD efforts on technology development, but, in 1996, outlined a strategy to pursue the development and deployment of an NMD system by 2003 if the threat warranted and the technology was ready. In January 1999, the Administration announced that it had adjusted this program to permit deployment in 2005, and would decide in Summer 2000 whether to proceed with deployment of up to 20 at a single site. This was modified in February 2000 to allow for 100 interceptors.

Many in Congress disagreed with the Clinton Administration's approach arguing that the threat justified the more rapid deployment of an NMD system. Other analysts argued that the United States should modify a Navy theater missile defense system so that it would have the capability to defend against long-range ballistic missiles. Still others argue that the United States should focus on arms control and nonproliferation strategies, rather than missile defenses, to counter the threats from missile proliferation.

The Clinton Administration identified several factors regarding deployment of an NMD system. These included an assessment of the threat to the United States from long-range ballistic missiles, an assessment of the maturity of the technology and the feasibility of deploying an effective system, consideration of the implications for the ABM treaty and the possibility of gaining Russian agreement on amendments, the potential costs of the prospective system, and the environmental implications of deployment.

Many in Congress questioned the Administration's commitment to NMD funding and deployment. Some argued that additional funds could have speeded the development and deployment of the program. And, in an effort to press the Administration to deploy an NMD, both the House and the Senate passed legislation on NMD deployment.

Most Recent Developments

Secretary of Defense Rumsfeld recently confirmed that the Bush Administration will add $1 billion to the proposed missile defense budget. Details as to how exactly how that money will be allocated within the missile defense account are not yet available.

Leading missile defense advocates in Congress have urged the Bush Administration to avoid moving ahead prematurely on building an NMD system in Alaska. Senator Jon Kyl and Representative Curt Weldon wrote President Bush on March 7 asking him to examine the Alaska option in the context of a much broader NMD deployment. Meanwhile, Secretary Rumsfeld similarly has indicated he does not want to move forward with the Alaska option until he has a chance to review several ground, sea, and space-based NMD options. Both he and the President have added in recent weeks that they are examining options that would also seek to defend all of the United States, U.S. allies and friends, and U.S. troops in the field.

Technical problems continue to challenge the pace of NMD development. A recent Defense Department report to Congress (Operational Test and Evaluation office) remains somewhat critical of the NMD flight test program. Furthermore, the next NMD flight test continues to be delayed again, first from March to November 2000, then April and June 2001; now it is delayed until perhaps August 2001. At the end of March, industry and Pentagon officials announced there were problems with the rocket that is supposed to carry the NMD interceptor. Gen. Willie Nance, the NMD Program Manager, wrote in a Jan. Quarterly report that these delays in the rocket program have prohibited the collection of critical data needed to support the NMD program. He added that the contractor's (Boeing's) "cost and schedule performance continues to worsen."

The Operational Test and Evaluation office also informed Congress that the U.S. Navy could not field a sea-based system within the next five years because of technical challenges in upgrading the necessary radar, missiles, and warheads.

BACKGROUND AND ANALYSIS

Introduction

Many in Congress and outside government have a strong interest in deploying a ballistic missile defense (BMD) system to protect the United States from attack. The collapse of the Soviet Union in 1991, Iraq's use of Scud missiles in the 1991 Persian Gulf War, and the proliferation of ballistic missile technologies, all added to concerns about the risks to the United States. Two events in the summer of 1998 served to amplify these concerns. First, in July, a congressionally-mandated panel chaired by former Secretary of Defense Donald Rumsfeld (now Defense Secretary again) concluded that nations seeking to develop long-range ballistic missiles might be able to achieve that objective within 5 years of deciding to do so, and that the United States might have little warning before the testing and deployment of such missiles. And, second, at the end of August, North Korea flight tested a 3-stage ballistic missile. Although the third stage of this missile apparently failed in flight, and this missile would not have had the range to reach the continental United States. North Korea demonstrated that it had developed the technology for "staged" missiles, a milestone considered critical to the development of longer-range ballistic missiles.

Both the Clinton Administration and Congress reated to these developments. In January 1999, the Administration announced that, for the first time, it had allocated funding in its Future Years Defense Plan (FYDP) for the deployment of a National Missile Defense (NMD) system, even though it would not decide whether to deploy such a system until Summer 2000 And, in March 1999, Congress passed by a wide margin legislation declaring it the policy of the United States to deploy an NMD.

This issue brief provides an overview of the current debate on NMD. It begins with a brief summary of the provisions of 1972 ABM Treaty and a short history of U.S. NMD efforts. It then reviews approaches to NMD development and deployment, describing current NMD strategy and major alternative views on how the United States should address missile threats to its territory. The Issue Brief then identifies and describes the factors that the Clinton Administration considered in its September 2000 decision to delay NMD deployment. Finally, the Issue Brief summarizes current debate in Congress about NMD, focusing on budget issues and legislation.

THE 1972 ANTI-BALLISTIC MISSILE (ABM) TREATY

The 1972 U.S.-Soviet Anti-Ballistic Missile (ABM) Treaty prohibits the deployment of ABM system for the defense of the nations' entire territory. It permits each side to deploy limited ABM systems at two locations, one centered on the nation's capital and one at a location containing ICBM silo launchers. A 1974 Protocol further limited each nation to one ABM site, located either at the nation's capital or around an ICBM deployment area. Each ABM site can contain no more than 100 ABM launchers and 100 ABM interceptor missiles. The Treaty also specifies that, in the future, any radars that provide early warning of strategic ballistic missile attack must be located on the periphery of the national territory and oriented outward. The Treaty bans the development, testing, and deployment of sea-based, air-based, space-based, or mobile land-based ABM systems and ABM system components (these include interceptor missiles, launchers, and radars or other sensors that can substitute for radars).

HISTORY OF NMD IN THE UNITED STATES

The Sentinel and Safeguard Programs

The United States has persued research and development into anti-ballistic missile (ABM) systems since the early 1950s. In the mid-1960s it developed the Sentinel system, which would have used ground-based, nuclear-armed interceptor missiles and would have been deployed around a number of major urban areas to protect against Soviet attack. In 1969, the Nixon Administration renamed the system "Safeguard" and changed its focus to deployment around offensive missile fields, rather than cities, to ensure that these missiles could survive a first strike and retaliate against the Soviet Union. The Senate almost approved an amendment halting construction of the system in 1969, but the program continued when Vice President Agnew broke a tie vote. Nevertheless, sentiment against ABM deployments and in favor of negotiated limits on ABM systems was growing. The United States and Soviet Union concluded negotiations on the ABM Treaty in 1972. The United States completed its ABM site near Grand Forks, North Dakota. It operated for 9 months in 1974 and 1975, then was shut down because it proved to be not cost-effective. Russia continues to operate a modernized ABM site around Moscow. U.S. research and development into ABM systems, especially for ICBM protection, continued, albeit at lower budget levels through the late 1970s, before rising again during the Carter Administration.

The Stragetic Defense Initiative (SDI) and Global Protection Against Limited Strikes (GPALS)

In March 1983, President Reagan announced an expansive effort to develop non-nuclear ballistic missile defenses that would protect the United States against a full-scale attack from the Soviet Union. Although the Strategic Defense Initiative (SDI) remained a research and deployment effort, with little testing and no immediate developments, President Reagan and the program's supporters envisioned a large-scale defensive system with thousands of land-, sea-, air-, and space-based sensors and interceptors. As cost estimates and technical challenges increased, the Reagan Administration announced it would begin with more limited deployment of land-based and space-based sensors and interceptors that would seek to disrupt, rather than defeat, a Soviet attack. The former Bush Administration further scaled back the goals for U.S. missile defense programs, in part as a result of the demise of the Soviet Union and the changing international political environment. Instead of seeking to protect the United States against a large-scale attack, the United States would seek to deploy a defensive system that could provide Global Protection Against Limited Strikes (GPALS). This type of ballistic missile defense would have sought to protect the United States, its forces, and allies against an accidental or unauthorized attack from the Soviet Union or an attack by other nations who had acquired small numbers of ballistic missiles.

National Missile Defense (NMD) Technology Development Program

After the 1993 Bottom Up Review (a DOD-wide review of U.S. military plans and programs), the Clinton Administration decided to emphasize theater missile defense (TMD) development and deployment efforts, and to focus NMD on technology development. Secretary of Defense Les Aspin noted that these program changes reflected an assessment that the regional ballistic missile threat already existed, while a ballistic missile threat to the United States *per se* might emerge only in the future. Many in Congress disagreed with this assessment and continued to press for the development and deployment of an NMD system. In 1996, the Clinton Administration adopted the 3 + 3 strategy to guide the development and potential deployment of an NMD system that could defend the United States against attacks from small numbers of long-range ballistic missiles. This strategy envisioned continued development of NMD technologies during the first 3 years (1997–2000), and, if the system were technologically feasible and warranted by prospective threats, deployment in the second three year period (2000–2003). The Administration modified its strategy in January 1999 by adding $6.6 billion to the FY 1999–2005 FYDP to support the possible deployment of an NMD system and moving the planned deployment date from 2003 to 2005. But the

Administration emphasized that an NMD deployment decision still would not be made until Summer 2000. On September 1, 2000, President Clinton announced that he had decided not to authorize deployment of a National Missile Defense (NMD) system at this time because he did not have "enough confidence in the technology, and the operational effectiveness of the entire NMD system." Research and development would continue, as would discussions with the Russians about modifications to the ABM Treaty, but the planned deployment date would slip until 2006 or 2007. The President further stated that the final decision on deployment would be left to the next Administration.

APPROACHES TO NMD

Clinton Administration Program

Program Design and Architecture. The Clinton Administration granted a contract to Boeing North America to serve as the "lead system integrator" for the NMD program. Boeing serves as the prime contractor, and will integrate elements of the program developed by different companies into an NMD system. Boeing also will execute the test program. (Boeing has contracted to provide 20 GBIs for deployment, as well as five spares. It must also build another 14 missiles for flight tests prior to deployment, and another 36 for follow on test and evaluation flights.)

BMDO initially described 3 notional architectures: C1 (Capability 1); C2; and C3. The C1 architecture might deploy up to 20 interceptors at one site to defend against a very limited threat, such as a small-scale accidental or unauthorized launch, or a small-scale deliberate attack. President Clinton's September 2000 decision against deployment would delay this initial system by a year or two. Currently, the FYDP provides funding for 100 interceptors and the support sensor and weapon infrastructure. This new architecture has been called C-1 Prime.

At the present time, the prospective NMD system architecture consists of: (1) the Ground-Based Interceptor, which includes a booster rocket, kill vehicle, and ground-based command and launch equipment; (2) a Ground Based Radar that will perform acquisition, tracking, discrimination, and kill-assessment functions; (3) the Battle Management, Command, Control, and Communications system that will be used to identify and assess attacks and authorize the launch of interceptor missiles; (4) and space-based sensors for early warning of attack (i.e., Defense Support Program/Space Based Infrared System and the Space and Missile Tracking System/ Space Based Infrared System Low Earth Orbit). Other candidate sensors include Upgraded Early Warning Radars, which will provide enhanced capability for the United States to detect and track missile launches, as well as other radars.

Congressional Reaction to Administration Program

Many in Congress disagreed with the Clinton Administration's NMD strategy. Some also argued that the threat from uncertainties in Russia and missiles in rogue nations exists now. Some also argued that the United States may have too little warning to respond to emerging threats with the deployment of a missile defense system. And some argued that the Clinton Administration placed the ABM Treaty above U.S. national security, maintaining it at all costs in spite of the demise of the Soviet Union. And many were particularly concerned about the Administration's refusal to commit to deploy an NMD system immediately. Conversely, some, including Senator Biden, argued that the new NMD strategy represents a turning away from long-term U.S. arms control objectives and non-proliferation policy.

After the Clinton Administration altered its NMD program in January 1999, some Members praised the Administration for adding deployment funds to the budget. Senator Jon Kyl stated, "I'm delighted. I think reality finally caught up with them." But some continued to question the Administration's commitment to NMD and they expressed concerns about the delay in the deployment date. For example, Representative Curt Weldon said he remained skeptical because the program still lacked a firm commitment to deployment and senator Robert Smith noted that he did not see a commitment to deployment that matched the rhetoric from the Administration. Nevertheless, in the report that accompanied the Senate Armed Services Committee's version of the FY2000 Defense Authorization Bill (S.1059), the committee praised the Administration for fully funding the development and deployment of an NMD system.

A few Members of Congress argued previously that the Clinton Administration's approach to NMD would have provided too little protection against the range of threats faced by the United States. Some would like to see a program that includes space-based sensors and interceptors. Others believe a sea-based NMD can provide more robust coverage sooner and for less money than the Administration's program (this concept is discussed below). And some Members believe that the United States should continue to pursue the development of a missile defense that can protect the united states from a large-scale attack by Russia. They note that Russian missiles still threaten the United States, and changes in Russian leadership could restore the adversarial relationship between the two nations.

Despite the failed intercept in July 2000, congressional sentiment appeared to support efforts to continue keeping the program on track and pushing forward with a summer 2000 deployment decision. However, a growing number of Members had argued that President Clinton should delay the decision until the next Administration. When the President announced such a delay on September 1, 2000, many Members praised his move. Most Democrats and some Republicans appeared to agree that the technology had not yet proved to be feasible and that further testing should be completed before a final deployment decision. Some Republicans, however, viewed the President's announcement as further evidence that the Clinton Administration was not serious about missile defense and had done little to protect the American public Senator Trent Lott referred to the decision as "another example of the Clinton-Gore Administration's legacy of missed opportunities. Representative Curt Weldon stated that the President's "misguided decision" would leave Americans "completely unprotected against the weapon of choice for rogue nations and terrorist groups—the missile."

Prospective Bush Administration Plan

Most experts agree that the Bush Administration is likely to conduct an extensive review of the NMD program before outlining any specific changes or proposals. President Bush issued directives to begin this review in mid-February 2001.

Although the outcome of this review is not yet known, candidate Bush outlined strong support for the deployment of an NMD system during the election campaign. In a press conference in May 2000, then-Governor Bush stated that the United States "must build effective missile defenses based on the best available options at the earliest possible date." He also stated that the NMD system must be designed to protect "all 50 states and our friends and allies and deployed forces overseas..." In other comments, then President-elect Bush indicated he would prefer a more robust defense system than the one outlined by the Clinton Administration and that it could possibly include sea-based and space-based components. Secretary of Defense, Donald Rumsfeld, apparently supports more robust defenses as well. He outlined this support during his nomination hearing and in a speech at the Munich Conference on European Security Policy. At that event he stated that the United States intends to develop and deploy a missile defense designed to defend our people and forces against a limited ballistic missile attack..." He said that the United States would consult with its allies about this deployment and that it had "every interest in seeing that our friends and allies... are defended from attack." General Colin Powell, the Secretary of State, also expressed support for the deployment of an NMD during his nomination hearings, but he noted that the United States must still resolve issues related to this deployment and the ABM Treaty with Russia and U.S. allies.

Sea-Based NMD

Some NMD supporters, and increasingly senior Navy military leaders, have advocated an alternative sea-based NMD program. The Heritage Foundation, for instance, examined current and future ballistic missile threats in 1995 and 1996 and proposed a sea-based NMD to meet these threats. The Foundation's most recent (March 1999) report, *Defending America: A Plan to Meet the Urgent Missile Threat,* outlined a plan "to achieve the most cost effective, most affordable global anti-missile protection in the shortest time." The plan, supported by other conservatives as well, calls for deploying an NMD system based aboard the U.S. Navy's Aegis ships. Currently, the United States has about 27 Aegis cruisers and about 26 Aegis destroyers (by about 2008, there will be 57 destroyers).

There was some movement in 1999 on this issue. In the report that accompanied the Senate Armed Services Committee's version of the FY2000 Defense Authorization Bill (S. 1059), the Committee called on the Secretary of Defense to prepare a new report evaluating options for supplementing a land-based NMD architecture with sea-based assets. It mandated that the report address the engineering steps that would be needed to develop a sea-based NMD system and that it evaluate requirements, performance benefits, design trade-offs, operational impacts, and refined cost estimates for sea-based NMD assets. Meanwhile, the Navy has proceeded to examine more closely some of the many technical and cost hurdles. But a recent, comprehensive review (*Taking National Missile Defense to Sea: A Critique of Sea-Based and Boost-Phase Proposals,*) counter supporters' claims that a sea-based NMD system would be inexpensive and easy to deploy quickly.

Boost-Phase NMD

By mid-2000, a growing number of analysts and critics of the Administration's NMD program, from across the political spectrum, had begun to argue that the United States should pursue boost-phase, rather than mid-course ballistic missile defenses. A boost-phase defense would attack an enemy's missiles early in flight, before they had left the atmosphere and before they had time to deploy multiple warheads or decoys. The interceptors could be deployed at sea, on land, or in space, as long as they were close enough to intercept an enemy's missiles within the first few minutes of its launch. Some critics, such as Richard Garwin, argued that this type of defense would be the only way to protect the United States against missile attack because a land-based, mid-course NMD would not be able to distinguish between decoys and actual warheads. Others, including then Governor George Bush, argued that the United States should pursue boost-phase defenses as a part of a more robust system, because that would give the United States multiple opportunities to intercept attacking missiles.

Officials in Russia have also argued for the development of boost-phase defenses. In early June, President Putin proposed that the United States and Russia cooperate on the development of boost-phase defenses that could "put a cap" on rogue nations and their missiles. He also proposed that Russia share its technology for these missiles with nations in Europe. He stated that this type of defense would not violate the ABM Treaty because it could be directed against theater-range ballistic missiles. The Clinton Administration was skeptical of the Russian proposal because it lacked details. Furthermore, the Clinton Administration argued that this would not replace the U.S. NMD program because it could not protect against long-range strategic ballistic missiles.

The Clinton Administration did not deny the potential for boost-phase defenses for NMD, but noted that the technologies for this type of system were not as advanced as the technologies for mid-course defenses, and that the United States would not be able to deploy such defenses until years after the current 2005 goal for NMD deployment. Furthermore, some critics have argued that, because the defenses would have to respond instantaneouly to the launch of an enemy missile, the United States would have to trust computers, rather than human beings, to interpret events and initiate a conflict.

Focus on Arms Control and Nonproliferation Strategies

Some Members of Congress and analysts outside government argue that the United States does not need a national missile defense to address the threat of missile attack from rogue nations. Some believe that the United States will not be able to develop and deploy a cost-effective NMD because of daunting technical challenges and certain high costs that would be associated with such a complex weapon system. Others argue that rogue nations with weapons of mass destruction could attack the United States with lower cost, and less obvious, means than ballistic missiles. They note that a BMD system would do nothing to stop cargo ships, small aircraft, or other unconventional or simpler means of delivery. Some also argue that a U.S. NMD could actually intensify missile threats to the United States if Russia slows or stops its offensive force reductions in response to U.S. proposals for changes in the ABM Treaty. They note that the strategic arms reduction treaties will eliminate thousands of warheads that could destroy the United States, while an NMD would only attempt to defend against a few dozen warheads.

Most critics of proposals to deploy an NMD do not dispute that some nations hostile to the United States may be seeking long-range ballistic missiles. They would, however, address these threats with a combination of diplomatic, arms control, and nonproliferation tools. They believe that economic, political, and military incentives, could help persuade nations not to pursue missile technologies or sell them to countries of concern. And they argue that a strong international nonproliferation regime could bring more pressure to bear on rogue nations than a U.S. NMD. And if cooperative methods are less than successful, many note that the United States could still deter missile attacks from rogue nations with its overwhelming military superiority in nuclear and conventional forces. They believe that no nation, even one led by a leader with less-than-rational objectives, would risk attacking the United States if it believed that its own survival would be threatened in response.

Factors Affecting an NMD Deployment Decision

The Clinton Administration identified four broad criteria to consider in its Deployment Readiness Review: an assessment of the threat, an assessment of the arms control and strategic environment, a technical assessment of the program, and an assessment of the cost of the NMD system. Additionally, however, an environmental impact assessment was prepared. These are discussed further below. The degree to which these may be applied to NMD deployment plans in the Bush Administration has not been made clear.

Threat Assessment

In 1995, Intelligence Community concluded in its November 1995 report, *Emerging Missile Threats to North America During the Next 15 Years. NIE 95–19,* that "no country, other than the major declared nuclear powers, will develop or otherwise acquire a ballistic missile in the next 15 years that threaten the contiguous 48 states." Some Members of Congress disputed this finding, noting that it did not address threats to Alaska and Hawaii, and did not consider the possibility that nations might accelerate missile programs by buying technologies, or full missile systems, from other nations. Some in Congress argued that the Administration had directed the report's findings to support the slow pace of its NMD program. Congress mandated that an independent panel review the underlying assumptions and conclusions of NIE 95–19. This panel, known as the Gates Commission, noted that the study may have been conducted in haste and that its conclusions were politically naive because they did not examine the entire range of issues associated with foreign missile developments. However, it concluded that the study had not been politicized with a result directed by the White House.

In 1997, the intelligence community reaffirmed that the United States would not face a new long-range missile threat for 10–15 years. Members of Congress, however, continued to question this conclusion, and in the FY1997 Defense Authorization Act, Congress mandated that the CIA appoint an independent panel to review the emerging missile threat to the United States. In July 1998, this panel, chaired by former Secretary of Defense Donald Rumsfeld (now Defense Secretary again), reported that a threat to the United States could emerge sooner than 2010, and that countries such as North Korea or Iran might have long-range missiles within 5 years of deciding to develop such systems. In January 1999, the Clinton Administration appeared to accept the Rumsfeld Commission's conclusions. Secretary Cohen noted that "there is a threat, and the threat is growing, and... it will soon pose a danger... to Americans here at home." He highlighted North Korea as a potential source of this threat.

At around the same time, the intelligence community appeared to alter its assessment of the threat from North Korea. In late 1998, Robert Walpole, the National Intelligence Officer for Strategic and Nuclear Programs spoke about the results of an assessment completed in October 1998. This study concluded that North Korea's Taepo Dong II missile, which is still under development, might have the range needed to reach most of the United States, albeit with an inaccurate and very light payload. And, in testimony before Congress in late February 1999, General Lester Lyles, the director of the Ballistic Missile Defense Organisation, stated that North Korea might acquire that capability by the year 2000. The Director of Central Intelligence, George Tenet, also noted in testimony in February that North Korea's Taepo Dong II missile might have the capability to reach Alaska and Hawaili with a larger warhead and the rest of the United States with a smaller, inaccurate warhead.

In early September 1999, the intelligence community released a new estimate of the projected ballistic missile threat to the United States. This report indicates that Russia, China, and North Korea are all likely to have ICBMs that can reach U.S. territory in the next 15 years, that Iran probably will have such a capability, and Iraq possibly may have that capability. The report indicated that Russia will have the most robust force, but, because of economic constraints, its force levels are likely to decline below the levels permitted by existing arms control agreements. China may also have tens of missiles armed with nuclear warheads that could target the United States, and that the Chinese threat would, in part, be influenced by technology gained through espionage. The report also stated that North Korea might test its Taepo-Dong II missiles at any time, and that this missile could have the capability to deliver an early-generation nuclear weapon to U.S. territory. The Taepo-Dong I missile, which was tested in August 1998, might also reach U.S. territory, but only with a lighter chemical or biological weapons payload, and with significant inaccuracies.

Technical Feasibility

The meaning of technical feasibility as a criteria for deployment has been relatively open to interpretation. In the NMD debate, it generally carries two meanings. First, there is a political connotation. Many in Congress and elsewhere who want an NMD system deployed as soon as technologically possible tend to believe that this criteria would be met as soon as the United States develops and tests all the components of a prospective system. This generally means that when a system can be built, it should be built. A second meaning of technical feasibility refers to specific criteria established within the Defense Department in order for a weapon system to proceed toward deployment. Until recently, these included a number of precise and technical criteria to be achieved within the program before a positive recommendation for NMD deployment could be made to the White House.

The NMD program office in the Pentagon has stated that

two successful test intercepts will be required to move the program forward. Site construction contracts can be awarded after one successful intercept, but two successes must be achieved before actual site construction can begin. Additionally, a new NMD milestone was established called the "site authority to proceed." This requires that the Secretary of Defense authorize the start of site construction in April 2001 based on the decisions the United States has made regarding the ABM Treaty. (A decision at this time is necessary to meet the scheduled 2005 NMD fielding date.) Last year, the number of flight tests that could occur before the Deployment Readiness Review (DRR) was reduced from four to three. The pace of the program has caused senior technical experts in and outside of the Pentagon to warn that significant program risk exists, which could lead to negative program developments down the road. They warn that the program is being schedule, rather than event driven.

Recent intercept attempts confirm that unambiguous success remains elusive. On October 2, 1999, BMDO reported it had successfully intercepted an intercontinental ballistic missile over the Pacific Ocean. Reportedly, the test demonstrated the "hit-to-kill" technology being purused in the current NMD program. But, reports of test anomalies surfaced in Jan. 2000, which DoD officials confirmed were true, but who argued nonetheless that the kill vehicle "worked in spite of that." On January 18, 2000, a second test failed to destroy its target over the Pacific Ocean as planned. Defense officials pointed out, however, that other test objectives such as system integration were achieved. Preliminary analyses suggested that the two infrared sensors on the kill vehicle failed in the last seconds of the test, causing it to miss the target. Then, on July 7, 2000, the kill vehicle failed to separate from the booster rocket, so the test of its capabilities never occurred.

In February 2000, additional criticism of the NMD program surfaced from within the Pentagon's Operational Test and Evaluation directorate, warning of undo pressure placed on the NMD program to meet an artificial decision point in the development process. This echoed similar criticism from a November 1999 Pentagon sponsored panel of technical and national security experts (the Welch panel). Some critics outside the government have focused on the system's ability to discriminate between warheads and decoys on an attacking missile. They note that adversaries are likely to deploy decoys in an effort to defeat the system, and, therefore, the system will be ineffective as soon as it is deployed. Some conclude that this weakness means the United States should not proceed with the development and deployment of NMD; others conclude that the United States should pursue more robust and advanced NMD technologies, including advanced space-based sensors and boost-phase interceptors.

By July 2000, a growing number of analysts and Members of Congress had called on the Clinton Administration to delay its NMD deployment decision. Some argued that the technology had not proven feasible; others wanted the decision to be made by a new President in January 2001. In late August, 2000, Philip Coyle, the Director of Operational Testing at the Department of Defense, stated that the United States would not be able to deploy an NMD system by the target date of 2005 because testing of the system's components had fallen behind schedule. He contended that a more aggressive testing program would be needed to achieve a deployment date of 2005.

By late July and early August, reports indicated that Secretary of Defense Cohen was likely to advise the President to proceed with early steps in the contradicting process for the construction of the X-band radar in Alaska. This construction would have to begin by Spring 2001 to support a 2005 deployment date. But the process could be stopped, before construction began, if the next President decided to pursue a different path on NMD. However, President Clinton did not accept this recommendation, and, when he announced that he would not authorize deployment of an NMD system, he cited the test failures and questions about technical feasibility as his primary concerns.

Arms Control and Strategic Environment

In January 1999, Secretary of Defense Cohen stated that NMD deployment "might require modifications to the [ABM] Treaty and the Administration is working to determine the nature and scope of these modifications." In late February 1999, Deputy Secretary of State Strobe Talbott met with Russian officials in Moscow to begin discussions about ABM Treaty modifications. The U.S. team sought to reassure Russia that the planned NMD would not interfere with Russia's strategic nuclear forces and that the United States still views the ABM Treaty as central to the U.S.-Russian strategic balance. The Russians were reportedly unconvinced, and continued to argue that the United States overstated the threat from rogue nations so that it could build a defense capable of intercepting Russian missiles. When discussions resumed in mid-August 1999, the two sides again reaffirmed that the Treaty is the "cornerstone of strategic stability," but Russian officials continued to reject the idea that the treaty could be amended and argued that any changes to the treaty would upset strategic stability, undermine Russia's national security, and undermine the whole offensive arms control process. In November 1999, President Yeltsin warned that any U.S. attempt to move beyond the existing limits in the ABM Treaty would "have extremely negative consequences" for other arms control treaties.

In February 2000, Secretary of State Albright reported a slight change in Russia's response to U.S. proposals after meetings with then-acting President Putin. However, the Russian position remained firm throughout the year. When the Russian parliament approved ratification of the START II Treaty in April 2000, it indicated that U.S. withdrawal from the ABM Treaty could be considered an extraordinary event that would lead to Russia's withdrawal from START II. Furthermore, in June 2000, Defense Minister Sergeyev repeated Russia's contention that the U.S. NMD system could be easily expanded and, therefore would undermine Russia's nuclear deterrent. He argued that United States would use its NMD system along with its offensive forces to achieve superiority over Russia and China. Presidents Clinton and Putin discussed ABM Treaty issues at their summit meeting in Moscow in June 2000. However, they made little progress on resolving their differences. In a Joint Statement on the Principles of Strategic Stability, they agreed that the ABM Treaty remains the "cornerstone of strategic stability," but that it could be modified in response to changes in the international security environment. They also agreed that the international community faces a growing threat from the proliferation of weapons of mass destruction, but Russia did not agree that this justified any change in the ABM Treaty.

President Clinton sited the continuing impasse with Russia on ABM Treaty modifications when he announced that he would not proceed with NMD deployment at the present time. A delay in the start of construction at Shemya Island would, according to the President, give the United States more time to pursue discussions with Russia in an effort to "narrow our differences" on the nature of threat and the U.S. interest in NMD. In late November, 2000, President Putin stated that Russia would be willing to reduce its offensive forces below 1,500 warheads if the United States remained committed to the ABM Treaty. This proposal was unlikely to break the deadlock because the United States had shown little interest in such deep reductions in offensive forces, and U.S. officials have stated that the United States would only accept Russian proposals for deep cuts if Russia were to accept U.S. proposals to modify the ABM Treaty.

Although the Bush Administration has indicated that it would discuss U.S. NMD plans with Russian officials, it has not set an agenda or a timeline for negotiations on modifications to the ABM Treaty. Officials in the Administration have, however, referred to the ABM Treaty as "ancient history" and "no longer relevant to the new strategic environment." Through these and other comments, Administration officials have signaled a willingness to withdraw from the ABM Treaty if Russia is unwilling to modify it or replace it with an agreement that would permit the deployment of more robust defenses. Some analysts believe that a U.S. announcement of withdrawal would compel Russia to agree to modifications: others argue that Russia's acquiescence or opposition is not important because the United States should simply proceed with the defenses it deems necessary.

In addition to considering the arms control objectives, U.S. officials have also considered the effect that NMD deployment would have on relations with NATO allies and China. Within these countries there is little enthusiasm for the United States deploying an NMD system, and in some cases (including NATO countries), there are strong negative reactions. President Clinton also acknowledged the opposition from U.S. allies when he announced his decision not to proceed with NMD deployment, noting the United States must have allied support because key components of the system would be on their territories. He expressed a willingness to consult with U.S. allies about NMD, even though his Administration did not begin these consultations until months after it began to plan for NMD deployment.

President Bush has also recognized that China and U.S. allies have expressed opposition to NMD. Officials from the Administration have simply stated that China has nothing to fear from U.S. NMD because it would not be directed against China's missiles. The Administration has, however, taken a more active role in consulting with U.S. allies about NMD and in ensuring the allies that the United States would include them in its missile defense efforts. This active effort appears to have erased the allies' concerns. Although many remain skeptical about the threat and concerned about the arms control and arms race implications of a U.S. withdrawal from the ABM Treaty, many have begun to accept the fact that the United States intends to proceed with NMD.

Budget Issues

There has never been a clear, consensus cost figure for deploying an NMD system. For several years, the Clinton Administration estimated that a limited NMD system would cost $9 to $11 billion to develop, test, and deploy. In January 1999, the Administration estimated that an initial system of 20 interceptors would cost about $ 10.6 billion. In February 2000, the Administration provided a life-cycle cost estimate of $26.6 billion for an initial system of 100 ground-based interceptors, presumably in Alaska. A couple of months later, the Pentagon provided a life-cycle estimate of $30.2 billion for the NMD system ($FY 1991). By May 2000, the General Accounting Office reported a cost figure of $36.2 billion (GAO/NSIAD-00-131), which number BMDO also apparently was using.

A late April 2000 study by the Congressional Budget Office (CBO) estimated that it would cost about $29.5 billion to develop, build, and operate and initial NMD system (the expanded Capability 1 system) through 2015. The total cost was comparable to the Administration's estimate of $30.2 billion (now apparently $36.2 billion). CBO estimates it will cost another $19 billion through 2015 to expand the initial system of 100 interceptors and build what is called a Capability 2 and Capability 3 system designed for greater numbers of more sophisticated potential missile threats. Additional space-based sensors would bring the total costs for NMD to around $60 billion through 2015. NMD critics argue that the true costs will be even higher, perhaps as much as $120 billion, to include other items some NMD supporters want: space-based and naval-based NMD interceptors.

Environmental Issues

In November 1998, the Administration filed a Notice of Intent in the *Federal Register* that BMDO would begin to hold public scoping hearings in conjunction with its plan to conduct an environmental impact analysis of potential locations for elements of an NMD system (*Federal Register* 63915–16). Thus far, these locations include only Alaska and North Dakota, with Alaska being chosen for the first phase.

The purpose of the public scoping hearing was to gather information from interested parties regarding specific environmental concerns. This input was considered in a draft Environmental Impact Statement (EIS). More public meetings were held prior to the final EIS in the spring of 2000.

In late September 1999, the draft EIS was reported to include language for a possible two-site deployment of NMD interceptors—Alaska and North Dakota. It suggested that up to 100 interceptor silos could be located in one location or up to 100 could be deployed in both one site in Alaska or North Dakota. This appears to represent a change from the original focus on one NMD site.

NATIONAL MISSILE DEFENSE IN CONGRESS

Budget Issues

Despite the addition of $6.6 billion to last year's FYDP for NMD deployment, some continued to express doubts about the Clinton Administration's commitment to NMD. Some supporters argued that an NMD system could be deployed earlier than 2005 if the Administration allocated more money. But program managers in DOD and BMDO believed little more could be done without introducing significant program risk. Time and engineering effort, not more money, will lead to effective NMD development as soon as possible, according to this view. This year, an additional $2.2 billion was added to the FYDP.

Legislative Debate

Although many in Congress disagreed with the Administration's plan for NMD, they were not able to enact legislation that would mandate the deployment of nationwide ballistic missile defenses until March 1999. President Clinton vetoed the Defense Authorization Bill for FY1996, in part, because it contained such a mandate. In 1996 and 1997 Congress considered, but failed to pass, independent legislation that would mandate the deployment of an NMD system. On April 21, 1998, the Senate Armed Services Committee approved the American Missile Protection Act of 1998 (S. 1873, S. Rept. 105–175). This legislation called for the deployment of a national missile defense system as soon as the technology was ready. When the bill came to the floor in May 1998, Democrats succeeded with a filibuster. The effort to invoke cloture failed by one vote, 59 to 41, with only 4 Democrats joining all 55 Republicans in support of the legislation. The Senate failed, again, to invoke cloture, in a vote held on September 9, 1998. Once again, the vote was 59–41.

Senator Cochran introduced this bill again in January 1999 (S. 257). After failing to win changes in the language, the Administration reportedly threatened to veto the legislation because it would only use the state of technology as the measure for deployment, and would ignore considerations about cost, threat, and treaty-compliance. Nevertheless, the Senate Armed Services Committee approved the legislation, by a vote of 11–7, on February 9, 1999. The full Senate approved the bill, by a vote of 97–3, on March 17, 1999. Democrats dropped their opposition to the Senate bill, and the White House withdrew its threat of a veto, after the Senate approved an amendment stating that it is U.S. policy to continue to negotiate with Russia on reductions in offensive nuclear weapons and an amendment noting that NMD programs remained subject to annual authorization and appropriations for funding.

Representative Curt Weldon introduced similar legislation in the House on August 5, 1998 (H.R. 4402) and, again, in early February 1999 (H.R. 4). This legislation simply states that it is "the policy of the United States to deploy a National Missile Defense." Although it does not specify when or how much missile defense the United States should deploy, supporters argued that it would produce a major change in U.S. policy because although Administration policy at the time supported development, it left a deployment decision for the future. This legislation passed the House Armed Service Committee, by a vote of 50–3, on February 25, 1999, and the full House, by a vote of 317–105, on March 18, 1999.

The Senate took up H.R. 4 on May 18, 1999. It struck all but the enacting clause with the language of S. 257, then approved the modified bill by unanimous consent. The House debated the new version of H.R. 4 on May 20, 1999, and approved the bill with the Senate language by a vote of 345–71. Congress sent the legislation to the President on July 12, 1999, and the President signed in on July 23. Some Members of Congress were angered by the Administration's interpretation of the legislation. They noted that Administration was not prepared to implement the law because it still planned on deciding whether to proceed with NMD deployment after the program review in Summer 2000. Members, including Representative Weldon, argued that the legislation eliminated the need for this decision by indicating that the United States would proceed with deployment as soon as the technology was ready. Yet, in a statement issued when he signed the law, President Clinton noted that "by specifying that any NMD deployment must be subjected to the authorization and appropriation process, the legislation makes it clear that no decision on deployment had been made."

For Additional Reading

CRS Products

CRS Report RS20052. *National Missile Defense: The Alaska Option,* by Steven A. Hildreth.

CRS Report RS20062. *National Missile Defense and the ABM Treaty: Overview of Recent Events,* by Amy F. Woolf.

CRS Issue Brief IB98028. *Theater Missile Defense: Issues for Congress,* by Robert Shuey.

2

The President's NMD Decision and U.S. Foreign Policy

President Clinton's senior adviser on arms control says that the key "to managing the diplomacy of NMD (National Missile Defense) deployment is Russia."

Not only is Russia the other signatory of the 1972 Anti-Ballistic Missile (ABM) Treaty, but it still has many thousands of nuclear warheads, according to former Arms Control and Disarmament Agency Director John Holum.

Holum told an audience at Stanford University on March 3 that Russia's approach to U.S. efforts to adapt to the ABM Treaty "will have a significant impact on the reactions of other states." While the United States must recognize "that Moscow has legitimate fears about any NMD deployment," he also said the Russians must be ready to negotiate on adaptation "in good faith."

In a speech designed to explain President Clinton's NMD Decision this summer on whether or not to proceed with NMD, and to describe some of the international reaction to proposed U.S. national and theater missile defenses, the senior State Department official said the U.S. is laying "the groundwork for reaching agreement, if, and when, the Russians make a political decision to negotiate Treaty changes." U.S. officials are seeking to address Russian concerns on NMD and ABM Treaty adaptation "through invigorated U.S.-Russian cooperation on measures related to the ABM Treaty, as well as missile defense," Holum said.

Since both the United States and Russia face threats from ballistic missiles, he said, cooperative programs between the two "should reap tangible security benefits." Right now, he said, the U.S. is still assessing how recent Russian leadership changes, including the Duma elections, "might affect the ABM/NMD negotiations."

Holum also emphasized the importance of Europe to NMD diplomacy. Allied concerns must be addressed effectively, he said. U.S. officials, he said, believe that missile defense programs, including a limited NMD, can enhance the ability of the United States "to fulfill its NATO and global security commitments."

Finally, Holum said he has worked hard to establish a regular strategic dialogue with the Chinese on the subject of missile defense in an effort to allay their concerns. Part of the problem, he said, is trying to overcome the low information level the Chinese have about NMD.

Just as deterrence works in the context of the U.S.-Russian relationship, so too, does it with the U.S. and China, he said. The United States does not consider China "to be a rogue state," Holum said, nor does it envision any future that would involve American NMD protection being used against China.

"We need to manage our dialogue with China so they will not view a U.S. decision to deploy a limited NMD as evidence of hostility or an effort to undermine their security," he added. Additionally, he said, "We don't want NMD to give China incentives to go beyond the ongoing strategic modernization program they had planned before NMD became an issue."

In concluding his remarks, Holum said the United States believes that NMD "can be carried out in conformance with the core purpose of the ABM Treaty, with further strategic reductions, with a stable strategic environment, and with continued progress against proliferation."

Following is the text of Holum's remarks as delivered:

Presentation by the Honorable John D. Holum
Senior Adviser for Arms Control and International Security
U.S. Department of State
Conference on International Reactions to U.S. National and Theater Missile Defense Deployments
Stanford University
March 3, 2000

I'm delighted to have this opportunity to step outside the

Washington beltway and talk about national missile defense (NMD) and its impact in a broader international context. On an issue of this significance, it's not only important, but imperative, for us in Washington to avoid "group-think" and to expose ourselves to the thinking in the outside world. You come at this issue from a wide range of backgrounds and perspectives, and I trust our exchange will be enlightening for us all.

I've also prepared for this conference by conducting another round of meetings on NMD, the ABM Treaty and START III with Yuri Kapralov and his Russian team earlier this week in Geneva. Those meetings always provide a healthy dose of reality. The best description I can offer is that on ABM amendments we persist in interpreting the Russian "nyet" as a contraction of "not yet," while they, with force and persistence, tell us we couldn't be more wrong.

The Fourth Criterion

The Administration takes the foreign policy implications of a possible NMD deployment decision very seriously. You are all familiar with the four criteria the President will consider, especially the first three—the threat, technology, and cost. Today I want to focus specifically on the fourth one, which has not been as fully examined.

Since the fourth criterion was first articulated we have become increasingly mindful not only of direct arms control considerations, but of the broad international dimension of an NMD deployment decision. The December 1999 White House document "A National Security Strategy for a New Century" articulates the fourth criterion as "the implications that going forward with NMD deployment would hold for the overall strategic environment and our arms control objectives."

In a meeting with members of the Senate a couple of weeks ago, Strobe Talbott and I were challenged on why the U.S. is even considering the views of Russia and other countries as part of our NMD deployment decision. I would not have thought to look to the Founding Fathers to help frame a response, but as they did on so many other issues, they captured the essence of the argument beautifully. Ironically, it is found in Federalist Paper 63, which justified the Senate's creation.

The author, probably Hamilton or Madison, argues that,

without a more stable body of government, the esteem of foreign powers could be forfeited by unenlightened and variable policy, and that only the Senate would possess a sensibility to world opinion and merit international respect and confidence. Then the author explained why attention to the opinion of other nations is important, in these words:

"An attention to the judgment of other nations is important to every government for two reasons: the one is, that, independently of the merits of any particular plan or measure, it is desirable, on various accounts, that it should appear to other nations as the offspring of a wise and honorable policy; the second is, that in doubtful cases, particularly where the national councils may be warped by some strong passion or momentary interest, the presumed or known opinion of the impartial world may be the best guide that can be followed."

Secretary Albright will be very focused on the fourth criterion when she provides her input into the President's deployment decision this summer. Under this criterion she will consider at least six elements — the impact of NMD deployment on our arms control objectives, our non-proliferation objectives, and our relations with European allies, with Pacific allies, with Russia, and with China. These are the elements I want to focus on tonight.

In particular, I want to talk about how we are taking the views of Russia, our friends and allies, and China, into account and, at the same time, seeking to shape their reactions to NMD. We aren't just being good listeners; we want a dialogue. We want to persuade others that a deployment decision would be the "offspring of a wise and honorable policy," and we need to have our views challenged to convince ourselves that the President's decision will not be based on "some strong passion or momentary interest."

Such a dialogue imposes a heavy burden on the United States to clearly articulate the purpose of proceeding with NMD, including our view of the threat; the details of our NMD program; and how we see it fitting into a larger worldview, including its impact on the current arms control and non-proliferation regimes, and strategic stability more broadly.

But a constructive dialogue also places burdens on other countries. They must move beyond their natural resistance to any disruption to the status quo and be prepared to face up to changes in the strategic environment. They must get past a tendency to "worst-case" the impact of any adaptation of the ABM Treaty, or assume that any change represents a "slippery-slope" leading inevitably to the Treaty's destruction.

In short, our friends and allies, Russia and China, must come to this dialogue with open minds and be prepared for a rational discussion. It's not enough to just say "No" in the face of a U.S. need to address what we believe is a real threat to our security. "No" is not a dialogue, and no country will ultimately have a veto over NMD deployment if the President concludes such a system is necessary to protect the American people.

The Key to Managing NMD Diplomacy is Russia

The key to managing the diplomacy of NMD deployment is Russia. It is the other Party to the ABM Treaty. It still has many thousands of nuclear warheads. And Russia's approach to adapting the Treaty will have a significant impact on the reactions of other states.

Our own approach is cooperative. We want to avoid forcing the President to a choice between the ABM Treaty and an NMD system that he decides is necessary to protect the American people. But to avoid this, the Russians must be prepared to negotiate in good faith. At the same time, we need to recognize that Moscow has legitimate fears about any NMD deployment.

As I mentioned, I flew to San Francisco just having completed the fourth in a series of meetings with my Russian counterparts on START III and the ABM Treaty. A parallel dialogue is under way between Deputy Secretary Talbott and DFM Mamedov. Secretary Albright is also fully engaged on these questions, and considerable time was devoted to these issues during her recent talks in Moscow. We are laying the groundwork for reaching agreement if and when the Russians make a political decision to negotiate Treaty changes.

We are addressing Russian concerns in three broad areas. First, we need to reassure Moscow that in deploying a limited NMD system we are not seeking to change the core foundation of our nuclear relationship, that is, that a limited NMD will not threaten Russia's strategic deterrent. Accordingly, we are seeking only those Treaty changes that we believe will be necessary to address threats as we project they will emerge.

We believe this phased approach will maximize our chances of reaching agreement with Russia on ABMT adaptation, as well as on START III.

Based on objective analysis, neither our Phase I, nor even Phase II, architecture would pose a threat to Russia's strategic deterrent. Russian officials have, in fact, stated repeatedly that they have the capability to overwhelm any NMD. Late last year, General Yakovlev, the Commander of the Strategic Rocket Forces, said that the SS-27, which will form the backbone of Russia's ICBM force under START II and III, "is able to breach any anti-missile system that exists in the world and any which will be built in the near future."

I have been struck by the fact that in our discussions, the Russians' critique of NMD has not focused on the impact of Phase I or Phase II deployments on their deterrent but, rather, on their concern that such deployments would establish an infrastructure allowing future breakout. So one of our negotiating challenges will be to ensure continuing Russian confidence that a U.S. NMD system remains a limited one, fielded within the agreed terms of an amended ABM Treaty.

I believe we can accomplish this through confidence-building and transparency measures—an approach we used in negotiating the ABM/TMD demarcation agreements—and possibly through enhancements to the ABM Treaty's verification regime, which now relies solely on national technical means. We have been putting forward some ideas along these lines.

Russia views the capabilities of a limited NMD system in the context of a surprise, disarming U.S. first-strike. We tend not to understand that countries—Russia and China, in particular—tend to look at NMD in a larger context; they connect the dots. Thus, its not totally surprising that the Russians see a more threatening environment when they link, for example, NMD with NATO expansion; intervention in Kosovo without United Nations imprimatur; and a general decline in Russian military power. While the thought of a bolt-out-of-the-blue nuclear strike now seems anachronistic to us, it may not seem so to the Russian military which, after all, is paid to consider the implications of such dire scenarios.

We have been explaining to our Russian counterparts in considerable technical detail why, even under a worst-case scenario, NMD would not threaten Russia's deterrent. But the strategic arms reduction process can also help address this concern. One of the major accomplishments of START II—its ban on MIRVed ICBMs and, in particular, vulnerable fixed silo MIRVed ICBMs—is a large step toward eliminating any strategic advantage from a first strike. Negotiated in parallel with changes to the ABM Treaty to permit a limited NMD, a START III agreement would ensure that as Russian strategic force levels decline, as they will with or without arms control, U.S. forces will come down as well. In short, we are not seeking to combine NMD with numerically superior U.S. offensive forces.

We are also seeking to address Russian concerns through invigorated U.S.-Russian cooperation on measures related to the ABM Treaty, as well as missile defense. "Cooperation" describes not only our approach to negotiating ABM Treaty changes, but also our willingness to engage the Russians in a significant number of specific activities.

We have put on the table for discussion a wide range of ideas ranging from expanded discussion of missile threats, including the possibility of a "joint" intelligence assessment, to the expansion of current cooperative programs such as the ongoing TMD exercise program and RAMOS; to an even wider array of voluntary transparency measures, some of which could be carried out even before the conclusion of an ABM agreement; to assistance in restoring the Russian ballistic missile early warning network.

Both the U.S. and Russia face ballistic missile threats. Through cooperative programs, both should reap tangible security benefits. This will help both governments demonstrate that a cooperative approach on ABM is in our common interest, rather than a confrontation leading to the Treaty's possible demise.

We are still assessing how the change in the Russian leadership, as well as last December's Duma elections, might affect the ABM/NMD negotiations. Acting President Putin made some encouraging statements during Secretary Albright's recent visit to Moscow, but it is not possible to draw any conclusions at this point.

The Russians will ultimately have a calculation to make—whether it is better to accept the potential deployment of a limited U.S. NMD system and continue on the path of strategic arms reductions or, alternatively, to jeopardize the strategic predictability provided by the ABM Treaty and the START process at a time when they can least afford a new arms buildup. They may not make that calculation until after the Presidential election in March. The good news is that the acceleration of the election from June to March provides a wider window for negotiations before President Clinton faces the NMD deployment decision this summer.

The Europeans

As with the Russians, the key to NMD diplomacy with Europe is dialogue. Last November when Strobe Talbott offered the first extended briefing of U.S. thinking to the North Atlantic Council, our Allies "unloaded" their pent-up feelings on the first available American target. But I believe we are now well past the emotional stage in this discussion.

But the Allies have concerns that we need effectively to address. We are institutionalizing in NATO a process for addressing these issues in the months leading up to the Spring Ministerials and the President's NMD decision, so he will have the full range of Allied thinking. Meanwhile we will provide the information they need, correct any misperceptions, and articulate our considerations with respect to NMD and, in doing so, hopefully adjust their thinking.

Let me briefly address the key concerns our European allies have raised about our NMD policy.

First, the Allies fear NMD will undermine the NATO alliance's principle of "shared risk" and could ultimately lead to the "decoupling" of the U.S. from Europe.

To the contrary, we believe missile defenses, including a limited NMD, can enhance U.S. ability to fulfill its NATO and global security commitments. Defenses render less credible any rogue state attempts to use WMD-armed ballistic missiles to deter us from responding to aggression or otherwise meeting our security commitments. We should keep in mind, for example, that U.S. intervention in the Gulf War and in Kosovo faced considerable opposition in both the public and the Congress. What would the public opinion balance sheet have looked like if Sadaam or Milosevic could have threatened to use WMD-armed missiles against the United States if we intervened? At the NAC, Deputy Secretary Talbott has posed the question "Why would the U.S. be a better ally if we were exposed to a missile threat?" We haven't heard a good answer.

A second concern we hear is that NMD means giving up on deterrence. In fact, the core of deterrence is the ability to convince a potential aggressor that the risks far outweigh any potential gains. There are two parts of this equation. The threat of retaliation drives home that the negative consequences of aggression would be huge. But deterrence is also bolstered if we can reduce the chance that an attack would succeed in the first place. Ballistic missile defense does not undermine, but complements and reinforces, deterrence.

Third, some of our NATO allies are concerned that we are overstating the threat. This concern, I think, flows from outdated Cold War perspectives and, perhaps understandably, fails to account for the revolution in thinking sparked in large part by the Rumsfeld Commission Report. We don't think states like North Korea or Iran are likely to use their missile and WMD programs as operational weapons of war, prompting devastating retaliation. Rather, we have come to the view that such states seek missile and WMD programs primarily as weapons of coercive diplomacy, to complicate U.S. decision making or limit our freedom to act in a crisis by, say, coming to the defense of our South Korean ally.

So we have to avoid mirror-imaging. For coercive purposes, WMD-armed ballistic missiles need not be deployed in large numbers or be highly accurate and reliable. There is no need for robust test programs, or for deployment of large numbers of missiles in dedicated long-term deployment sites. That, combined with our uncertainties in assessing the threat (e.g., the limits on our intelligence collection capabilities, use of denial and deception, and uncertainties regarding the amount of outside help), means our warning times have sharply diminished. Only a few years ago, the U.S. intelligence community had high confidence that it could provide five years warning of a proliferant state ICBM. It now considers a threat to have emerged upon the first successful flight test, which could occur with perhaps a few months warning, if that.

Finally, our European allies are concerned that NMD will

lead to an unraveling of the arms control process, undermine strategic stability, and lead to a worsening of U.S./NATO relations with Russia and China. This concern has undoubtedly been reinforced by the Senate's vote on the CTBT and the Duma's refusal to date to ratify START II. Of course we recognize the historic relationship between offense and defense. The Clinton Administration, however, rejects the idea that limited modifications to the ABM Treaty are incompatible with further reductions under START and the maintenance of strategic stability. Objectively, a limited NMD will have no significant capability against Russia's strategic force, even at much lower levels. Our challenge, of course, is to demonstrate that convincingly to Russia.

NMD is also compatible with nonproliferation regimes. Our missile non-proliferation strategy has three elements: to prevent the threat from emerging in the first place, if it nonetheless does emerge to deter its use or, failing that, to defend against it. Each of these elements complements the others. Development of a limited NMD system should not be taken as a signal that we have abandoned our efforts to prevent proliferation or our ability to deter. But to the extent prevention does not entirely succeed, and to the extent we cannot be confident deterrence will work, defense also has a role.

Relations with Russia, and fears about NMD's impact on international arms control and non-proliferation regimes, probably head the list of Allied concerns. Those concerns should largely evaporate if we can reach agreement with Russia on ABM Treaty changes and START III.

In any event, we will be presenting these arguments to our European allies over the coming weeks and months in a regular series of briefings on our plans and our dialogue with Russia.

China

I've left the toughest case until last. While our dialogues with the Russians and our allies are well underway, the same cannot be said for China. I find this personally disappointing. I have worked for some time to establish a strategic dialogue with the Chinese. The accidental bombing of the Chinese embassy in Belgrade has been the most recent setback in our attempts at engagement, and it came just when the NMD issue was heating up. However, Deputy Secretary Talbott did lead an interagency team to Beijing on February 17-18 for wide ranging talks that provided our first real opportunity to engage the Chinese on ballistic missile defense issues.

We have a lot to overcome. The Chinese information level on NMD is very low (Strobe's trip offered the first opportunity to provide threat and architecture briefings to a wide audience); and the perceptual gaps are wide (the Chinese, like the Russians, connect dots and see NMD as part of a grand design aimed at China). That is not the case. We believe deterrence works in the context of the U.S.-China relationship, as with Russia; we do not consider China to be a rogue state; and we do not envision a future that would require NMD protection against China.

Nevertheless, the objective facts are that China today has a small strategic force, and the North Koreans live in the same neighborhood; thus even a limited NMD system aimed at the North Korean threat could also significantly erode China's deterrent capability against the U.S.

We need to manage our dialogue with China so they will not view a U.S. decision to deploy a limited NMD as evidence of hostility or an effort to undermine their security. We don't want NMD to give China incentives to go beyond the ongoing strategic modernization program they had planned before NMD became an issue. That could have repercussions for CTBT, the NPT Review Conference, and South Asia. We also need to make sure NMD does not give China a reason to curtail its adherence to existing arms control and nonproliferation norms and regimes, or a reason to limit its future cooperation with us.

In my personal view, China's response to NMD over time will likely depend on more than a simple calculus of the number of strategic warheads that can reach the U.S. Economics (and the importance of the U.S. to China's economic advancement); the status of cross-strait relations with Taiwan and U.S. Taiwan policy; China's bilateral relationship with Japan; and potential TMD deployments in the region are all likely to rank above NMD in China's near-term hierarchy of security considerations. In turn developments in these areas may well shape China's response to NMD. To the degree we can break China's perceptual linkages between NMD and both Taiwan and regional TMD issues, and convince them that these issues have different dynamics, that will help.

At this point, we are really at the informational level with China. We need a regular strategic dialogue to allay Chinese concerns. Where we go next, however, will likely depend on the overall tenor of our broader relationship.

Conclusion

What should you take away from my talk?

First, that the Secretary of State, Strobe Talbott and I all treat the fourth criterion very seriously, and that we view this criterion in a broad fashion to include the impact of NMD on all aspects of the "overall strategic environment."

Second, our intention is to ensure that the President has before him all of the relevant considerations when he makes a decision on NMD deployment this summer.

Third, no country will hold a veto over NMD deployment. In the end, with the fullest possible information on all the costs and benefits before him, the President will have to make a decision based on U.S. security and the best interests of the American people.

But fourth, with friends and allies, with Russia and China, we will listen, to be sure, but we also intend a vigorous dialogue. We believe our approach to national missile defense can be carried out in conformance with the core purpose of the ABM Treaty, with further strategic reductions, with a stable strategic environment, and with continued progress against proliferation. We intend to make the case, in the spirit of Federalist Paper 63, that it is, indeed, "the offspring of a wise and honorable policy," and deserves international understanding and support.

3

History of the Ballistic Missile Defense Organization

Tonight, consistent with our obligations under the ABM Treaty and recognizing the need for close consultation with our allies, I am taking an important first step. I am directing a comprehensive and intensive effort to define a long-term research and development program to begin to achieve our ultimate goal of eliminating the threat posed by strategic nuclear missiles... Our only purpose—one all people share—is to search for ways to reduce the danger of nuclear war.

—President Ronald Reagan, 23 March 1983

The Ballistic Missile Defense Organization (BMDO) traces its roots to the Strategic Defense Initiative (SDI) program that President Ronald Reagan started in March 1983. Overseen by the Strategic Defense Initiative Organization (SDIO), Reagan's program was to explore the technical feasibility of missile defenses in the hope that such defenses, if feasible, might provide the basis for a shift from offense-dominated deterrence to a form of deterrence that relied increasingly on strategic defenses. By 1987, there was sufficient progress in the SDI program to establish an architecture designed to defeat a major attack by Soviet Strategic Rocket Forces.

Since the Cold War ended during the administration of President George Bush, he shifted the goal of the SDI program to the development of a new architecture that would protect the United States from limited missile attacks and defend deployed American forces and U.S. allies against attacks from theater missiles. The trend toward greater emphasis on Theater Missile Defense (TMD) in this new architecture continued into the presidency of William Clinton, which changed the name of SDIO to BMDO in May 1993. During the early years of the Clinton Administration, the lion's share of Ballistic Missile Defense (BMD) funding went to TMD, with National Missile Defense (NMD) relegated to second priority and receiving only a quarter of the funding provided for TMD. By the end of President Clinton's second term, however, NMD was overshadowing TMD.

Laying the Foundation for Today's Missile Defense Program

The SDI program spawned a number of significant technological advancements that underpin today's missile defense program. This is especially true with regard to hit-to-kill (HTK) technology which is the basis of all interceptors employed in today's missile defense systems. In 1984, shortly after the SDI Organization was chartered, the Army's Homing Overlay Experiment demonstrated the feasibility of intercepting a reentry vehicle in mid-course with a hit-to-kill (HTK) interceptor. Building on the Army's success, SDIO carried out a number of successful HTK programs. Included here are the small radar homing interceptor technology program, which became SDIO's Flexible Lightweight Agile Guidance Experiment, and the Exoatmospheric Reentry Vehicle Interceptor System. These programs clearly demonstrated the practicality of kinetic kill technology. Furthermore, because of the tremendous energy released when an HTK interceptor strikes its target, this approach has been judged most effective in destroying missiles armed with nuclear, chemical, and biological warheads.

Capitalizing on the directed energy weapons (DEW) work of the Advanced Research Projects Agency and the Air Force, SDIO pushed back the frontiers of laser development to where it was possible to test a fully integrated laser system. Among SDIO's other DEW accomplishments were the development of mirror coatings that eliminated the need for heavy cooling systems and the advancement of deformable mirrors which astronomers use extensively today.

SDIO's success in miniaturizing components in virtually all areas of missile defense technology has been fundamental to progress in missile defense systems over the past decade. One example of this miniaturization is SDIO's development of small rocket motors that weighed little more than eleven pounds yet produced over ten thousand pounds of thrust.

Through its accomplishments, SDI shifted the U.S.-Soviet rivalry from ballistic missile technology where the Soviets were at least on a par with the United States to the development of missile defenses where America's edge in high technology was a decisive advantage. In the process, SDI renewed Western hope that there was an alternative to mutual assured destruction and forced Soviet leaders to recognize that they could not keep pace with U.S. missile defense efforts. As a result, restricting the SDI program became a central goal of Soviet arms control negotiators. Soviet obsession with SDI gave the United States powerful leverage in arms talks during the final years of the Cold War.

By the fall of 1987, SDIO had developed a national missile defense concept called the Strategic Defense System Phase I Architecture, which was composed of a space-based interceptor, a ground-based interceptor, a ground-based sensor, two space-based sensors, and a battle management system. With its interceptors based on HTK technology, this architecture was to destroy a given percentage of warheads in a massive Soviet missile attack against the United States. Later phases of the architecture would increase the system's operational effectiveness.

BMDO TECHNOLOGY MAKES COMMERCIAL SENSE

Many corporation have incorporated BMDO-funded technology—which includes some of the most advanced invocations in the world—into their product lines, giving them the competitive edge in what is now an extremely dynamic international marketplace.

- Atleast 64 companies have spun off from Federal laboratories, private companies or universities to commmercialize BMDO-funded technology.
- Roughly 393 new commercial products have resulted from BMDO-funded technologies.
- 27 companies funded by the BMDO Small Bussiness

Innovation Research program have gone public after BMDO has funded them.

- Over 555 ventures have been formed using BMDO-funded technology as a basis.
- At least 687 patents have resulted from BMDO-funding with 220 more pending.

Transitioning to the Post-Cold War Era

The end of the Cold War during the presidency of George Bush brought a relaxation of tensions between America and the Soviet Union and reduced concerns about nuclear war. However, a major new threat emerged: the spread of ballistic missile technology and weapons of mass destruction throughout the world. In early 1991, this new and dangerous security environment prompted President Bush to replace the SDI Phase Architecture with a system known as GPALS (Global Protection Against Limited Strikes). The principal goal of GPALS was to defend America against limited missile attacks and protect deployed U.S. forces and American allies against shorter-range ballistic missiles. GPALS was an integrated architecture with three components: a global, space-based system of Brilliant Pebbles interceptors; a force of ground and sea-based theater missile defenses; and a limited, ground-based national missile defense element. All interceptors in GPALS were based on the HTK principle. President Bush's decision to reorient the U.S. missile defense program was validated by the Gulf War, with its battles between Patriot and Scud missiles.

The emphasis on theater missile defenses that was part of the GPALS system was sustained under the administration of President William Clinton, but not the GPALS architecture that integrated national, theater, and space-based systems into a single architecture. As part of the new direction the Clinton administration took with regard to missile defense, on 13 May 1993, Secretary of Defense Les Aspin changed the name of SDIO to the Ballistic Missile Defense Organization (BMDO). A few months later, a new orientation for the missile defense program emerged from the Bottom-Up Review (BUR), a major study of U.S. defense requirements for the post-Cold War era. Published in the fall of 1993, the BUR laid out a missile defense program with three components that were prioritized by means of funding.

A former anti-missile site in Nekoma, North Dakota.

- The top priority of the BUR program was theater missile defense, which was to receive $12 billion over the course of five years. Three projects constituted the core of this component: improvements to the Army's Patriot missile system (known as Patriot Advanced Capability-3 or PAC-3), a modification to the Navy's Aegis air defense system to give it the capability to intercept theater ballistic missiles (later known as Navy Area Defense or NAD), and a new Army missile defense system known as Theater High Altitude Area Defense (THAAD).
- Second priority went to national missile defense, which was to receive about $3 billion over five years. This "technology readiness" program was designed to shorten the time required to field an effective national defense in case a new missile threat to the U.S. homeland should suddenly materialize.
- Third priority was assigned to a five-year development program to produce advanced technologies that could improve both national and theater defenses. A total of $3 billion was earmarked for this third BUR component.

The BUR Evolves: TMD and International Programs

In addition to the three core TMD programs already mentioned, the BUR called for a fourth major program that would emerge from a competition between three projects: Corps-SAM (Surface-to-Air Missile), Navy Upper Tier, and a boost phase intercept option (such as the Air Force's airborne laser program). When Corps-SAM changed into an international program known as the Medium Extended Air Defense System (MEADS), it increased in importance and was designated a major defense acquisition program (MDAP). [1]Where Navy Upper Tier was concerned, it evolved into the Navy Theater Wide (NTW) program after it was elevated to MDAP status. The addition of MEADS and NTW to NAD, PAC-3, and THAAD meant that the BMDO TMD program now included five MDAPS instead of the four originally called for in the BUR. This produced funding strains in the overall BMD program that were aggravated by cost growths within the TMD programs themselves and by the occasional addition of smaller, unfunded requirements.

Central to Navy Theater Missile Defense, a Standard missile launches from USS Antietam

While pursuing its own TMD programs, BMDO also conducted a number of cooperative TMD programs with America's allies and friends. The longest running and most significant of these is the U.S.-Israeli Arrow missile program, which has its roots in a 1986 agreem ent between the United States and Israel. The missile developed through this program is a key element in the national missile defense system the Israelis are fielding as the year 2000 comes to an end. A second international program known as RAMOS (Russian-America Observation Satellite) evolved through several stages from a 1992 project. By the year 2000, RAMOS called for the Russians to build two satellites, each of which were to be fitted with U.S. sensors. These satellites would then be used to gather various phenomenological data that the two countries would share. In addition to providing valuable technical information, the project aims to help the U.S. and Russia move beyond the confrontational spirit of the Cold War. A third program grew out of U.S.-Japanese talks that began in December 1993. In response to a growing regional threat, Japan and the

United States signed an August 1999 memorandum of understanding that defined four joint developmental projects related to the interceptor for the Navy's NTW program.

The BUR Evolves: NMD

Pressure for changes in the BUR's NMD program developed rather quickly after Republicans, strong supporters of national missile defense, gained control of Congress in 1994. Additional impetus came from intelligence estimates of threats against the American homeland. Responding to these forces, DoD announced in February 1996 that NMD was being changed from a technology readiness program to a deployment readiness program. Known as the "three-plus-three" program, this new approach called for BMDO to complete three more years of developmental work leading to a systems integration test in 1999. Following this test, the United States would be ready to field a national missile defense in three more years if the threat warranted such a deployment. If a deployment were not warranted in 1999, BMDO would continue improving and refining the NMD components under development, but would always be able to deploy a system in three years following any decision to do so.

The Ground Based Interceptor.

As concern about the threat to the America continued, Secretary of Defense William Cohen announced in January 1999 that DoD was adding $6.6 billion to the NMD program to ensure that the U.S. could support a June 2000 decision to deploy. He also stated that the target date for deployment would be shifted from 2003 to 2005 to reduce program risk. The system that was to be fielded by 2005 would include twenty interceptors, a new X-band radar on Shemya Island in the Aleutians, up-grades to already existing early warning radars, operational space-based sensors, and a command and control system. Two years later, the system would be upgraded with the addition of eighty more interceptors, allowing it to deal with a larger threat. Other planned changes would further enhance NMD's operational performance.

By the time of Secretary Cohen's announcement, a number of important developments had already occurred in the NMD program. DoD and BMDO had established the NMD Joint Program Office, which had selected Boeing North American to serve as the Lead System Integrator (LSI) to manage the integration of service developed systems. Furthermore, two highly successful tests of the candidate sensors for NMD's exoatmospheric kill vehicle (EKV) had prompted the LSI to make an early selection of the Raytheon EKV without holding the planned fly-off with Boeing's own competing EKV. The early down-selected decision saved about $100 million, which was used to insert another test in the NMD program. This meant that there would be three intercept tests before DoD conducted an NMD Deployment Readiness Review in the summer of 2000 as a precursor to a presidential decision on the possible deployment of national missile defenses. After succeeding in its first intercept flight test in October 1999, the Raytheon EKV failed to hit its target in its next two tests, the last one coming on 8 July 2000. While top DoD officials believed that there was enough data from the five tests to conclude that the NMD system was conceptually and technically sound, the two straight test failures raised doubts at the higher levels of government about the readiness for deployment of the NMD system. These doubts were compounded by strong international opposition to an NMD deployment based upon its possible impact on the ABM Treaty.

The ABM Treaty and the President's Decision not to Deploy NMD

While the Defense Department was pushing forward with its NMD program, the State Department had been negotiating intensely with the Russians to gain acceptance for an amendment to the ABM Treaty of 1972 that would permit the United States to deploy an NMD site in Alaska. This treaty had emerged from the first round of the Strategic Arms Limitation Talks (SALT) that had begun in November 1969 and lasted two and a half years. The basic treaty limited the U.S. and Soviet Union to two missile defense sites, each having no more than one hundred interceptors. In 1974, a protocol to the treaty reduced to one the number of sites each side could deploy. Once a country deployed a defensive system at a given location, it could not deploy at any other location, even if it closed the original site. In the 1970s the Soviet Union established its one ABM facility at Moscow, a facility that Russia continues to operate. The United States established Grand Forks, North Dakota, as its one site, but closed its Safeguard NMD system in February 1976, a few months after the system first became operational.

Under the Reagan and Bush administrations, American arms negotiators had used the so-called broad interpretation of the ABM Treaty as a wedge for opening negotiations with the Soviets on a possible regime of arms agreements and cooperative programs to pave the way for a transition from offense-dominated nuclear deterrence to a deterrence paradigm based increasingly on strategic defenses.[2] The Clinton administration opted for another approach. It dismissed the broad interpretation of the treaty in 1993 and focused its energies on "strengthening" the ABM Treaty, which, the administration emphasized, was a cornerstone of strategic stability in the post-Cold War world. In pursuit of this policy, American diplomats negotiated the multilateralization of the ABM Treaty and secured a demarcation agreement that provided criteria for distinguishing TMD systems (not covered in the original treaty) from NMD systems.

By 26 September 1997, when these two changes were finally agreed to, the Administration's policy and negotiating efforts had aroused strong opposition in the Republican-dominated Congress. The Senate demanded the right to offer its advice and consent on the amendments and almost certainly would have rejected the agreements had they been submitted for approval. Furthermore, in fiscal year 1999 and again in fiscal year 2000, Congress passed measures requiring presidential certification that the demarcation and multilateralization agreements were not being implemented before funds could be expended to support U.S. participation in the Standing Consultative Commission that had been established by the ABM Treaty.

By the time Congress moved to block the implementation of the multilateralization and demarcation agreements, the time was approaching when it would be necessary to initiate long lead time activities if the U.S. were to have an NMD system operational in time to meet the projected threat from rogue nations such as North Korea. Since NMD plans called for constructing a new X-band radar on Shemya Island and deploying an NMD site in Alaska, the United States would have to negotiate with Russia to amend the ABM Treaty.

When the Clinton administration began its efforts to amend the treaty, it met strong opposition from the Russians, who protested that the treaty was the cornerstone of strategic stability and could not be amended. In their protests, the Russians were supported strongly by elements of the international community, including China, France, and the United Nations. Furthermore, during the summer of 2000, as the deadline approached for President Clinton's decision on whether or not to initiate an NMD deployment, the Russians played their trump card. Under the leadership of newly elected President Vladimir Putin, the Russian Duma approved in quick succession the START II strategic arms agreement and the Comprehensive Test Ban Treaty. The former had been agreed to by Presidents George Bush and Boris Yeltsin in 1993 and approved by the U.S. Senate in 1996. From this putative "moral high ground" the Russians now threatened to scrap the entire arms control structure if the United States insisted on changing or withdrawing from the ABM Treaty.

Stout Russian resistance to amending the ABM Treaty and NMD test failures were important considerations in intense, high-level government deliberations that were carried out in the weeks following the IFT-5 test. These deliberations involved representatives of the State Department, the Department of Defense, and the National Security Council and included the proceedings of DoD's own Deployment Readiness Review of the NMD program. Based on the advice that flowed from these deliberations, President Clinton decided not to initiate an NMD deployment, announcing his decision in a 1 September 2000, speech at Georgetown University. In his remarks, the President noted that the world was, indeed, becoming in some ways a more dangerous place so that pursuing an NMD system was rational. Nevertheless, given the fact that the NMD program was still showing signs of technological difficulties and that all of America's security measures, including arms control, must complement each other, he had decided that the time was not right for a deployment. Moreover, given the technical difficulties, he believed that his decision to defer the NMD decision to the next President would not significantly delay the operational date of an American NMD system.

Conclusion: A Way Ahead

Over the past fifteen years, America's national security requirements have changed dramatically as the world moved through the final decade of the Cold War and into a multi-polar world marked by the proliferation of ballistic missile technologies. Throughout this time, BMDO and its predecessor organization have led a focused, concerted effort to develop missile defenses that could match America's changing security requirements.

As a result of these efforts, the United States is positioned technologically to meet the challenges of a new strategic environment that includes growing threats from improved theater ballistic missiles and the spread of ICBMs to hostile nations that previously posed no strategic threat to the U.S. homeland. The United States already has available Patriot PAC-2 missiles that have been improved considerably since the Gulf War. The Israeli Arrow missile is becoming operational as the year 2000 draws to a close. The first Patriot PAC-3 unit, equipped with an all new hit-to-kill interceptor, will be fielded during the final quarter of FY2001. Within two years of PAC-3's operational debut, the first Navy Area Defense unit is scheduled to be deployed. In the more distant future, THAAD and Navy Theater Wide will be coming on line, adding a second, overarching, protective layer to the defenses already provided by NAD and PAC-3. At the same time, work on national missile defenses continues apace so that BMDO is prepared to move this program in whatever direction the new President selects

Looking ahead into the uncertainty of the twenty-first century lends a special poignancy to the words of America's patriarch, George Washington: "To be prepared for war is one of the most effectual means of preserving peace." Because of the important advances in missile defenses over the past decade and a half, the United States can look forward with hope to a new world of peace and prosperity while remaining confident that its defenses are ready for any conflict the future might bring.

Endnotes

1. In order to be an MDAP, an acquisition program must either be designated by the Under Secretary of Defense for Acquisition, Technology, and Logistics as an MDAP or estimated by the USD(AT&L) to require an eventual total expenditure for research, development, test, and evaluation of more than $355 million in FY 1996 constant dollars or, for procurement, a total expenditure of more than $2.135 billion in FY 1996 constant dollars. Once a program is designated an MDAP it is managed through a defined process that includes several phases such as concept exploration and definition, demonstration and validation, and engineering and manufacturing. Before an MDAP can pass from one phase of the process to another, the program must meet established exit criteria such as the successful completion of a given number of tests. Transitions between phases are known as milestones and are designated by capital Roman numerals. For example, MSI marks the transition from concept exploration and definition to the demonstration and validation phase.
2. The expression, broad interpretation of the ABM Treaty, derives from an intense debate in the 1980s over the interpretation of certain provisions in the treaty pertaining to futuristic systems that were based on technologies not used in the components and systems described and controlled in the ABM Treaty. These futuristic systems were said to be based on inother physical principals.lo Supporters of the ihbroadlr interpretation argued that the treaty anticipated the development of futuristic systems and did not agree to restrain research, development, and testing associated with these new systems. Advocates of the i.narrowlo or irrestrictivel. interpretation held that the treaty prohibited the development, testing, and fielding of all but fixed land-based ABM systems, regardless of the technologies upon which they were based. The

debate raged throughout much of the eighties and was never really resolved before the end of the Cold War, since the administrations of both President Ronald Reagan and President George Bush adhered to the narrow interpretation. For one discussion of the broad-versus-narrow issue by a participant in the SALT I talks, see Paul H. Nitze with Anna M. Smith and Steven L. Rearden, From Hiroshima to Glasnost: At the Center of Decision (New York: Grove Weidenfeld, 1989), p. 414.

Ballistic Missile Defense Organization,
External Affairs
7100 Defense Pentagon
Washington, D.C. 20301-7100
(703) 697-8472

4

The Ballistic Missile Defense Organization

Introduction

The Ballistic Missile Defense Organization (BMDO) manages, directs, and executes one of the most technologically complex programs ever undertaken by the Department of Defense (DoD). Partnered with all of the Military Departments, other federal agencies, the private sector, and major research institutions, BMDO's role is to facilitate the integration of leading edge and emerging technologies into an effective acquisition policy for missile defense.

The Director of the BMDO is appointed by the Secretary of Defense and reports to the Under Secretary of Defense for Acquisition, Technology and Logistics (USD/AT&L). As the Ballistic Missile Defense Acquisition Executive (BMDAE), the BMDO Director is charged with developing defensive systems to counter an evolving theater and strategic ballistic missile threat, with its attendant threat of the employment of Weapons of Mass destruction (WMD) on the U.S. and its allies.

As a result of these factors, the BMDO mission is complex and multifaceted. BMDO must develop options for, and deploy when directed, a ballistic missile system that is capable of providing effective defense of the U.S. against limited attacks of ballistic missiles, whether accidental, unauthorized, or deliberate. BMDO must enable deployment of an effective and transportable advanced theater missile defense (TMD) capability to protect forward-deployed and expeditionary elements of the U.S. Armed Forces, as well as its friends and allies. Doing so requires the BMDO to manage programs of basic and applied research to develop follow-on technologies, for both near-term and technology insertion options, for enhancing future BMD systems.

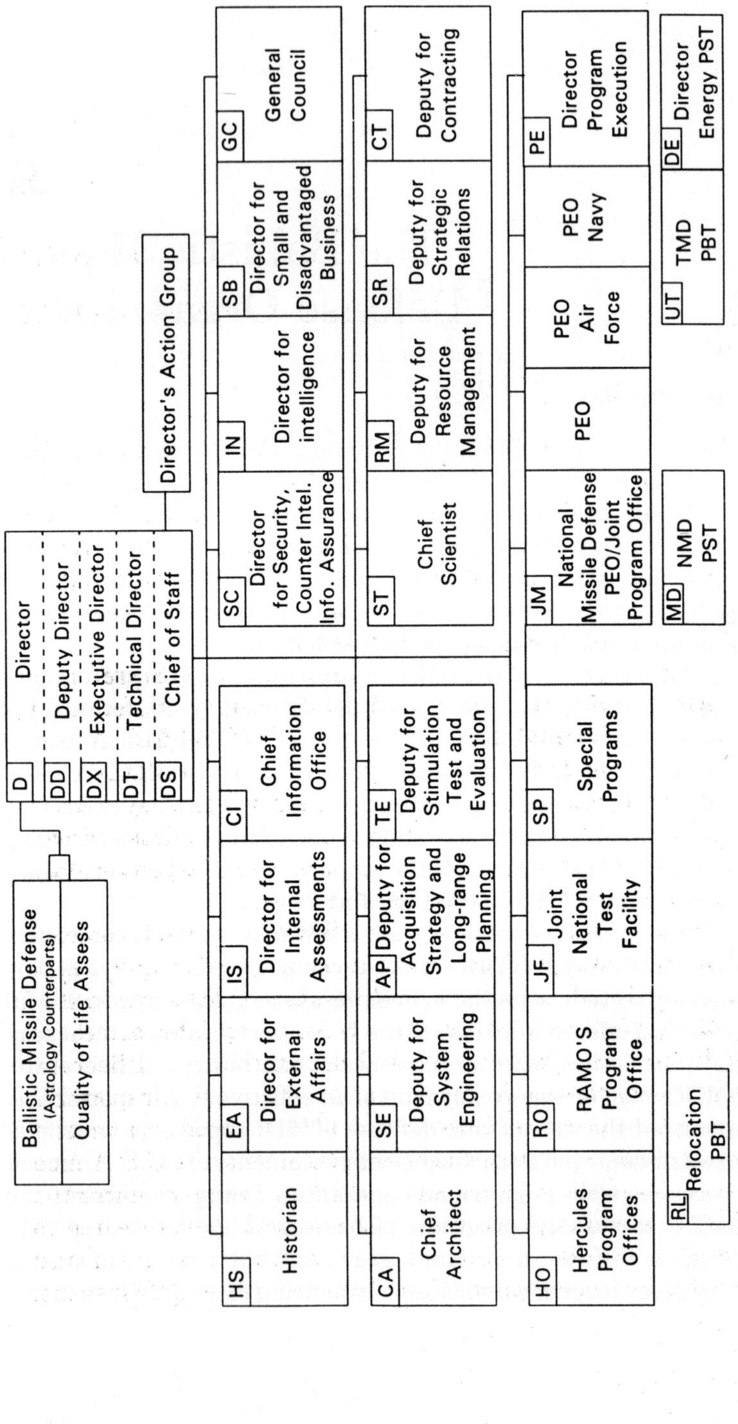
Ballistic Missile Defense
(Astrology Counterparts)
Quality of Life Assess
D Director
DD Deputy Director
DX Exectutive Director
DT Technical Director
DS Chief of Staff
Director's Action Group
HS Historian
EA Direcor for External Affairs
IS Director for Internal Assessments
CI Chief Information Office
SC Director for Security, Counter Intel. Info. Assurance
IN Director for intelligence
SB Director for Small and Disadvantaged Business
GC General Council
CA Chief Architect
SE Deputy for System Engineering
AP Deputy for Acquisition Strategy and Long-range Planning
TE Deputy for Stimulation Test and Evaluation
ST Chief Scientist
RM Deputy for Resource Management
SR Deputy for Strategic Relations
CT Deputy for Contracting
HO Hercules Program Offices
RO RAMO'S Program Office
JF Joint National Test Facility
SP Special Programs
JM National Missile Defense PEO/Joint Program Office
PEO
PEO Air Force
PEO Navy
PE Director Program Execution
RL Relocation PBT
MD NMD PST
UT TMD PBT
DE Director Energy PST

Background

The BMDO program is a key element of the overall U.S. defense strategy for the 21st century. Its mission reflects the necessity to provide operational commanders with interoperable systems that can be integrated effectively in defending against ballistic and cruise missiles. Air and missile defense systems must have the capability to operate simultaneously in the same battlespace. The nature of the threat requires that systems be interoperable to a sufficient degree not only to enhance mission success, but also to minimize fratricide. These complex facts-of-life and operational parameters shape the functions and organization of BMDO, as the organization has oversight of all the Services' systems and acquisition programs for missile defense and air defense against both theater and national threats.

These threats have not remained static and continue to proliferate as more sophisticated weapons are developed or distributed to potentially hostile nations.

BMDO, therefore, must balance the need to develop new technologies to counter future threats while preparing to respond to immediate and near-term defensive requirements. BMDO's role is increasingly carried out within constraints related to budget, long timelines for developing new technologies and systems, and the realities of the acquisition process. At the same time, BMDO must be aware of operational and program risks, domestic and international politics, as well as treaty considerations.

Even though the BMDO mission has evolved and reflects the practicalities of these boundaries, defending against ballistic missiles has been a sustaining BMDO vision. Operating on the cutting edge of missile and information technology, BMDO is not merely a technology user, but by necessity, a technology innovator. This spirit of innovation permeates BMDO operations and the way its mission is carried out.

Mission Essential Tasks

- Develop for Deployment a Limited National Missile Defense
- Implement the Upper-Tier Acquisition Strategy for Regional Defense
- Field Lower-Tier TMD
- Ensure an Integrated and Interoperable Missile

Defense
- Technology Investment to Pace the Threat/Avoid Surprises
- Foster International Cooperation
- Focus BMDO and Organization for success

Source: The BMDO Playbook, April 2000

BMDO Program Areas

Director's Action Group [DAG]: Provides specialized staff support to the Director. Provides an integrated team function approach to managing and scheduling the Director's top priority issues, both internal and external. Provides functional support to Director for speeches/briefings.

Historian [HS]: The Historian is responsible for conducting the official BMDO history program in support of the Director and staff to preserve the history of the most extensive weapons development program ever undertaken in the history of the United States. The Historian's responsibilities also encompass the history of the BMDO's predecessor, the Strategic Defense Initiative Organization, and general missile defense history.

External Affairs [EA]: Serves as the principal advisor to the Director for planning, coordinating, facilitating, and implementing all congressional and media-related/public affairs actions.

Internal Assessments [IS]: Serves as the principal advisor to the Director on all matters relating to the ability of the organization to meet its chartered responsibilities in the acquisition of ballistic missile defense systems and technology. Assesses how well the organization is doing in fulfilling the leadership priorities established by the Director.

Chief Information Officer [CI]: Responsible to the Director for the management of overall policies, plans, and procedures for Ballistic Missile Defense (BMD) management and information technology.

Security, Counterintelligence, and Information Assurance [SC]: Serves as the principal advisor to the Director on all matters relating to overall BMDO security and counterintelligence policy, plans, programs, and procedures.

Intelligence **[IN]:** Serves as principal advisor to the Director on all matters relating to BMDO relations with the Intelligence community.

Small and Disadvantaged Business Utilization **[SB]:** Responsible to the Director and serves as BMDO's principal advisor on the BMDO. Small Business and Small Disadvantaged Business Utilization Program.

General Counsel **[GC]:** The General Counsel serves as the principal legal advisor to the Director and senior BMDO officials. The General Counsel establishes and coordinates legal positions for the Director and exercises functional responsibilities and authorities on all legal matters pertaining to the BMD program.

Chief Architect **[CA]:** The Chief Architect serves as the organization's senior technical advisor to the Director for joint systems architecture development, to include architectures for National Missile Defense (NMD), Theater Air and Missile Defense (TAMD), and cruise missile options. Responsible for the design and implementation of the various architectural disciplines and new initiatives leading to acquisition milestone decisions in the Agency's BMD programs. The Chief Architect shall exercise functional responsibilities and authorities for the architecture and analysis of the overall BMD program for the purpose of reaching an informal internal conclusion that the system will perform as intended with a low level of risk within stated schedules and cost parameters.

System Engineering **[SE]:** The Systems Engineer serves as the principal advisor to the Director for the systems engineering, integration, and interoperability of the BMD program, to include NMD, TAMD, and cruise missile options. Ensures system engineering function, supports architecture analysis, and cost effectiveness trades. Develops and manages a program for overall systems integration to achieve interoperability among BMD systems; ensures the integration for all Service and weapon system elements, including Battle

Management/Command, Control, Communications, Computers and Intelligence (BM/C4I).

Acquisition Strategy and Long Range Planning **[AP]:** Responsible to the Director for the management of BMD acquisition strategy, to include NMD, TAMD, and cruise missile options. Ensures that balanced, realistic requirements (i.e., weapons, sensors, and BM/C4I components) for BMD systems are properly reflected in long-range acquisition strategies to meet overall BMD mission requirements. Translates DoD and other Federal agency policies to ensure compliance when developing strategic plans. Serves as BMDO's liaison to the Joint CINCs for requirements integration, planning, wargaming, exercises, and operation assessments.

Test, Simulation, and Evaluation **[TE]:** Serves as the principal advisor to the Director for test, simulation, and evaluation (T&E) resources, civil engineering, and environmental planning and compliance for the BMD program, to include NMD, TAMD, and cruise missile options. Responsible for the overall planning, programming, budgeting, and execution of the T&E infrastructure and the modeling and simulations program.

Science and Technology **[ST]:** Serves as the Chief Scientist to the Director for the management of BMD Technology and Technical Core Competency Programs. The Chief Scientist exercises functional responsibilities and authorities for the overall management, within the BMDO, of BDM Technology and Technical Core Competency programs and projects necessary to implement policies, program guidance, and program strategy.

Resource Management **[RM]:** Responsible to the Director, and serves as the principal advisor for planning and control, cost estimating and analysis, and financial management. Focal point for collecting financial and programmatic data. Develops policies, procedures, and formats for cost estimating and analysis for all BMD acquisition programs. Supports cost and operation effectiveness analysis. Develops cost estimates in support of BMD program and budget exercises. Ensure budgeting for the BMD Program focus is maintained, OSD-directed fiscal requirements are met, and cost, schedule, and performance standards are maintained consistent with the program baseline and Program

Management Agreements. Serves as the focal point for the BMDO Selected Acquisition Report and the Defense Acquisition Executive Summary. Also serves as the focal point for performance management and measurement activities. Administers manpower, personnel, and organizational planning programs, training, special emphasis/affirmative action programs, morale/welfare programs, incentive awards programs, the Career Acquisition Workforce program, facility management, and travel operations.

Strategic Relations **[SR]:** Responsible to the Director for developing the analysis, planning, and implementation of all international relations of the organization. Serves as the principal advisor to the Director for international participation in the BMD program, relations with other government agencies, and Congress on international relations issues. Responsible for coordinating policy and programs regarding international security, arms control negotiations, international agreements, and ancillary documents.

Contracting **[CT]:** Serves as principal business advisor to the Director on all contractual matters pertaining to the BMD program.

Joint National Test Facility [JNTF]: Serves as the Commander, Joint National Test Facility (Schriever Air Force Base, Colorado Springs, CO) reporting to the Director. The key mission is to provide missile defense related analysis, system level engineering, integration, and test and evaluation support for the development, acquisition, and deployment of missile defense systems and architectures.

National Missile Defense Joint Program Office **[NMD JPO]:** The NMD Joint Program Office (JPO) has the responsibility to develop, demonstrate, and deploy (when directed) a system to defend the United States against a limited strategic ballistic missile threat by a rogue nation.

Program Suppor Terms

National Missile Defense Program Support Team: Serves as the Program Support Team (PST) for the NMD JPO. Manages the development of plans and policies, the definition of resource requirement, and the program specifications for the core NMD programs. Implements program guidance and program strategies required to demonstrate, validate, integrate, and make available for fielding the NMD capabilities.

Upper Tier/Lower Tier PST: Serves as the PST for the TAMD Upper and Lower Tier acquisition programs. Manages the development of plans and policies, the definition of resource requirements, and the program specifications for the core Upper and Lower Tier programs. Implements program guidance and program strategies required to demonstrate, validate, integrate, and make available for fielding the Upper Tier capabilities.

Forward Defense PST: Serves as senior advisor to the Director on all matters related for planning and implementing functions for boost phase defenses attack operations, and related special projects.

Ballistic Missile Defense Organisation,
External Affairs
7100 Defense Pentagon
Washington, D.C. 20301–7100
(703) 697–8472

5

Ballistic Missile Defense—Program Focus

Introduction

> "We've seen since the 1991 Gulf War a proliferation of ballistic missile capabilities throughout the world, both through technology and system transfers and indigenous development. Over twenty countries now have ballistic missiles of theater range. Some two dozen countries have, or are capable of developing, weapons of mass destruction. The pairing of these capabilities is a dangerous trend that demonstrates that ballistic missiles are rapidly becoming the weapon of choice among regional powers."

Lt. General Ronald Kadish
Director, Ballistic Missile Defense Organization
March 30, 2000

For over fifty years ballistic missiles have been a threat to the United States and its military operations. During the Cold War, the strategic balance and deterrence between Soviet and U.S. forces held this threat to our national security in check. In the absence of a deterrence calculus between superpower rivals, however, national security is again at risk.

Deterrence may not work when facing rogue states and terrorists equipped with ballistic missiles. When combined with the spread of weapons of mass destruction (WMD), the threat to American security is compounded. During the Gulf War, SCUD attacks on Coalition forces demonstrated the need to protect our troops overseas. The U.S. government considers the proliferation of longer range ballistic missiles to be one of the greatest dangers to both national security and global security.

Program Areas

The Ballistic Missile Defense Organization (BMDO) has three broad program areas: National Missile Defense (NMD), Theater Missile Defense (TMD), and the Ballistic Missile Defense Technology Program. Key programs consist of NMD and five TMD programs: PATRIOT Advanced Capability-3 (PAC-3), Navy Area, Navy Theater Wide, Theater High Altitude Area Defense (THAAD), and Medium Extended Air Defense System (MEADS) systems. The core programs represent the bulk of BMDO's budgeted funding for research, development, test and evaluation (RDT&E) and procurement. The variety of scenarios and threat characteristics (e.g., maximum/minimum ranges, reentry vehicles, and radar cross sections) and the characteristics of the defended areas (e.g., military forces, population centers, and ports of debarkation) require complementary systems for complete, cost-effective defense. Additionally, BMDO supports advanced research through its Ballistic Missile Defense Technology to advance and preserve America's technological edge.

National Missile Defense

The National Missile Defense (NMD) program anticipates the need to field a missile defense system to defeat a limited ballistic missile strike against the US homeland. With the increasing proliferation of both medium- and long-range ballistic missiles and weapons of mass destruction to rogue states and terrorist organizations, it is important to develop a means to defend the American homeland that does not rely on deterrence alone. The decision to proceed to build and deploy a system depends will be made by the President after the Deployment Readiness Review. The deployment readiness approach incorporates assessments of the threat of attack, the cost of development, our international treaty obligations, and the technological readiness of the system. The NMD program also consists of preparing options for rapid deployment with contemporary technology in case a sudden threat emerges.

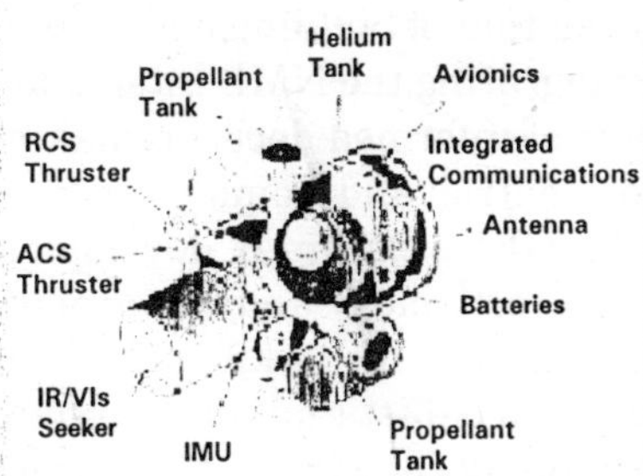

KV Characteristics

- Multispecial Passive Long Wavelength Infrared Seeker
- Guidance and Navigation
  - Interferometric Fiber Optic Gyroscope Inertial Measurement Unit
  - Solid-state Accelerometers
- Divert Propulsion
  - Liquid Bipropellant
  - High Acceleration
- Cold Gas Attitude Control System

Key NMD components include a Ground-Based Interceptor (GBI), featuring the Exoatmospheric Kill Vehicle (KV), an X-Band Radar (XBR), Upgraded Early Warning Radar (UEWR), Battle Management/Command, Control and Communications (BM/C3), and space sensor technology.

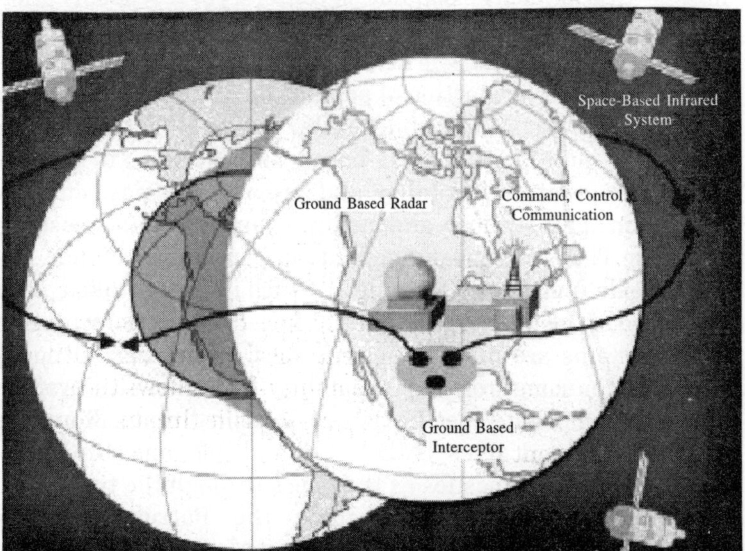

The NMD XBR is designed to provide target tracking and discrimination. Currently, NMD program developers are constructing a testbed radar to resolve several technical issues and to participate in the system testing. Upgrades to the current Early Warning Radar network will provide the existing forward-based attack warning system the capability to augment the operation of a NMD system. These radars can be modified quickly and at a cost significantly less than that of building new radars. The BM/C3 project focuses on integrating the NMD interceptor and sensor operations in support of informed decision-making and the best NMD command, control and communications architecture for the system. The GBI program is developing, demonstrating and validating the technology and components for a state-of-the-art and cost-effective hit-to-kill missile to intercept and destroy intercontinental ballistic missiles targeted against the United States. Developing the GBI is the highest priority in the NMD program. This program consists of two efforts, the KV and the booster. The KV efforts are currently concentrating on the technical issues of the interceptor seeker.

The purpose of Theater Missile Defense (TMD) systems is to protect U.S. forces, allies and other countries, as well as geographical areas of vital interest to the U.S., from theater missile attacks such as population centers, ports of debarkation, and military forces and facilities. TMD concentrates on the more immediate ballistic missile threat posed to U.S. forces. The TMD mission includes protection of population centers, fixed civilian and military assets and mobile military units. BMDO is working to develop both land- and sea-based TMD systems to give our forces the greatest flexibility and provide the most effective protection against short- and medium-range ballistic missiles.

The TMD arena is divided into upper- and lower-tier. The tiers are defined by the altitude at which intercept takes place, the speed of the interceptor and the speed of the enemy missile. TMD systems are built to operate best in one tier, although there may be some crossover capability. This allows the systems to match and negate specific types of missile threats. Moreover, this arrangement gives TMD forces multiple opportunities to destroy incoming missiles as they pass through the tiers.

Lower-tier programs include the Patriot Advanced Capabilities 3 (PAC-3), Navy Area, and Medium Extended Air

Defense System (MEADS). Upper-tier programs include the Theater High Altitude Area Defense system (THAAD) and Navy Theater Wide Defense (NTW). Finally, the Airborne Laser (ABL) program development focuses on destroying the missile shortly after launch. Taken together, these programs provide American and Allied forces with layered defenses capable of engaging incoming theater ballistic missile attacks during all phases of flight. Because it offers more intercept opportunities, and thereby increases the chance for a successful intercept, a strategy of layered defense presents a more comprehensive shield against attack.

THAAD, NTW, Navy Area and PAC-3 are TMD Core programs. THAAD, Navy Area Defense and PAC-3 are Major Defense Acquisition Programs (MDAPs), while NTW is pre-MDAP. MEADS is an international program in the Program Definition-Validation Phase in conjunction with Italy and Germany. Finally, ABL is an Advanced Concept.

Theater Missile Defense In-Depth

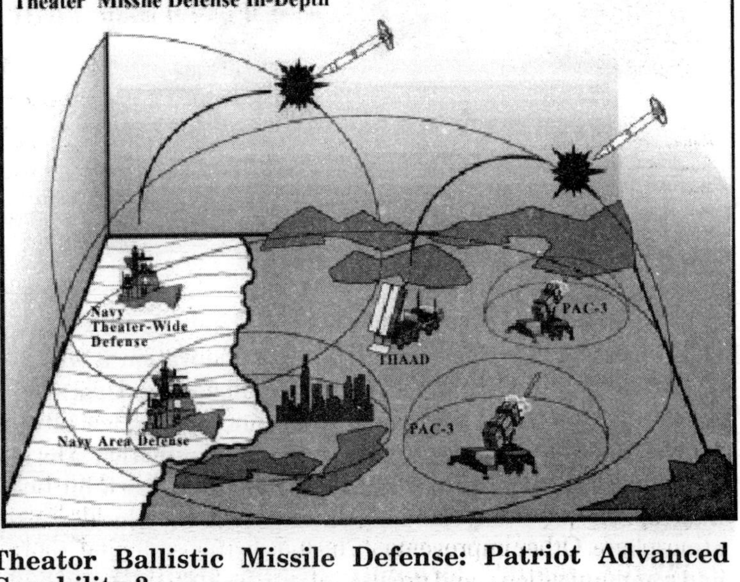

Theator Ballistic Missile Defense: Patriot Advanced Capability-3

PATRIOT Advanced Capability-3 (PAC-3) system development consists of three increasingly sophisticated upgrades called configurations. During 1995 and 1996, the two initial configurations were deployed to provide a missile defense to our troops as quickly as possible. PAC-3 is the most recent version of the famous PATRIOT air defense employed during the 1991 Gulf War. By FY 2001, the first PAC-3 units will be deployed to defend against ballistic missiles inside the atmosphere. This mission includes defending troops and fixed assets from short- and medium-range ballistic missiles, cruise missiles, and other air breathing threats such as fixed or rotary wing aircraft. The PAC-3 Fire Unit has three main components: the ground radar set, the Engagement Control Station, and eight missile launchers. Designed to be deployed anywhere in the world, PAC-3 can be transported aboard C-17 or C-5 aircraft.

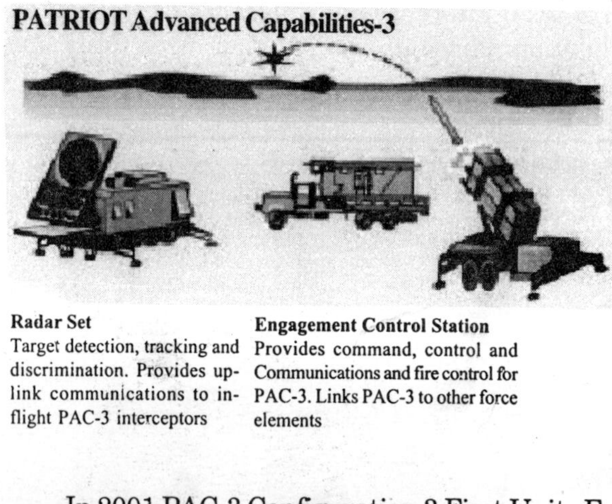

PAC-3 Missile
Hit-to-Kill, single state interceptor destroys targets in endoatmospheric (in the atmosphere) interceptions

PAC-3 Launcher
Protects and launches PAC-3 missiles. Canister provides easy re-loading of up to 16 missiles

Radar Set
Target detection, tracking and discrimination. Provides up-link communications to in-flight PAC-3 interceptors

Engagement Control Station
Provides command, control and Communications and fire control for PAC-3. Links PAC-3 to other force elements

In 2001 PAC-3 Configuration 3 First Units Equipped (FUE) will reach the field. The final PAC-3 Configuration 3 will field improvements to virtually all system components. Upgrades to the ground radar will improve its multifunction and low altitude capabilities, threat detection, and threat discrimination. The new PAC-3 missile will destroy targets by endo-atmospheric hit-to-kill interception - physically ramming the target while it is inside Earth's atmosphere. Other improvements include better command, control, and communications, and greater interoperability.

Theator Ballistic Missile Defense: Navy Area

The Navy Area system is based on the Navy's AEGIS cruisers

(*Ticonderoga* class) and destroyers (*Arleigh Burke* class), which form the backbone of the U.S. Fleet. With relatively minor modifications, these ships can be adapted to the ballistic missile defense role. The changes include upgrading the ships' AN/SPY-1 radar and AEGIS Combat System computers, as well as the computer programs. The STANDARD Missile (SM-2) Block IV will also be modified to optimize its performance against both cruise and ballistic missiles, including the addition of an infrared seeker to improve intercept accuracy. These improvements will provide theater commanders with a defensive capability against short- and medium-range theater ballistic missiles (TBMs) in the atmosphere during their descent phase. These ships will not need additional personnel to take on this mission, and the Navy already has the infrastructure in place for training and logistics.

Navy Area

AEGIS Ships:
These ships will provide defensing against cruise missiles, aircraft and theater ballistic missiles. They are especially well-suited to protect arriving forces, as well as cruicial sea ports, air fields, and other critical assets.

STANDARD Missile (SM-2) Block IV
Blast-fragmentation warhead, fired from the Vertical Launch System, and guided by the ship's SPY-1 radar system and the missiles infrared sensor.

Sea-based TMD offers several advantages to the nation. They can be stationed offshore near potential crisis "hot spots" where land-based TMD forces could not be readily deployed. As ships equipped with the Navy Area system can operate in international waters, there is no requirement to secure approval from a foreign government for deployment of the system. By acting as offshore TMD platforms, ship-based TMD systems can reduce the demands placed on airlift and sealift assets to transport land-based TMD defenses with ground forces. The Navy will receive its First Unit Equipped (FUE) with production software, hardware modifications, and SM-2 Block IVA missiles in 2003.

Theater Ballistic Missile Defense: Navy Theater Wide

Like Navy Area, Navy Theater Wide (NTW) builds on modifications to AEGIS ships and the STANDARD missile. The NTW system will modify the STANDARD missile for ascent, midcourse, and descent phase exo-atmospheric intercepts. The AEGIS Weapon System will be modified to support the increased battle space required for the improved, longer-range interceptor.

In 1996 the Navy Theater Wide (NTW) program became a "core" TBMD program. NTW was also designated a pre-Major Defense Acquisition Program (pre-MDAP).

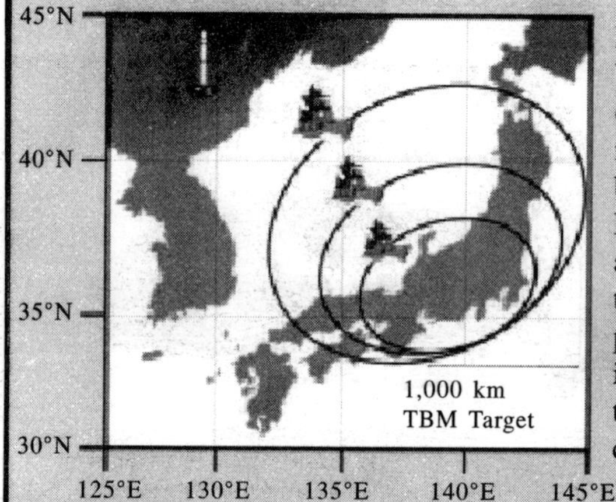

Navy Theater Wide capitalizes on the inherent mobility offered by Navy ships. By positioning a ship closer to the threat launch point, a significant increase in the defended area can be realized.

In 2000, NTW conducted additional flights as part of its flight demonstration program. NTW flight demonstration will occur in the AEGIS LEAP Intercept (ALI) phase. The ALI has a series of controlled test vehicles and flight test rounds scheduled from 1997 to 2001. The ALI test series employs the follow-on to the STANDARD Missile 2 (SM-2), known as the STANDARD Missile 3 (SM-3), and will test the four phases of the SM-3's flight: first stage boost, second stage endo/exo-atmospheric midcourse, third stage/KW separation, and guidance, leading to an intercept of TBM targets during various stages of their trajectory. These flight demonstration events will be followed by a series of more stressing threat representative test shots prior to deploying the tactical system.

Theater Ballistic Missile Defense: Theater High Altitude Area Defense

Development of the THAAD system started in 1992 and will be fielded by the Army in the 2007 time frame. The Theater High Altitude Area Defense (THAAD) system provides a ground-based, upper-tier component to the TMD architecture. THAAD engages TBMs at higher altitudes and longer ranges than lower tier systems, supporting both exo and endo-atmospheric hit-to-kill engagements. THAAD's range provides it sufficient battlespace, under most scenarios, to engage a threat, assess the success of the engagement, and, if necessary, fire a second missile.

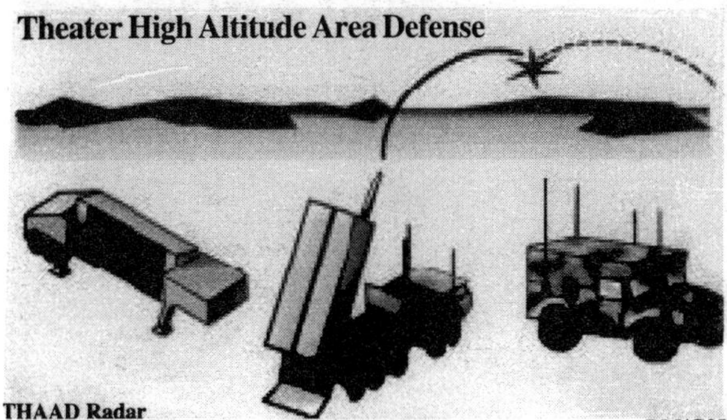

THAAD Missile
Single stage, solid propellant missile provides hit-to-kill accuracy in endo- and exo-atmospheric engagement

THAAD Radar
Provides surveillance, detection, tracking, threat classification and in-flight communications uplink with the THAAD missiles.

THAAD Launcher
Based on the standard U.S. Army Palletized Load System, Transports, portects, and launches THAAD missile.

BM/C3I
Provides engagement operations and communication links to the remainder of the force and launch control.

Comprised of a ground-based, X-band radar, THAAD launcher, THAAD missile (booster and kill vehicle), and battle management/ command, control, communications, and intelligence (BM/C3I) segments, THAAD can engage nearly all elements of the TBM threat spectrum. THAAD's ability to intercept incoming TBMs at a distance makes it a key element of the TMD architecture. The ability to do exo-atmospheric intercepts minimizes the effects of warheads of mass destruction on the ground, and prevents post-intercept debris from falling on our troops.

Theater Ballistic Missile Defense: Medium Extended Air Defense System

MEADS, an outgrowth of the U.S. CORPS/SAM program, began as a result of a 1990-92 "Program Cooperative Opportunity Survey." The U.S. Under Secretary of Defense (Acquisition and Technology) (USD(A&T)) invited the French, German, and Italian Governments to cooperate with the United States to develop a medium-range air and missile defense system. Of the three, Germany and Italy continue to work with the United States in a cooperative partnership to develop the system.

MEADS will be a lower-tier component of the Theater Missile Defense active defense pillar that will provide low-to-medium altitude air defense, anti-tactical ballistic missile defense, and cruise missile defense. MEADS units will be lightweight and modular in order to be highly transportable (C-130) and mobile. MEADS units will provide protection for maneuver forces and point defense for critical assets through decisive operations against multiple, simultaneous, 360° attacks by various classes of tactical missiles, Unmanned Aerial Vehicles, and air-breathing threats. Initially, the PAC-3 missile will be utilized as the MEADS interceptor. Eventually, when the threat warrants, a new interceptor will be developed.

All system components will be employed in a distributed architecture using high-capacity tactical communications. Since each battle element/battery can operate autonomously, one battle element/battery can be moving with the maneuver forces while other batteries are defending vital assets. MEADS will be compatible and interoperable with other Army, Joint Service, and allied systems expected to participate in joint/combined operations.

Ballistic Missile Defense Technology Program

Hit-to-kill technology remains the backbone of Ballistic Missile Defense. It is necessary, however, to continue to hone the technological edge that the United States currently enjoys. To this end, the Ballistic Missile Defense Technology Program supports research on new technologies and provides options for improvement to existing systems. These new ideas include technologies such as the kinetic energy interceptor, advanced surveillance and tracking sensors, and directed energy systems. This program is essential to keep the U.S. ballistic missile defense program ahead of the increasingly sophisticated global missile threat.

Conclusion

The Ballistic Missile Defense Organization (BMDO) continues to work to provide the United States and American armed forces with viable, cost-effective defenses against the threat of ballistic missile attack. By working to develop National Missile Defense and lower and upper tier Theater Missile Defense systems, BMDO's core programs provide a network of interoperable systems capable of engaging ballistic missile threats at multiple stages of flight to increase engagement opportunities and thereby provide the necessary protection

Ballistic Missile Defense Organization, External Affairs
7100 Defense Pentagon
Washington, D.C. 20301-7100
(703) 695-8743

6

National Missile Defense Program

Introduction

> *...We are affirming that there is a threat, and the threat is growing, and that we expect it will soon pose a danger not only to our troops overseas but also to Americans here at home... On August 31st, North Korean launched a Taepo Dong 1 missile.... The Taepo Dong 1 test was another strong indicator that the United States in fact will face a rogue nation missile threat to our homeland against which we will have to protect the American people.*
>
> —*William S. Cohen, Secretary of Defense, January 20, 1999*

> The primary mission of the NMD system being developed is the defense of the U.S.—all 50 states—against a limited strategic ballistic missile attack such as could be posed by a rogue nation. Such a system also would provide some capability against a small accidental or unauthorized launch of strategic ballistic missiles from more nuclear-capable states.
>
> —*William S. Cohen, Secretary of Defense, February 2, 1999*

The U.S. traditionally has relied on the wide expanses of the Atlantic and Pacific oceans to keep our homeland at arms length from the turmoil of global conflict. However, the proliferation of long range ballistic missiles and weapons of mass destruction of third world countries may negate much of this advantage and possibly deliver a serious blow to the national security of the United States.

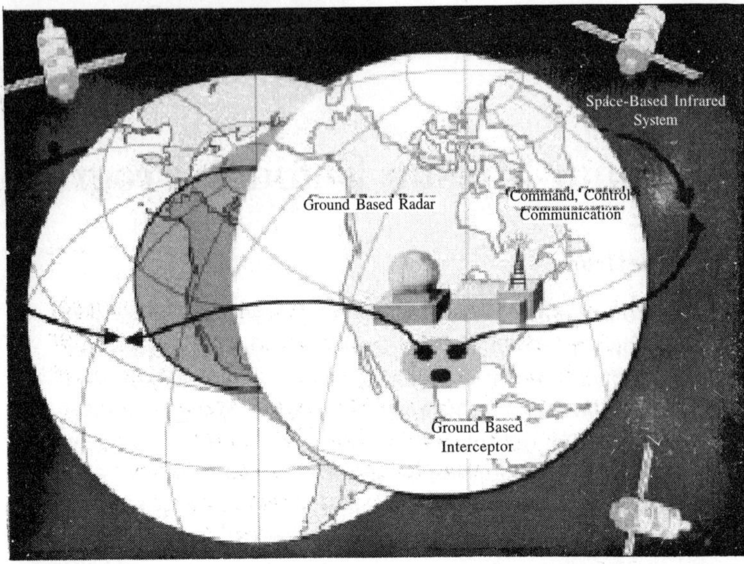

Proliferation

A present, only a few countries possess missiles that can strike the U.S. but the possibility that this number will increase cannot be ignored. Today, technology is spreading around the world at an astonishing rate, including technology dealing with ballistic missile development and, more ominously, with weapons of mass destruction.

Complementing this growing technological capability is the continuing intent among some regimes to harm the international system, particularly the U.S. and its allies. Furthermore, it is impossible to predict whether traditional notions of deterrence will operate under future conditions.

NMD Mission

The Ballistic Missile Defense Organization (BMDO) has balanced technological development, affordability, the potential threat, international treaty considerations and competing national defense priorities to establish the National Missile Defense (NMD) program. BMDO established an NMD Joint

Program Office (JPO) to manage the multiple-Service components of the NMD system and oversee their integration into an effective architecture.

The NMD program is a Major Defense Acquisition Program designed to develop and deploy an NMD system. Expected Initial Operational Capability (IOC) is in 2005. The decision to deploy the NMD system will be taken at a Deployment Readiness Review in 2000. The initial deployment. Capability 1 (C1) will be limited to 20 missiles. Increasingly capable deployment options after C1 will add further capability to the NMD system.

If deployment is required, the NMD system could protect the U.S. against limited attack by long range missiles. However, it would not be capable of repelling massed attacks or attacks by short range missiles.

Development of an NMD system may reduce the strategic value of long range ballistic missiles before they become commonly viewed as an essential component of international power and prestige and thereby present a strong incentive against these missiles.

NMD System

Although no deployment has been authorized, the NMD Deployment Readiness Program is completing technology development and initial system integration with the goal of maturing the key components enough to field as a system. The key NMD components include a ground based interceptor (GBI), an X-band radar (XBR), Upgraded Early Warning Radars (UEWR), Battle Management/Command, Control, and Communications (BM/C3) and space sensor technology.

The GBI program is developing, demonstrating and validating the technology and components for a state-of-the-art, cost-effective, lightweight, nonnuclear, hit-to-kill missile to intercept and destroy intercontinental ballistic missiles targeted against the United States. Developing the GBI is the highest priority in the NMD program. This program consists of two efforts: the Kill Vehicle (KV) and the booster. The KV efforts are currently concentrating on the technical issues of the interceptor seeker.

The NMD XBR is designed to provide target tracking and discrimination. Currently, NMD program developers are constructing a tested radar to resolve several technical issues and to participate in the system testing.

Upgrades to America's Early Warning Radar network will provide the existing forward-based attack warning system the capability to augment the operation of a NMD system. These radars can be modified quickly and with a cost that is significantly less than the cost of building new radars.

The BM/C3 project is focused on integrating the NMD interceptor and sensor operations in support of informed decision making. Currently, TRW is building the BM/C3 element to develop the best NMD command, control and communications architecture for the entire NMD system.

On 1 May 1998, BMDO awarded Boeing the contract to perform the responsibilities as the Lead System Integrator. Boeing's role will be that of the NMD Program "prime" contractor which will require them to integrate the development of the element programs into a system and successfully execute a test program leading to an integrated system test (IST) prior to the Deployment Readiness Review in Summer 2000. Under government oversight, Boeing will integrate the Raytheon kill vehicle into an off the shelf booster stack which was selected earlier this year. Boeing will also develop alternative architectures that could be deployed to counter a wide spectrum of potential threats.

Other components vital to NMD are the multiple components of the Space Based Infrared System. Although not funded by BMDO, these systems play critical roles in theater and national missile defense by providing surveillance, warning, and track data to overall missile defense operations.

Program Schedule

Currently, flight tests are being conducted at the Kwajalein

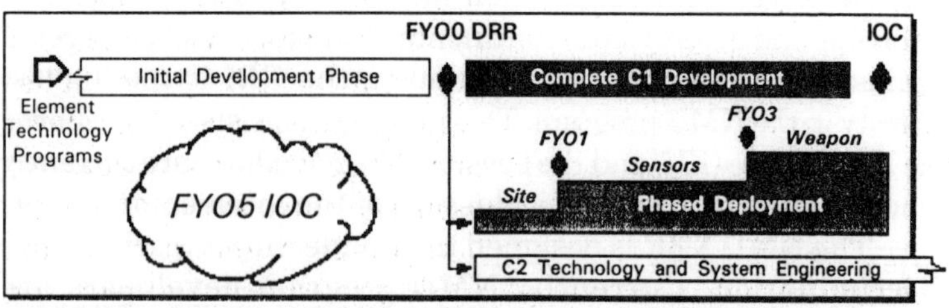

Missile Range in the Pacific Ocean. First, the elements will be

tested individually, and then eventually as a system. If successful, these tests will indicate that an effective and affordable NMD system can be built if so directed. The program has already conducted two successful sensor tests and one successful "hit to kill" intercept test. The NMD program is scheduled to conduct two more intercept tests prior to the Deployment Readiness Review, scheduled for Summer 2000.

Ballistic Missile Defense Organization, External Affairs,
7100 Defense Pentagon
Washington, D.C. 20301–7100
(703) 695–8743

7

National Missile Defense

Introduction

National Missile Defense (NMD) is a deployment readiness program that integrates and tests the key components (called Elements) of a National Missile Defense system. If deployed, NMD will protect all 50 states from limited attack by ballistic missiles from states of concern. As the result of the evolving threat, the Ballistic Missile Defense Organization (BMDO) designed the NMD program to be flexible and evolutionary.

The Ground Based Interceptor

The U.S. traditionally has relied on the wide expanses of the Atlantic and Pacific oceans to keep our homeland at arms length from the turmoil of global conflict. However, the proliferation of long range ballistic missiles and weapons of mass destruction to third world countries may negate much of this advantage and possibly deliver a serious blow to the national security of the United States.

History

At present, only a few countries possess missiles that can strike the U.S., but the possibility that this number will increase cannot be ignored. Today, technology is spreading around the world at an astonishing rate, including technology dealing with ballistic missile development and, more ominously, with weapons of mass destruction.

Complementing this growing technological capability is the continuing intent among some regimes to harm the international system, particularly the U.S. and its allies. Furthermore, it is impossible to predict whether traditional notions of deterrence will operate under future conditions.

The need for flexibility in Defense Programs is not new. Since the 1970s, changes in defense missions and in the systems designed to implement them have occurred every few years. The evolution of the program through the last four changes (from 1987 to 1999) has changed NMD missions from a deterrence enhancing role against a massive threat, requiring large numbers of defense interceptors, to a protection role against small numbers of threats.

In 1996, the Department of Defense (DoD) established as a Major Defense Acquisition and Deployment Readiness Program. To execute the program, BMDO established the NMD Joint Program Office (JPO) in 1997. With significant Army, Air Force and BMDO material contributions, the goal of the JPO is to integrate the various elements into a cost effective and operationally sound system designed to protect all 50 states from a ballistic missile attack.

National Missile Defense—What We Do

The initial protection program (in the late 1990s), called "3 + 3," was to develop, in three years, a NMD system capable of being deployed within three years after a deployment decision was made. In January 1999, the Secretary of Defense announced that the threat criteria established to trigger a deployment, would soon be met. Funds were programmed to move NMD from the development phase to a deployment phase should the program be directed to do so. The primary criteria for ordering the deployment include, but are not limited to: threat; technological readiness of a National Missile Defense system; and funding.

National Missile Defense—Who We Are

Since the National Missile Defense currently includes significant Army, Air Force and Ballistic Missile Defense Organisation elements, DoD policy established a Joint Program Office (JPO) to provide the program manager with unambiguous authority and responsibility and to create the management structure necessary to achieve multi-service interoperability.

The JPO consists of personnel from all the military services, as well as Defense Department civilian employees.

The JPO is a federated organization that has a "flat" structure. Each project manager works directly for NMD JPO Program Executive Officer (PEO). The NMD PEO then reports directly to the Director of BMDO.

The JPO provides the NMD program with a centralized management facility to oversee its current phase. Given the variety of participating organizations, the JPO's existence is a vital element in ensuring the success for NMD. The JPO will provide the DoD and BMDO with the means to coordinate activities between the Services, allow for integration of new developments, and provide a balanced, joint approach to the entire program.

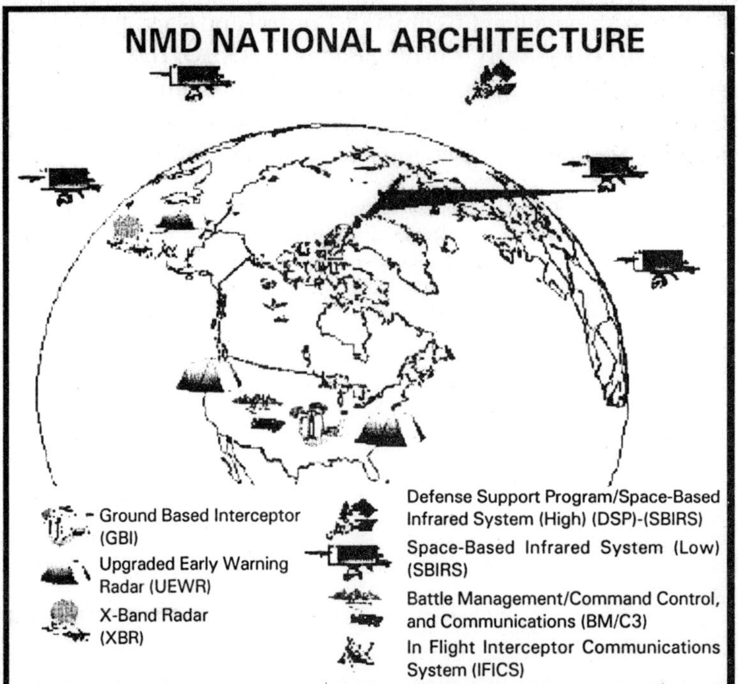

As a result of being a program that has high level visibility with the Administration and Congress, the JPO has been purposely elevated within the Office of the Secretary of Defense structure. Not only does this enable the JPO to be flexible and provide the most efficient centralized management, but it also facilitates the formation of the best available teams. These teams manage the NMD program and have the ability to incorporate new and future subsystems developed by the Services. This system ensures an objective, balanced view that avoids single Service solutions while managing an acquisition/contracting strategy through the Lead System Integrator.

National Missile Defense—Where We Are

JPO provides the NMD program with a centralized management facility in Washington DC to oversee its current development phase. The overall management and integration function focus is key as the program elements are located all over the United States. The ground systems are an Army contribution to the program and are located in Huntsville, AL. The Battle Management/Command, Control and Communications element to include Early Warning Radar and Space-Based Infrared System (SBIRS) is a combination US Space Command and Air Force contribution with Element locations in Boston, MA, Colorado Springs, CO; Los Angeles, CA and Huntsville.

Ballistic Missile Defense Organization,
External Affairs
7100 Defense Pentagon
Washington, D.C., 20301–7100
(703) 697–8472

8

National Missile Defense Architecture

Introduction

While the end of the Cold War greatly reduced the threat of global conflict and large-scale attacks on the United States, the proliferation of weapons of mass destruction (WMD) and the means to deliver them pose a major threat to the security of the United States. Over 20 nations, some with interests inimical to the United States, possess or are developing nuclear, biological, or chemical weapons. Ballistic missiles have also proliferated widely and have been used extensively in regional conflicts. The future may bring the proliferation of longer-range missiles, which can be used to attack or threaten the United States. National Missile Defense (NMD) is the focus of the U.S. response to these threats. The current NMD program of the Department of Defense is developing and planning to deploy, if directed, a ground-based missile defense system designed to protect the United States against limited ballistic missile threats from states of concern.

How will the NMD System Work?

All elements of the NMD system will work together to respond to a limited ballistic missile attack directed against the United States. The U.S. Early Warning System, consisting of Defense Support Program (DSP) satellites, and its follow-on capability, the Space Based Infrared System (SBIRS) satellites, will detect the launch of enemy missiles and then track these missiles while simultaneously gathering critical data. After confirmation, this information will be passed to the Battle Management/Command, Control, and Communications (BM/C3) system while ground-based radars acquire and track the incoming missile. This information will then be used to make an engagement decision. When defense engagement authority is granted, one or more interceptors will be launched on command to engage the threat. The BM/C3 system will continue to process radar and other system data in order to provide more information to the interceptor so it, in turn, can better discriminate between debris, false objects (penetration aids), and real warheads. The interceptor will use its on-board sensor to acquire the threat, select the target warhead, and guide itself to a direct, high-speed collision using on-board computers and divert propulsion systems. During and after the engagement, the radars continue to collect data and observe the intercept results in order to provide "kill assessment" information which evaluates the interceptor's success or failure.

Elements of the NMD System

As part of the NMD system, the Ballistic Missile Defense Organization (BMDO) is developing, testing, and integrating five major components, or elements. These five elements include: the Ground Based Interceptor (GBI); Upgraded Early Warning Radars (UEWR); Forward Deployed and/or U.S.-based X-Band Radars (XBR); Battle Management/Command, Control, and Communications (BM/C3); and the Space Based Infrared System (SBIRS) in high and low earth orbit.

Ground-Based Interceptor (GBI). The GBI and its associated components provide the "weapon" of the NMD system. Its mission is to strike high-speed ballistic missile warheads in the midcourse or exo-atmospheric phase of their trajectories and destroy them by force of impact. The GBI consists of several components. The missile payload is called the kill vehicle (KV). This component has its own sensors, propulsion, communications, guidance, and computing functions which all work together to complete the intercept. Next, is the booster that will propel the KV toward an approximate intercept location enabling the KV to perform terminal maneuvers and impact the incoming warhead. In addition to the missile payload, there is also ground command and launch equipment that is needed to launch the interceptor. This consists of the hardware and software for interface with the BM/C3 system, human-in-control interfaces (consoles) and interceptor storage sites (silos), in order to accomplish daily maintenance and readiness functions in addition to providing the launch of the interceptor upon command.

X-Band Radar (XBR). The XBR of the NMD program is a forward deployed ground-based, multi-function radar. In the NMD role, it performs acquisition, tracking, discrimination, and kill assessment of incoming warheads. The XBR uses high frequency and advanced radar signal processing technology to improve target resolution, which permits the radar to perform more effectively against closely-spaced warheads, debris and penetration aids.

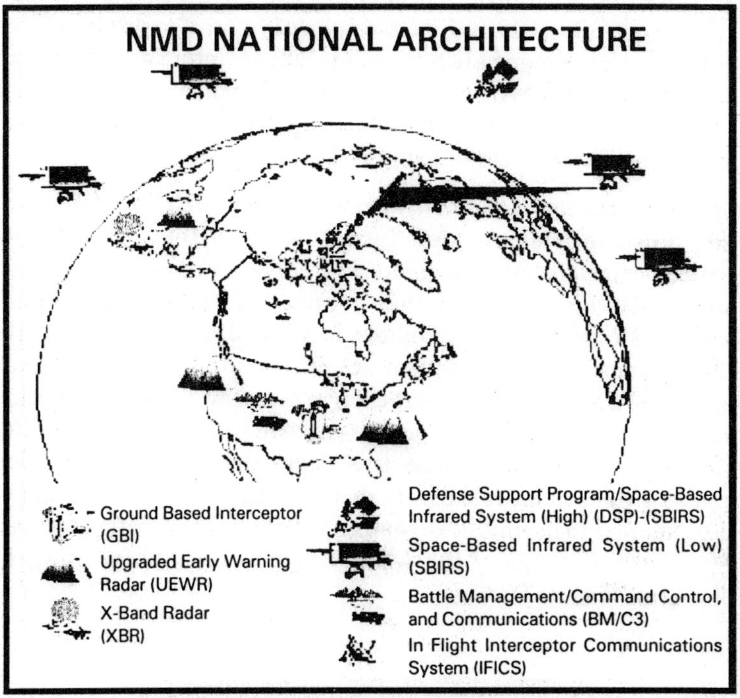

Upgraded Early Warning Radar (UEWR). U.S. early warning radars are large, fixed, phased-array surveillance radars used to detect and track ballistic missiles directed into the United States. Upgrades to America's Early Warning Radar network will provide the existing forward-based radars with the capability to support the NMD surveillance function. Prior to deployment of the SBIRS (Low) satellites, the UEWRs will be used to detect and track objects during their midcourse phase, primarily to cue the more precise X-Band Radar.

Battle Management/Command, Control and Communications (BM/C3). The BM/C3 element is the "brains" of the NMD system. In the event of a launch against the United States, the Commander-in-Chief of the North America Aerospace Defense Command (NORAD) will control and operate the NMD system through the BM/C3. This element supports the Commander-in-Chief with extensive decision support systems, battle management displays, and situation awareness information. In addition, it supplies the means to plan, select, and adjust missions and courses of action; and it disseminates defense engagement authorization (DEA) and other command decisions to the NMD system elements. The in-flight Interceptor Communications System (IFICS) is the BM/C3 communications link to the interceptors during flyout.

The Space-Based Infrared System (SBIRS). SBIRS is an additional element that future NMD systems will utilize. SBIRS (High) is being developed by the Air Force as part of the early warning system upgrade, which will replace the Defense Support Program (DSP) satellites. In its NMD mission, the SBIRS (High) constellation of sensor satellites will acquire and track ballistic missiles throughout their trajectory. This information will provide the earliest possible trajectory estimate to the BM/C3 element. By providing this "over-the-horizon" precision tracking data to the NMD system, the effective NMD battle space is expanded to permit interceptors to be launched before threats come within range of the XBR, which is critical for effective National Missile Defense.

Ballistic Missile Defense Organization,
External Affairs
7100 Defense Pentagon
Washington, D.C. 20301-7100
(703) 697-8472

9
National Missile Defense Program Evolution

Introduction

The Ballistic Missile Defense Organization (BMDO) has designed the United States Nation Missile Defense (NMD) to be flexible and evolutionary. To execute the program, BMDO established an NMD Joint Program Office (JPO) to manage multiple-Service participation. Initial deployment of NMD is expected in 2005. This first deployment, Capability 1 (C1) will be a limited capability of only about 20 interceptor missiles in response to a threat which also is currently projected to be limited. However, the NMD JPO will continue to improve technologies and integrate improved elements into the system if the threat increases. This degree of program flexibility is essential in the present world situation; we do not know who will threaten us or with what kinds of ballistic missiles.

History

The need for this kind of defense program flexibility is nothing new. Since the 1970s, changes in defense missions and in the systems designed to implement them have occurred every few years. The evolution of the program through the last four changes, which took place from 1987 to 1999, is summarized below. During that decade, NMD missions evolved from a deterrence enhancing role against a massive threat, requiring large numbers of defense interceptors, to a protection role against small threats.

The NMD Program

To meet the challenge of uncertainties about the threat characteristics and time scale extant in 1996, DoD established NMD as a Major Defense Acquisition Program and Deployment

NMD Program	*Mission*	*Defense*
Phase 1 (1987–1989)	Enhance distance of a Soviet First Strike	1000s of interceptors, ground and space based
Global Protection against Limited Strikes (GPALS) (1989–1992)	Protect against accidental or unauthorized launch	100s of interceptors, ground and space based
Technology Readiness (1993–1995)	Prepare technology to reduce deployment time	Ground based system, deployment not considered
Deployment Readiness-"3 + 3" (1996–2005)	Integrate systems; prepare to deploy three years after a future decision	10s of interceptors, ground based only
NMD Acquisition (1999–2005)	Prepare for initial deployment in 2005	10s of interceptors, ground based only

The first four programmatic re-directions occured three to four years apart and resulted in major program changes–but no deployment decision.

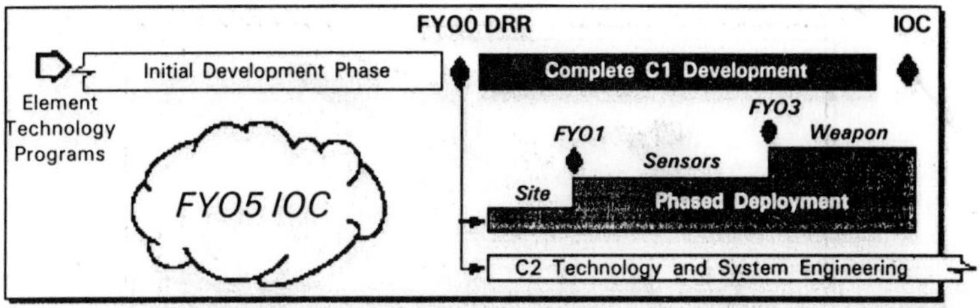

Readiness Program. The program, called "3 + 3," was to develop a NMD system capable of being deployed within three years after a deployment decision at a Deployment Readiness Review (DRR) in 2000. The DRR criteria are: existence of a threat and technological capability to proceed. In January 1999, the Secretary of Defense announced that the threat criteria would soon be met. Funds are now programmed to move NMD from the development phase to a deployment phase should we be directed to do so, as shown in Fig. 1. To reduce program risks, the NMD now projects initial deployment in 2005 rather than 2003. As before, the decision to deploy will be made at the DRR in 2000.

Architecture

Shown on previous page is the initial architecture to be developed within the NMD program which is associated with the deployment decision in 2000. It will be deployed in a configuration that is designed specifically for the threat it will have to defend against.

Ballistic Missile Defense Organization, External Affairs
7100 Defense Pentagon
Washington, D.C. 20301-7100
(703) 695-8743

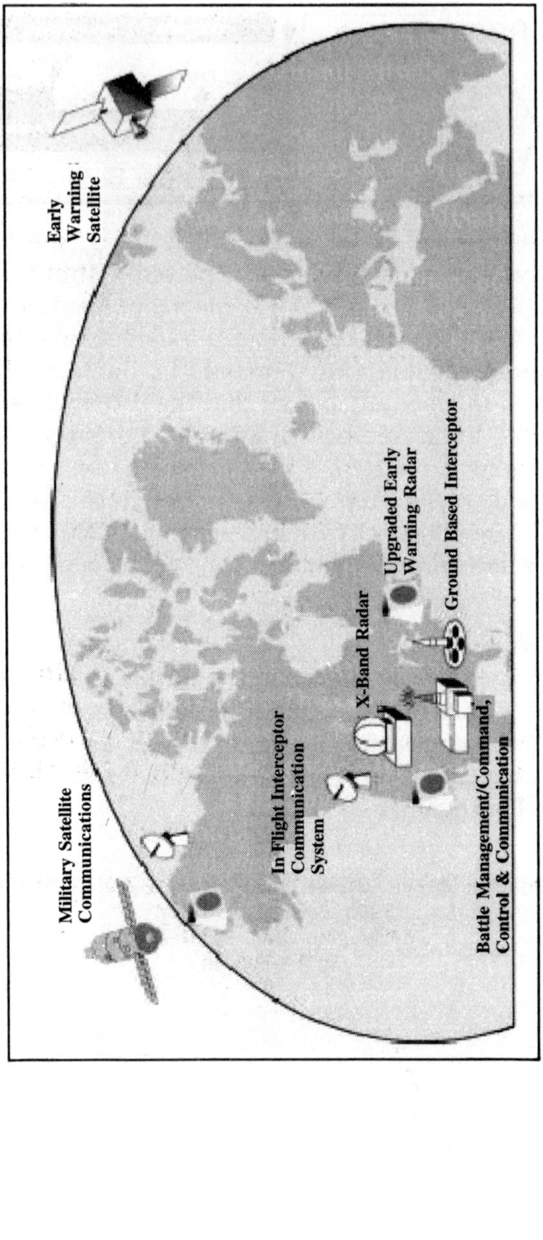
Early
Warning
Satellite
Military Satellite
Communications
In Flight Interceptor
Communication
System
X-Band Radar
Upgraded Early
Warning Radar
Ground Based Interceptor
Battle Management/Command,
Control & Communication

10

National Missile Defense Weapon Element

Introduction

The weapon element forms the core of the National Missile Defense (NMD) system. Its mission is to engage high-speed ballistic missile warheads in the midcourse (exoatmospheric) phase of their trajectories and destroy them by force of impact. The weapon system consists of:

- An interceptor component consisting of a booster vehicle and a kill vehicle (KV) to conduct the engagement;
- The ground based command and launch equipment needed to fire the interceptor; and
- The support equipment needed to deploy and maintain the interceptor.

The Role of The Ground Based Interceptor

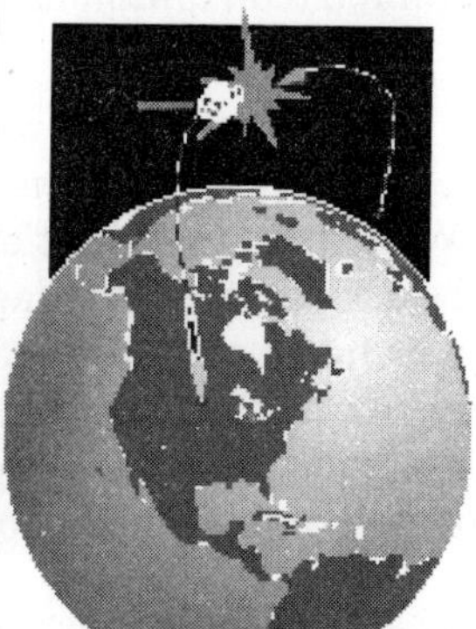

MISSION

PROVIDE NON-NUCLEAR HIT-TO-KILL INTERCEPT OF AN INCOMING REENTRY VEHICLE

DESCRIPTION

- WEAPON ELEMENT FOR NMD
- HIT-TO-KILL NON-NUCLEAR EXO-ATMOSPHERIC INTERCEPTOR OF ICBM REENTRY VEHICLES
- DORMANT, FIXED-BASED INTERCEPTOR

Operational Concept

The Ground Based Interceptor launches in accordance with a weapon tasking plan from the Battle Management, Command, Control and Communications (BMC3) element and flies toward the target's predicted location. Aided by one or more in-flight target updates (IFTUs) from the BMC3 element, the interceptor kill vehicle uses onboard sensors to acquire the threat cluster. It then uses its onboard discrimination capability, alone or fused with a threat object map (TOM) obtained from the BMC3 element, to determine which object is the designated target. The GBI KV then adjusts its trajectory to collide with the target. Both the kill vehicle and the target are demolished in the collision.

The Exoatmospheric Kill Vehicle (EKV). The EKV is the intercept component of the GBI. The EKV has its own seeker, propulsion, communications, guidance, and computers to support intercept targeting decisions and maneuvers. The EKV must accomplish a variety of complicated tasks to achieve a hit-to-kill collision. It will use an onboard communications system to transmit messages to and receive messages from the earthbound BMC3 element. The EKV also uses a multiple-waveband seeker to acquire and track targets. This seeker is comprised of focal plane arrays and a cryogenic cooling assembly attached to an optical telescope, supported by processing hardware and software. The EKV may use a combination of onboard navigation and target selection capabilities, as well as uplinked transmissions, to zero in on a target and destroy it.

Booster Development. In 1998, the Lead Systems Integrator, Boeing, began developing a dedicated weapon system booster using off-the-shelf motors. With slight modifications, the Graphite Epoxy Motor (GEM) will be used for the first stage, and the Orbus 1A will be used for the second and third stages. The kill vehicle contractor will supply an adapter to interface the kill vehicle with the booster. Upon assembly, the interceptor is housed in a canister designed to provide a controlled environment over the deployment life.

Performance of the GEM/Orbus/Orbus booster vehicle will be demonstrated in three booster verification (BV) flight tests. BV-1 and 2 will be conducted from Vandenberg Air Force Base,

California, to demonstrate performance of the three stage booster. BV-3 will be conducted from Kwajalein Missile Range,

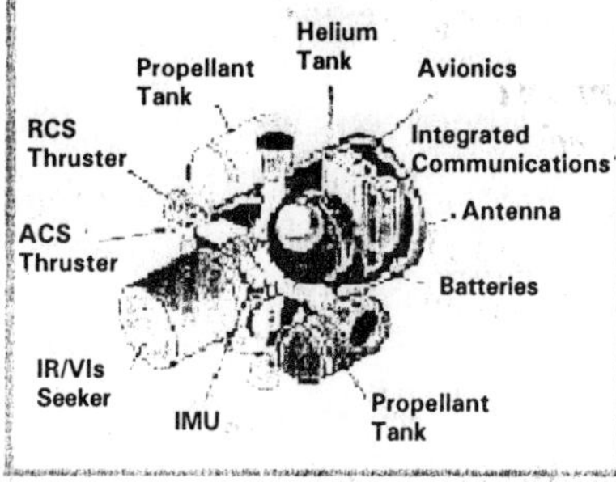

KV Characteristics

- Multispecial Passive Long Wavelength Infrared Seeker
- Guidance and Navigation
  - Interferometric Fiber Optic Gyroscope Inertial Measurement Unit
  - Solid-state Accelerometers
- Divert Propulsion
  - Liquid Bipropellant
  - High Acceleration
- Cold Gas Attitude Control System

in the central Pacific Ocean, to demonstrate the booster's interfaces with a simulated kill vehicle.

Payload Launch Vehicle (PLV). Until the off-the-shelf booster is available, flight tests are conducted using the Lockheed Martin PLV. The PLV consists of the second and third stages of retired Minuteman II boosters, modified as necessary to function as first and second stages. PLV performance is adequate for testing, but is insufficient for single-site coverage of all 50 states.

The Ground Based Interceptor

Weapon Support System (WSS). The WSS consists of the command, launch, readiness, training, and maintenance equipment used to support interceptor deployment and testing. The WSS acts as the interface between the BMC3 element and the interceptor before launch. It also supports the physical and environmental needs of the deployed interceptor.

Frequently Asked Questions:

How much does the PLV cost?

The Payload Launch Vehicle (PLV) is a component of the Ground-Based Interceptor (GBI) and ranges in cost between $12M–$18M.

How much does the EKV cost?

The Exoatmospheric Kill Vehicle (EKV) is a component of the GBI and ranges in cost between $30M–$35M.

How much does the Target Array cost?

The Target Array ranges in cost between $20M–$25M. The current configuration of the Target Array includes such things as the validated GBI Target (Minuteman II with the front section MSLS payload), PLV Booster, and support costs.

Summary

The evolutionary development of the NMD Weapon System element provides a low risk methodical approach to best address hit-to-kill intercept technical and performance issues. The planned test and evaluation program provides for periodic demonstrations of increased defense capability as hardware, software, and supporting NMD elements become available. The EKV represents a concerted effort by the Ballistic Missile Defense Organization to develop a viable defense against a limited ballistic attack using existing technologies.

Ballistic Missile Defense Organization
External Affairs
7100 Defense Pentagon
Washington, D.C. 20301-7100
(703) 697-8472

11

National Missile Defense Joint Program Office

Background

"Any acquisition system, subsystem, component, or technology program that involves a strategy that includes funding by more than one DoD Component during any phase of a system's life cycle shall be defined as a joint program."

—DoD Regulation 5000.2 (Section 3.3.5.3)

Since the National Missile Defense program currently includes significant Army, Air Force, and Ballistic Missile Defense Organization elements, DoD policy dictates the establishment of a Joint Program Office to provide the program manager with unambiguous authority and responsibility, and to create the management structure necessary to achieve multi-service interoperability. The JPO consists of personnel from all the military services, as well as Defense Department civilian employees.

On April 9, 1996, in a memorandum to the Director of the Ballistic Missile Defense Organization (BMDO), the Undersecretary of Defense for Acquisition and Technology (USD(A&T)) designated National Missile Defense (NMD) as a Major Defense Acquisition Program (MDAP). The program was placed in acquisition category (ACAT) 1D. This ACAT designation means the Defense Acquisition Executive will be the milestone decision authority for the NMD program. Further, USD (A&T) tasked the Director of BMDO, in his role as the BMD Acquisition Executive (BMDAE), to establish an NMD Joint Program Office headed by a Program Manager reporting directly to the BMDAE. This task was accomplished on 1 April 1997.

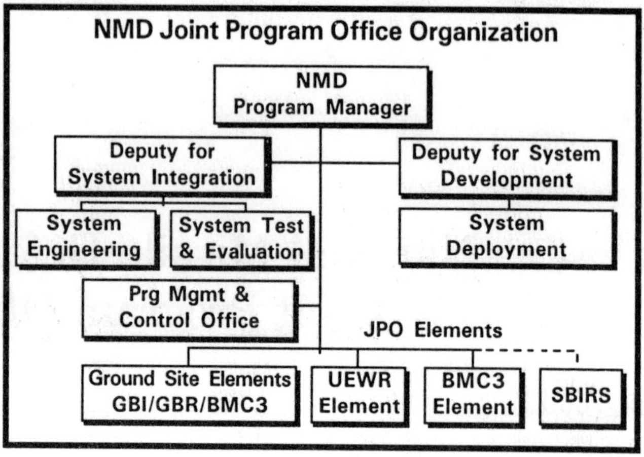

The NMD system is comprised of multiple-Service elements which include the Ground Based Interceptor (GBI), Battle Management/Command, Control, and Communications (BM/C3), X Band Ra-dar (XBR), Upgraded Early Warning Radar (UEWR), and the Defense Sup-port Program (DSP) and Space Based Infrared Systems (SBIRS) satellites, both Low and High. The goal of the JPO is to integrate these elements into a cost effective and operationally sound system designed to protect all 50 states from a ballistic missile attack.

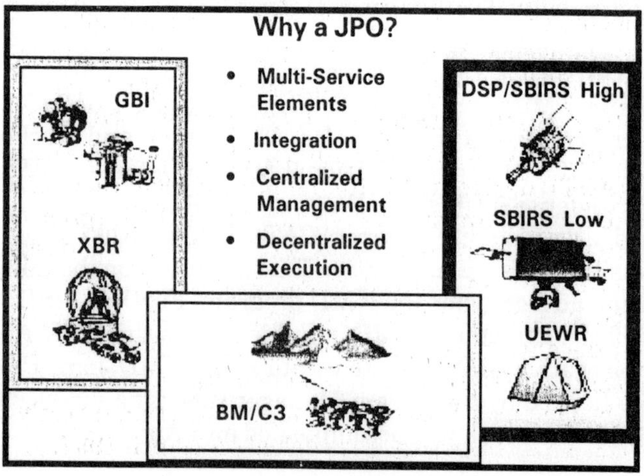

Reasons for JPO

- Provide centralized management for program efficiency with decentralized execution to obtain the best available teams to accomplish the program;
- Manage the NMD Program;
- Maintain flexibility to incorporate new or future subsystems developed by the Services;
- Ensure an objective, balanced view that avoids single Service solutions;
- Manage acquisition/contracting strategy through the Lead System Integrator.

JPO Organization

The JPO is a federated organization has a "flat" structure: Each project manager reports directly to the Joint Program Manager. The NMD Joint Program Manager works directly for the Director of BMDO in his role as the BMDAE. The JPO has overall management and integration as the main focus. The Army offices in Huntsville, AL, focus primarily on the ground systems. BM/C3 development is managed by the JPO and is executed jointly in Boston, MA; Huntsville; and Colorado Springs, CO, and SBIRS development is focused at the Air Force facilities in Los Angeles, CA.

Conclusion

Since its reception, the NMD JPO has overseen three successful NMD Integrated Flight Tests (IFTs). Currently the JPO is preparing for its fourth IFT, which will feature the second intercept attempt of a simulated threat.

Offices and Organizations Responsible for NMD Development

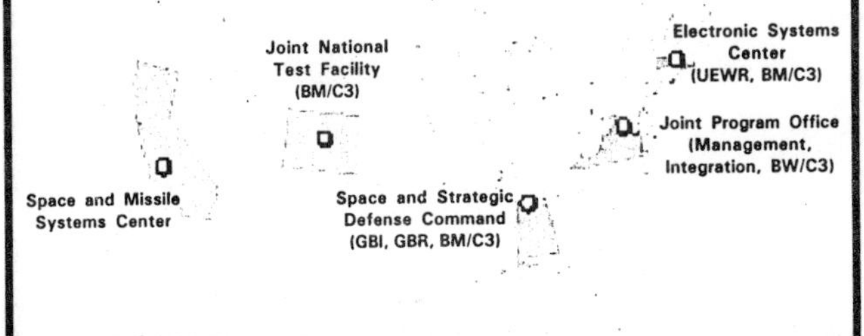

The JPO provides the NMD Program with a centralized management facility to oversee its current development phase. Given the variety of participating organizations, the JPO's existence is a vital element in ensuring the success of NMD. The JPO will provide the DoD and the BMDO with the means to coordinate activities between the Services, allow for integration of new developments, and provide a balanced, joint approach to the entire program. The JPO is an example of the DoD's commitment to joint activity within the military, combining Service resources to meet the challenges of the future.

Ballistic Missile Defense Organization, External Affairs
7100 Defense Pentagon
Washington, D.C. 20301-7100
(703) 695-8743

12

Senator Cochran Stresses Need for Missile Defense System

Missile Defense is needed in a world where some nations actively spread missile technology to regimes that are unfriendly to the United States, according to Senator Thad Cochran (Republican of Mississippi).

"If there were no missiles, there would be no need for a missile defense system," Cochran, the chairman of the Senate Governmental Affairs Subcommittee on International Security, Proliferation and Federal Services said in a February 14 speech to fellow lawmakers.

"The Australian Foreign Minister noted last week that until now, a lot of the debate has been directed at the United States," Cochran said.

"I frankly think an awful lot of the debate should instead be directed not only toward those countries that have got or are developing these missile systems but the countries that have been transferring that missile technology to others," he added.

Cochran, who authored the National Missile Defense Act of 1999, acknowledged that "not every nation welcomes our NMD plans."

"France still has not embraced the concept, and Russia and China continue their opposition," he said.

But that opposition "shouldn't change our plans to deploy missile defenses," he continued.

Implementing Missile Defense, he said, "threatens no nation, although it will create an obstacle" for those who would threaten America.

"Those who mean us no harm have nothing to fear from

this purely defensive system," Cochran said. "Those who do mean us harm will learn that the United States will no longer commit itself to continuing vulnerability."

Cochran observed that some opponents of Missile Defense deployment "point to diplomatic initiatives and political change as evidence that the threat is diminishing."

But despite North Korean leader Kim Jong Il's effort to present a more open face to the world, "little has actually changed with respect to North Korea's proliferation activities," Cochran said, citing recent testimony by Central Intelligence Agency Director George Tenet.

"The Bush administration's resolve to deploy missile defenses is an essential first step in modernizing our national security assets," he said.

Following is a transcript of Senator Cochran's February 14 speech from the Congressional Record:

National Missile Defense System
U.S. Senate
February 14, 2001

Mr Cochran: Mr President, I take this time to respond to those who are suggesting we put off, or even cancel, the deployment of a national missile defense system.

One reason the critics of the program are giving for delay is the alleged opposition of our allies, particularly those in Europe. Earlier this month at the Munich Conference on International Security, Secretary of Defense Donald Rumsfeld made a forceful case for deployment of a defense against strategic ballistic missiles. He explained the rationale for our missile defense program, and he also made it clear that this administration intends to deploy such a system as soon as possible.

He told those attending the conference that deploying a missile defense system was a moral issue because "no U.S. President can responsibly say his defense policy is calculated and designed to leave the American people undefended against threats that are known to exist."

Former Secretary of State Kissinger, who negotiated the 1972 Anti-Ballistic Missile Treaty, also spoke at the conference. He said a U.S. President cannot allow a situation in which "extinction of civilized life is one's only strategy."

The response from our European allies was very encouraging. For months, critics have been saying that our allies firmly oppose our plans to deploy missile defenses and would never go along with them. But the Secretary General of NATO, George Robertson, said: Now the Europeans have to accept that the Americans really intend to go ahead....... Now that the question of "whether" it's going to happen has been settled, I want an engagement inside NATO between the Americans and other allies about the "how" and the "when."

With respect to the threat, Secretary General Robertson said: The interesting point is that there is now a recognition by leaders—American, European, and even Russian—that there is a new threat from the proliferation of ballistic missiles that has got to be dealt with. The Americans have said how they're going to deal with it. The Europeans are being offered a chance to share in that.

Robertson also added: The concept of mutually assured destruction is obsolete. The old equation no longer works out: Russia and the United States in a balance of terror. Now there are groups and States acquiring missile technology and warheads with great facility. We are living in a dangerous new world.

Germany's views are also changing. Chancellor Gerhard Schroeder, addressing fellow Social Democratic Party members, said recently, "We should be under no illusions that there will be no difference of opinion with the new American leadership under President George W. Bush. First and foremost, it won't be about the planned National Missile Defense program but about trade policy issues. Differences over NMD are not the decisive factors in the German-American relationship." German Foreign Minister Fischer said that NMD "above all is a national decision for the United States." In Moscow this week, he said, "in the end, the Russians are going to accept it somehow."

Here in Washington last week, Britain's Foreign Secretary said, "On the question of what happens if national missile defense proceeds; if it means the U.S., feels more secure and therefore feels more able to assert itself in international areas of concern to us, we would regard that as a net gain in security." And the Prime Minister of Canada, who just a few months ago had joined Russian President Putin in calling for preservation of the ABM Treaty, said last week after consulting with President Bush, "Perhaps we are in a different era."

The Australian Foreign Minister noted last week that until now, a lot of the debate has been directed at the United States. I frankly think an awful lot of the debate should instead be directed not only toward those countries that have got or are developing these missile systems but the countries that have been transferring that missile technology to others. . . . If there were no missiles, there would be no need for a missile defense system.

Dr. Javier Solana of Spain, former Secretary-General of NATO and now the director of foreign policy for the European Union, said "The United States has the right to deploy" an NMD system. Of the ABM Treaty, the so-called "cornerstone of strategic stability," Dr. Solana said, "It is not the Bible."

The words we now hear from our European and other important allies are signaling changed attitudes. I think they have been influenced by the Bush administration's willingness to confront the NMD issue squarely, to consult fully with our allies, and to make clear a determination to protect this nation and its allies from long-range ballistic missile attack. The best ally is a strong one, and the actions of the Bush administration are an overdue reassurance that the United States will indeed be a strong alliance partner.

Of course, not every nation welcomes our NMD plans. France still has not embraced the concept, and Russia and China continue their opposition. But this shouldn't change our plans to deploy missile defenses. Our action threatens no nation, although it will create an obstacle for those who would threaten the U.S. Those who mean us no harm have nothing to fear from this purely defensive system; those who do mean us harm will learn that the United States will no longer commit itself to continuing vulnerability.

Another reason for proceeding as soon as possible to deploy missile defenses to protect the United States was highlighted last week in testimony presented to the Senate by the Director of Central Intelligence, George Tenet.

He said, "we cannot underestimate the catalytic role that foreign assistance has played in advancing . . . missile and WMD programs, shortening the development times, and aiding production." He noted that it is increasingly difficult to predict those timelines, saying "The missile and WMD proliferation problem continues to change in ways that make it harder to monitor and control, increasing the risks of substantial surprise." Director Tenet went on to say, "It is that foreign assistance piece that you have to have that very precise intelligence to understand, and sometimes you get it and sometimes you don't."

Because of the difficulty monitoring foreign assistance, Director Tenet added that "these time lines all become illusory."

He also noted that it is a mistake to think of nations who aspire to obtain missiles as technologically unsophisticated: "we are not talking about unsophisticated countries. When you talk about Iraq and Iran, people need to understand these are countries with sophisticated capabilities, sophisticated technology, digital communications."

And the danger does not stop when one of these nations acquires the technology that is now so freely available. Mr. Tenet warned about what he termed "secondary proliferation":

There is also great potential for secondary proliferation, for maturing state-sponsored programs such as those in Pakistan, Iran and India. Add to this group the private companies, scientists and engineers in Russia, China and India who may be increasing their involvement in these activities taking advantage of weak or unenforceable national export controls and the growing availability of technologies. These trends have continued, and in some cases have accelerated over the past year.

The Director of Central Intelligence added, "So you know, the kind of technology flows that we see from big states to smaller states and then the inclination of those people who do the secondary proliferation I think is what's most worrisome to me."

Some who oppose missile defense deployment point to diplomatic initiatives and political change as evidence that the threat is diminishing. For example, they point to recent efforts by North Korea's leader Kim Jong Il to present a more open face to the world. But according to the Director of Central Intelligence, little has actually changed with respect to North Korea's proliferation activities. For example, he testified, Pyongyang's bold diplomatic outreach to the international community and engagement with South Korea reflect a significant change in strategy. The strategy is designed to assure the continued survival of Kim Jong Il by ending Pyongyang's political isolation and fixing the North's failing economy by attracting more aid. We do not know how far Kim will go in opening the North, but I can report to you that we have not yet seen a significant diminution of the threat from North to American and South Korean interests.

Pyongyang still believes that a strong military, capable of projecting power in the region, is an essential element of national power. Pyongyang's declared military-first policy requires massive investment in the armed forces, even at the expense of other national objectives ..... [T]he North Korean military appears, for now, to have halted its near decade-long slide in military capabilities. In addition to the North's longer-range missile threat to us, Pyongyang is also expanding its short- and medium-range missile inventory, putting our allies at risk.

Similar claims about diminishing threats have been made about Iran. A year ago, those who oppose missile defense were suggesting that because of the election of reform-minded leaders we need no longer worry about that country obtaining more capable missiles. Here is what the Director of Central Intelligence had to say about Iran in his testimony last week:

Iran has one of the largest and most capable ballistic missile programs in the Middle East. It's public statements suggest that it plans to develop longer-range rockets for use in a space-launch program. But Tehran could follow the North Korean pattern and test an ICBM capable of delivering a light payload to the United States in the next few years .....

Events in the past year have been discouraging for positive change in Iran. Prospects for near-term political reform in the near term are fading. Opponents of reform have not only muzzled the open press, they have also arrested prominent activists and blunted the legislature's powers. Over the summer, supreme leader Khamenei ordered the new legislature not to ease press restrictions, a key reformist pursuit, that signaled the narrow borders within which he would allow the legislature to operate.

I hope that reformers do make gains in Iran, although senior CIA officials have testified that Iranian "reformers"—such as President Khatemi—are enthusiastic about acquiring ballistic missiles. I hope Iran will one day be a thriving democracy. But that day has not arrived, and our security policy cannot be based on hope.

We need missile defense not just because of the capabilities of particular countries, but because of the larger problem: The proliferation of missile technology has created a world in which we can no longer afford to leave ourselves vulnerable to an entire class of weapons. Remaining vulnerable only guarantees that some nation will seize upon this vulnerability and take the United States and our allies by surprise.

The Bush administration's resolve to deploy missile defenses is an essential first step in modernizing our national security assets. Because of the neglect our missile defense program has suffered over the last eight years, we now face a threat against which we will have no defense for several years. Because of decisions made by the previous administration, the only long-range missile defense we have in the near-term will be the ground-based system planned for initial deployment in Alaska. Additional resources must be provided so that other technologies and basing modes can be developed and tested. But now, we must move forward as fast as we can with the technology we have today. We must not prolong our vulnerability by waiting for newer and better technology. Therefore, it is important that the administration immediately begin construction of the NMD radar at Shemya, AK. Construction of the national missile defense radar at Shemya, AK, should begin immediately.

Construction of this radar was to have begun this May, but last September President Clinton postponed the decision to proceed, citing delays with other elements of the system and a lack of progress in convincing Russia to modernize the ABM Treaty to permit NMB deployment. However, construction of the Shemya radar is the so-called "long-lead" item in deployment of the NMD system; it is the step that takes the longest and must begin the soonest. Delaying construction of the NMD radar means delaying deployment of the entire system, and we cannot afford more unnecessary delays in this program.

There is still time to recover from the delays caused by President Clinton's postponement last fall. The radar design is complete, the funds have been appropriated, and any missile defense system we build will have to begin with an X-band radar at Shemya. So we should get on with it.

Beginning construction of the Shemya radar will be a demonstration of the determination of our government to fulfill its first constitutional duty, which is to provide for the security of our Nation. It will send an unmistakable signal to all—friend or potential foe—that the United States will not remain vulnerable any longer to those who threaten us with ballistic missiles.

13

Rumsfeld Deems Missile Shield System Feasible

U.S. Defense Secretary Donald Rumsfeld says the Bush administration is reviewing various options for the development and deployment of a missile defense system aimed at protecting the United States from a limited ballistic missile attack.

President Bush has concluded that "vulnerability for the American people is not an appropriate strategy," Rumsfeld said February 14 during an interview on the PBS television "NewsHour with Jim Lehrer."

Rumsfeld said that he is certain the technology to build and deploy such an anti-missile system is feasible, and imperative given that the proliferation of ballistic missiles across the world has become pervasive.

"We are not talking about a shield to deal with tens and hundreds of thousands of these things," he said, but a system to deal with limited attacks. He added that, in his view, Russia's concern about the proposed missile defense system "is not really serious" because Moscow has thousands of missiles "and we are talking about dealing with handfuls" of them.

Rumsfeld said he is not certain why Russian officials have objected so strongly to the proposed defense system, but he added:

"Let's be very honest about what Russia is doing. Russia is an active proliferator. They are part of the problem. They are selling and assisting countries like Iran and North Korea and India and other countries with these technologies which are threatening other people including the United States and Western Europe and countries in the Middle East."

Russia's concern about the United States seeking to protect

itself from missile attack seems misplaced, the secretary said, in light of that record of proliferation.

Rumsfeld also said he believes that U.S. allies in Europe can be convinced of the rationale for the proposed missile defense initiative. "They look at the degree to which proliferation is occurring and the spread of these capabilities is occurring — and I think that they will recognize, just as we do, that a position of vulnerability is not a proper policy," he said.

The Cold War is over and changes have occurred, Rumsfeld said of the new global threat environment. "We have to be attentive to the new threats," he said, and fashion deterrents that will contribute to a more peaceful and a safer world.

Following is the transcript of Rumsfeld's interview:

(Note: In the text, "billion" equals 1,000 million.)

DOD News Briefing
Secretary of Defense Donald H. Rumsfeld
Wednesday, February 14, 2001
Interview by Jim Lehrer on PBS NewsHour

Lehrer. Secretary of Defense Donald Rumsfeld, he has just begun his second tour in that position, having served earlier under President Ford. He is with us now for a Newsmaker interview. Mr Secretary, welcome.

Rumsfeld. Thank you very much.

Lehrer. First on the submarine tragedy at Pearl Harbor: is it true that VIP civilians were actually at these control stations when is this happened?

Rumsfeld. It is correct that there were — there was a group of civilians who were aboard which is a very normal thing for a situation like that. Whether, what they were doing during it is something that will be subject to the investigation. and that investigation is under with a —

Lehrer. There is no indication yet as to whether their being there had any effect that could have led to this tragedy?

Rumsfeld. None whatsoever. The investigation is in progress. And there is an admiral that is conducting it. In addition, there will be an investigation by the National Transportation

Safety Board and when those individuals complete their work, we'll know precisely what took place.

Lehrer. When do you think it will be finished? When will we know, do you think?

Rumsfeld. I don't want to put a deadline date on it — one of which is under the Department of Defense, but the other is not, and not —

Lehrer. That is the Transportation and Safety Board.

Rumsfeld. Exactly. But it is a tragic accident and I have spoken with the minister of defense of Japan and Secretary Powell has spoken with the foreign minister. And the president has spoken to the prime minister. Everything that can be — humanly done — is being done for the survivors and their families.

Lehrer. When you say it was normal to have 16 civilians on this submarine, what do you mean?

Rumsfeld. It's not unusual when a aircraft carrier, a submarine is steaming that they take distinguished visitors out who have been helpful to the Navy or helpful to one of the services. It's quite common.

Lehrer. It's public relations thing, is that it?

Rumsfeld. It is. It's a reward for work people have done to help the Navy or the Navy League—things like that.

Lehrer. But you don't know enough now to suggest that maybe this policy may be under review?

Rumsfeld. No, not at all. I think that we just have to let the investigation run its course.

Lehrer. Now, the Japanese want their sunken ship brought afloat. They want the United States to do it. Are we going to?

Rumsfeld. We have taken a submersible called the Scorpio is en route or it has arrived actually now. And it will go down to the bottom of the sea where the ship is and survey the site. It will take video pictures, and it has some arms and it could do modest recovery. When it finishes that site survey, we'll know an awful lot more about what the situation is actually down there.

Lehrer. The key to it is that the survivors want to know what happened to those nine people who are missing, is that correct?

Rumsfeld. That is certainly their interest and it is something we'll know a lot more about when the Scorpio has finished its work.

Lehrer. Mr Secretary, on more general terms, what is your reading? You been there, been secretary now, what three and a half weeks, something like that?

Rumsfeld. Barely. Barely.

Lehrer. What is your reading thus far of the state of the American military?

Rumsfeld. Well, there is no question it's the finest military on earth; that we know. It is also no question but that the world has changed dramatically since most of the capabilities of our current military were fashioned. Indeed, I find that most of the weapons systems were there when I was there. I approved the M-1 tank, and that is the main battle tank. I was at the roll out for the F-16 aircraft, and the F-15 was brand new, and I approved the B-1 bomber. That is all 25 years ago. These capabilities are what we have today in large measure. And they are good but they were designed for the Cold War. They were basically designed and fashioned and put forward because we had a major superpower on the face of the earth that was contesting the United States. The Soviet Union is gone today, and it is a very different world. Technologies have advanced tremendously. And it is time to — and the president uses the word transformation and I think properly so. If you think back in the Eisenhower period in our adult life times the last transformation really took place after World War II. And it was to move us into the Cold War. And we went from artillery pieces to ballistic missiles. We went from diesel submarines to nuclear submarines — from conventional aircraft carriers to nuclear aircraft carriers — from propeller-driven aircraft to jet aircraft. It was a significant change to overhead satellites for intelligence in communications. That was really the last major transformation.

Lehrer. And is this review that you've now been asked to do by the president; is it literally — do we really need big aircraft carriers anymore, do we really need these big tanks anymore?

Rumsfeld. Well, it is just starting. And we are clearly

going to look at, across the board and say, take a fresh look at the kind of world we are living in. And we are going to look at the — our circumstance in that world and then look at what are the kinds of threats, realistically the kinds of threats and problems and opportunities that exist given our country circumstance in the world. And they are very different from the Soviet Union period. They are quite different. We don't look to a massive tank attack across the North German plain today. We don't get up worrying about a strategic nuclear exchange, massive retaliation with the Soviet Union. The Soviet Union is gone. And the range of threats are quite different. So what we need to do is come to some conclusions about what that means for us. Now, the bulk of our force is going to be there for a long time because a ship lasts 20 years. You can only effect 1/30th, let's say you could effect 1/30th of that each year. And the same thing with aircraft; they're there a long time. But you must begin to change and transform the new things that are taking place.

Lehrer. You really mean transform. You don't mean just fix it around the edges and make the ships a little faster or smaller? You mean a major change in the way we go about this?

Rumsfeld. Well, time will tell. But I think that realistically the world has changed significantly. Technologies are advancing so rapidly. The kinds of threats we face —

Lehrer. Give me an example of something that I could understand that there is a, say that there is an existing weapons system that was, that maybe come on when you were there before, and that there is just no use for it now. What could replace that in a way? I don't mean you don't have to be too specific.

Rumsfeld. I would rather use the examples I used.

Lehrer. Okay.

Rumsfeld. The Eisenhower transformation; we went from ground communications and ground gathering intelligence to overhead satellites. Now, those same kinds of changes can take place.

Lehrer. Where would you go from overhead satellites? Is there another place to go beyond that that is a new technology that could replace overhead satellites?

Rumsfeld. Well, there are always things that you can do differently. I mean just think of what has happened recently when people went to fiber optics. We've gone from analog to digital. Take — give you an example that involved me. The M-1 tank came to me to make a decision. We always had diesel tanks and I made the decision to go to a turbine tank for the first time in the history of the world. Now, we also recently have taken that same main battle tank and gone from analog subsystems on that platform to digital subsystems. Instead of opening the top and looking out and seeing where you are going now you can receive things from satellites and targeting information and communications information. So that the same platform can leap forward in terms of utilizing advanced technologies.

Lehrer. Much has been made in the last, this week, the emphasis that the president has put on national security and defense. But much has been made over the fact that, "Wait a minute," he has said, "we are not going to spend any more money until Rumsfeld finishes this review" and Robert Kagan, a columnist for the *Washington Post,* and others have said that this really hurt Rumsfeld; he didn't know this was going to happen; he thought this was going to be more money.

Rumsfeld. Well, I don't feel hurt. The situation is first of all — just to tweak what you said — he did not say we are not going to spend any more money. He said we are not going to make big additions to the budget and I personally think that is a perfectly rational thing to do. It seems that it's not surprising that someone would want to engage their brain before they opened the taxpayers' wallets. And what we are going to do is take a look and have a review and make some judgments, and we've been in three weeks, so it's asking a lot to look at a massive department and situation like that, and a budget that is in the range of $300 billion, and then think you can quickly go before the Congress and be persuasive as to the kind of changes you want to make. So we do intend to do that review. We are going to do it fairly rapidly and I think we'll end up with some good thoughts. We'll also end up with additional reviews and work that has to be done later.

Lehrer. What do you say to those who say wait a minute, Mr Secretary, Bush the candidate says the United States military wasn't ready — there were a lot of readiness problems, it was in decline, it needed a lot of things, and now you all are saying no, no, nothing right now, we're going to review everything and it may be a while before we make changes?

Rumsfeld. Well, what you say is, look, the president is for a strong national defense. This week he is focused on quality of life and announced increases in pay and some housing improvements and some healthcare improvements for the men and women which are the heart of this whole system. People ask me what has changed in 25 years — well, what hasn't changed are the terrific humans beings that are in the armed forces of the United States. We are so fortunate they are there. So we went down to Fort Stewart and focused on that. The answer to it is that we will take a period of time and go before the Congress and make the case; the way he characterized it was what he was doing thus far is a down payment. I think that is a fair characterization.

Lehrer. Is it conceivable that — not probable but conceivable — that once you do your review, that you come back and say, wait a minute, we can do this on $300 billion; we don't need to increase defense spending — what we need to do is rearrange how we spend it — cancel this program — stop doing that and put it in new technologies and new things?

Rumsfeld. Well, I haven't done the review. But we do know that the Congressional Budget Office as a nonpartisan group has indicated they felt a significant increase was necessary just to maintain current level of capability. Harold Brown and Jim Schlesinger, two former secretaries of defense of both parties, have indicated they feel it will take an increase. I have not had that look. I simply have not had the opportunity to do it. What I do know is that savings tend to come later, not earlier; that is, for example, when you have to do things to rearrange yourself so you can save some money, you tend not to get the benefit of that — whether it's a company or a department of government — you don't get the benefit of that the first year. It tends to come in the second or third or fourth year.

Lehrer. We had a couple of retired generals on here the other night, this week, talking about this very subject. And they both said that the real problem over there — over there meaning the Pentagon, the thing you're in charge of — is that there is too much tied up in logistics and not enough in combat readiness. Like it has gone from 40 percent to 70 per cent of the expenditure — does that sound right to you?

Rumsfeld. I can't validate the numbers.

Lehrer. Sure.

Rumsfeld. But there is no question that you have to constantly be looking at your teeth to tail ratio, as they say. How much bite is there out there for what the support behind it is? And there are many articles that have suggested that the ratio has deteriorated over the years.

Lehrer. You don't have any reasons to question that at this point?

Rumsfeld. I'm in the process of looking at that type of thing.

Lehrer. Also you are going to go ahead with the missile defense system, are you not?

Rumsfeld. The president has indicated that he intends to deploy a missile defense system. We are internally now reviewing various options. He concluded — and I think fairly — that vulnerability for the American people is not an appropriate strategy.

Lehrer. Do you think a system can be developed that can do this, the technology is there?

Rumsfeld. I think that there is no question in my mind but that we will be able to evolve a system that will be able to deal with ballistic missiles. We know that the proliferation of these technologies across the globe is pervasive. We know that the Gulf War persuaded people they ought not to contest western armies and navies and — they are looking at weapons of mass destruction. Ballistic missiles, cruise missiles, terrorism and various and things where they can have an advantage, so-called asymmetrical advantage; and, therefore, it's appropriate that we develop the capability to deal with relatively small numbers of these things. We are not talking about a shield to deal with tens and hundreds of thousands of these things. And Russia's concern about it — it seems is me — is not really serious because they know for sure that they have thousands of these things (missiles) and we are talking about dealing with handfuls (of them).

Lehrer. So why have they objected?

Rumsfeld. Oh, I don't know. I don't climb in people's mind. Obviously it's to their advantage to express concern about it. There is the ABM Treaty, which they would have to adjust. I think before it's over, they will accommodate themselves. Of course, let's be very honest about what Russia is doing. Russia is an active proliferator. They are part of the problem. They are selling and assisting countries like Iran and North Korea and India and other countries with these technologies which are threatening other people including the United States and Western Europe and countries in the Middle East. So why they would be actively proliferating and then complaining when the United States wants to defend itself against the, the fruit of those proliferation activities, it seems to me, is misplaced.

Lehrer. What about the objections from Western Europe, our allies?

Rumsfeld. Well, I think what you've heard from the United States in recent years was that it was a — that the Russians didn't want to us do it. And that concerned Europe. I think Europe at this stage is going to accommodate and understand and feel the same kinds of threats that we do. I don't think that it's going to be a problem.

Lehrer. You've already been to Munich for your first meeting with your fellow defense ministers.

Rumsfeld. I have.

Lehrer. And what was your feel after the meeting? Can you win them over do you think?

Rumsfeld. Oh, I think so. I think they are realistic. These are our allies, these are people who are, you know, very rational people. They look at the nature of the threat. They look at the degree to which proliferation is occurring and the spread of these capabilities is occurring — and I think that they will recognize, just as we do, that a position of vulnerability is not a proper policy. We were comfortable during the Cold War with mutual assured destruction, with the threat of massive retaliation.

Change is hard — to go away and say, look, the Cold War is

over — it's hard for men who have spent their adult lives living with Cold War think in their mindset. And what we have to do is say, that chapter is there. We now live in a somewhat different world. There are evolving threats. Cyber warfare, information warfare, terrorism — these are things that are happening today. And we have to be attentive to the new threats and we have to fashion deterrents that will, in fact, help it contribute to a more peaceful and a safer world.

Lehrer. Personal question finally. Did you come here the second time to do this job with a particular goal or mission? What drove you to do this?

Rumsfeld. Well, I wasn't driven to do it. In fact, it came as an enormous surprise. I had no intention of coming back into government at all. And I was helpful and I was happy to be helpful.

Lehrer. You mean during the campaign?

Rumsfeld. During the campaign and then during the transition, giving him my thoughts. At some point the president decided that that is what he wanted to do and it came as a big surprise.

Lehrer. But I mean you don't have a, you didn't come with your own agenda?

Rumsfeld. Well, you know, I've not been living in a cellophane package these last 25 years, I been involved in a lot of things relating to government in terms of the use of space and the ballistic missile threat and various other — I was a Middle East envoy for President Reagan.

Lehrer. You were chair of the commission that looked at the missile threat.

Rumsfeld. I was, so I have a lot of interests and things that I think I think, but unless you get in there and have the responsibility for it, then you have to know that's what you think. And that is the process I'm engaged in.

Lehrer. All right. Mr Secretary, thank you.

Rumsfeld. Thank you.

14

Deputy Secretary-designate Wolfowitz on Defense Policy Goals

U.S. Deputy Defense Secretary-designate Paul Wolfowitz says the United States "must begin a long-overdue renovation and transformation of the armed forces" to preserve and extend peace into the 21st century.

Speaking February 27 at a confirmation hearing before the Senate Armed Services Committee, he said that Defense Secretary Donald Rumsfeld has designated three goals for the department:

- improve the quality of life, wages and morale of the U.S. armed forces as well as strike a balance among force levels, commitments and deployments;
- develop the capabilities to defend against missiles, terrorists, and threats to U.S. information systems and space assets; and
- take advantage of the technological revolution to create a 21st century military establishment.

New challenges face the United States and the global community that are quite different from the dangers of the Cold War, he said. "Amidst the peace that encompassed the developed world, ethnic conflict, regional thugs, failed states, terrorists, and the proliferation of missiles and weapons of mass destruction presented new challenges," he said. "The need, indeed the demand, for U.S. leadership increased as well."

To help in meeting those challenges, Wolfowitz said five key objectives have been set for the Defense Department—develop a deterrence for the new strategic environment; assure readiness and sustainability of the armed forces; modernize command and control, and space capabilities; reshape the defense establishment; and reform Defense Department structures, processes and organizations.

Wolfowitz said that despite declining defense budgets and a shrinking force structure, over the past 10 years the United States has increased military deployments for humanitarian and peacekeeping operations, which has added substantially to an already busy force. Renovation and transformation of the armed forces are necessary because of the challenges of the new era and the demands of a changing world, he said.

Wolfowitz, 57, has been nominated by President Bush to the number two position in the Defense Department. His nomination will be considered by the Senate Armed Services Committee, and if approved, would then go before the full Senate for approval.

Wolfowitz served in the first Bush administration as under secretary of defense for policy under then-Defense Secretary Dick Cheney from 1989-1993. He also served at Defense as deputy assistant secretary for regional programs from 1977-1980. He served in the Reagan administration as director of policy planning for the State Department and as assistant secretary of state for East Asian and Pacific Affairs. In 1986, he was appointed U.S. Ambassador to the Republic of Indonesia.

Wolfowitz is dean of the Paul H. Nitze School of Advanced International Studies at Johns Hopkins University.

Following is the text of Wolfowitz's remarks as prepared for delivery:

Prepared Statement of Dr Paul Wolfowitz for his Confirmation Hearing
Before the Senate Armed Services Committee
U.S. Senate
February 27, 2001

Senator Warner, Senator Levin, Members of the Armed Services Committee: It is an honor to appear again before this great committee, one that has done so much over the years to make our nation strong and the world more peaceful. I am grateful to the President and Secretary Rumsfeld for the confidence that they have shown in me by nominating me for a position of such great responsibility. When I think of the men and women who have sought confirmation here in the past, and the number of important laws like the Goldwater-Nichols Act that have originated with this committee, I feel truly humbled.

If confirmed by the Senate, this will be my third tour in the Pentagon. It is also the second time that I have come before this distinguished committee to seek confirmation for a senior position in the Department of Defense.

On the previous occasion, in 1989, it was a very different world. The Cold War was still a reality. Even in the heyday of Mr Gorbachev, the principal threat to our nation still came from a Soviet Union that was armed to the teeth with nuclear and conventional weapons.

We had well over 2 million men and women on active duty to deter and, if necessary, defend against this constant threat.

Twelve years ago, many observers believed that the United States was in a period of permanent decline, and many pointed to other nations as models for reforming the U.S. economy. Budget deficits were taken as a given, the personal computer was a toddler, and the Internet was a mere infant.

In the intervening years, the Cold War has become part of history, and we have fought and won a major war in the Persian Gulf. America did not decline, it prospered. We remain a vibrant world power, with a position that is in many respects unique in the history of the world.

Under these circumstances, it was only natural that our nation desired to reap a peace dividend. We reduced our defense budget by 40 per cent, and cut the force by nearly the same amount. Our defense budget was drawn down to the lowest percentage of our gross domestic product since the late 1930s.

But the world remained, in Secretary Rumsfeld's phrase, a "dangerous and untidy" place. Amidst the peace that encompassed the developed world, ethnic conflict, regional thugs, failed states, terrorists, and the proliferation of missiles and weapons of mass destruction presented new challenges. And, the need, indeed the demand, for U.S. leadership increased, as well.

Despite declining defense budgets and a shrinking force structure, in the past decade we drastically increased the number of military deployments for humanitarian and peacekeeping operations. This added greatly to the workload of an already busy force, one that was struggling to maintain its combat readiness with dedicated, but tired troops manning aging equipment. Today, as General Shelton has said, the force is "frayed."

We must begin a long overdue renovation and transformation of the Armed Forces in order to preserve and extend the peace well into the twenty-first century. President Bush has set this task as one of the highest priorities of his Administration. As the President has reminded us, peace is not ordained, it is earned; and it must be earned, in particular, by the hard and often dangerous work of our men and women in uniform.

The President has set three important goals for the Defense Department: First, we must strengthen the bond of trust with the American military. As General Creighton Abrams said when the All-Volunteer Force was first created, "people aren't in the Army, people are the Army" and the same is true of all the military services.

Building on the dedicated work of the House and the Senate, we must continue to improve military pay and quality of life. But good pay and fair allowances by themselves won't keep the best people in the service. Working with the Congress and with our allies, we must also reexamine the balance among force levels, commitments, and deployments. We will have to make sure that we are focused on the most important defense tasks, and not placing unreasonable demands on our men and women in uniform.

We will also have to acknowledge the relationship between morale and readiness. President Bush has said that "even the highest morale is eventually undermined by back-to-back deployments, poor pay, shortage of spare parts and equipment, and rapidly declining readiness." Our men and women in uniform must have first class equipment, adequate material for training and maintenance, decent barracks, modern family quarters, and suitable working conditions.

Second, we must develop the capabilities to defend against missiles, terrorists and the complex set of threats to our information systems and our all-important assets in space. U.S. power in the field is unparalleled. Many of our enemies have determined that in order to move against us, they must be able to strike us at home. Some have chosen to develop long-range missile systems. Others have chosen to support or direct terrorist attacks with conventional devices, weapons of mass destruction, or cyber weapons against our nation, our forces, or our diplomats abroad. We must do everything in our power to stop them.

Third, the Department of Defense must take advantage of the technological revolution to help us create a military for the 21st century. To this end, at the direction of the President, Secretary Rumsfeld has already launched a review of our defense strategy and programs designed to provide a sound understanding of the state of our Armed Forces and their readiness for the 21st century security environment. This work must be done quickly, and it must be done before we can know what our true defense resource requirements are. President Bush and Secretary Rumsfeld believe, as the Secretary puts it, that we need to "engage our brains before we open the taxpayer's wallet." I strongly support that approach and will work hard to shape a prompt and effective review.

In addition to that review, to support and make progress on the President's goals, the Secretary has set five key objectives for the Department of Defense:

First, we must fashion and sustain a new form of deterrence appropriate to the new strategic environment. The proliferation of missiles and weapons of mass destruction is a key element in the new strategic environment. We need new concepts and forms of deterrence to deal with it. We need a deterrence based less on massive levels of punishment or retaliation, and more on the use of both defensive and offensive means to deny our adversaries the opportunity and benefits that come from the use of weapons of mass destruction.

Second, we must assure the readiness and sustainability of our Armed Forces, now and into the future. This will require not only spending to bring up current readiness levels, but also investment in the re-capitalization and modernization efforts that our forces need to avoid being caught in the trap of making ever-increasing expenditures to maintain aging equipment.

Third, we must modernize our command and control, and space capabilities to support our 21st Century needs. Our command, control, communications, and intelligence infrastructure is the foundation of American military strength.

That infrastructure is essential for current operations and indispensable for adapting today's force to take advantage of new technology to meet 21st century challenges. As Secretary Rumsfeld has said, we must significantly improve our intelligence and space capabilities, as well as our ability to protect them against various forms of attack.

Fourth, we must begin reshaping the U.S. defense establishment to meet new challenges and take advantage of new opportunities. We face the demanding task of preparing for an uncertain future where there are many individual, unpredictable threats but no single major adversary to focus our efforts. We will have to make a stronger effort to define the key tasks and, begin to move, as President Bush has said, "beyond marginal improvements to replace existing programs with new technologies and strategies."

Building on the superb human capital of the current force, we must fashion a future force that is at once more agile, more lethal, and more rapidly deployable. It must be able to operate over increasingly longer ranges. It must integrate the capabilities of all of the services so that field commanders have the best possible combination of air, sea, and land weapons for each situation; and it must have the best technology that America can offer. Our dedicated soldiers, sailors, airmen, marines and coast guardsmen deserve no less. Finally, we must reform Department of Defense structures, processes, and organizations. We need to seek greater efficiencies not only to safeguard the taxpayer's money, but also because that will allow us to create better weapons systems and invest more in the cutting edge of our nation's defenses.

There is no more solemn responsibility that the American people entrust to the federal government than in the words of the Constitution "to provide for the common defense." There is no group of Americans who deserve more respect and honor from their fellow citizens than the men and women of our Armed Forces, who daily put themselves in harm's way for that constitutional purpose. It is both exciting and humbling to be asked again to help lead them in their work for the common defense.

Mr Chairman, it is more than just an honor to be nominated by the President to be Deputy Secretary of Defense, it is also a great responsibility. I appreciate the trust that President Bush and Secretary Rumsfeld have placed in me. If confirmed, I look forward to continuing to work closely with this committee to achieve our common goals. Indeed, I pledge to you that I will work with the Services, the Congress, and the defense industry to help the President and the Secretary prepare our Armed Forces to meet the challenges of the 21st Century.

Thank you. I look forward to your questions.

15

Rumsfeld: U.S. will Consult Closely with Allies on Missile Defense

The United States will consult closely with its allies on missile defense, Secretary of Defense Donald Rumsfeld said March 8.

"We've been spending a good deal of time reviewing the various options in respect to missile defense," said Rumsfeld, who held an impromptu media availability with German Defense Minister Rudolf Scharping after their meeting at the Pentagon.

"We perceive the American attitude as very valuable that there will be close and intensive conversations," Scharping said.

Following is the Defense Department transcript of the media availability, joined in progress:

U.S. Department of Defense
http://www.defenselink.mil
March 8, 2001
Impromptu Media Availability on Steps of Pentagon's River Entrance
Secretary Rumsfeld and Minister of Defense Rudolf Scharping of Germany

Rumsfeld: — Federal Republic of Germany and the United States. The minister of defense here is anxious to hear your questions and respond in full, and I will applaud.

Q: Are there any worries about the German defense budget?

Scharping: Are there American worries?

Rumsfeld: The subject really didn't come up in our discussions.

Q: But would you have any worries? There is definitely concern about that in Germany.

Scharping: There has been much debate about the budget 2001 in Germany, and I assured the defense committee and the (inaudible) finance minister that we need no additional monies this year. That was a remark only for this year. Now they are trying to find out if I can get some American support for the defense budget debate in Germany.

Rumsfeld: Then my initial instinct was correct. (Laughter) I'll leave the internal domestic discussions among the Germans.

Q: Mr. Secretary, can we talk about NMD? Any changes of opinion since you have been in Munich between the German and the American (inaudible)?

Rumsfeld: We did not get into those nuances. We did talk about the subject and I can tell you where we are. We've been spending a good deal of time reviewing the various options in respect to missile defense and have begun to develop some political rethinking about the (inaudible) National Security Council and the president, and that stage is ahead of us again. At which point then, we would very likely have discussions with the congress, and at the point where we think we have some ideas that fit the President's goal. We then, of course, would consult closely with our allies in Germany and others.

Q: [in German]

Scharping: With respect to my colleague I will answer in English, and then in German.

First of all, the German government continuously said there is enough time for intensive conversations within NATO and with others. And we perceive the American attitude as very valuable that there will be close and intensive conversations. We understood that the American administration has not changed the wording of it, because the real differences we are talking about — missile defense or about the national missile defense project which focused on the United States and territories.

Q: If the Germans want to participate from the American missiles system. [sic] They won't get it for free, so what do they expect from the German side regarding a ballistic missile system?

Rumsfeld: I think you're about eight steps ahead of where we are in our thinking.

People talk about theater missile defense and national missile defense. What's national depends on where you live. I don't really use the word national missile defense. I think (inaudible).

What we have is a world where the proliferation of these technologies, the weapons of mass destruction and the ability to deliver them is pervasive, and we know that. We know that these weapons are enormously powerful and can do great damage.

The United States and its friends and allies around the world as well as our deployed forces are all of interest to us. The kind of question you're properly probing for can only be answered at the point where we've completed the process I just described and then have an opportunity to talk to people about what kinds of things conceivably can be done over some period of time.

Q: What do you think that the Germans could offer?

Rumsfeld: That is impossible to answer that until you end up, as I say, complete the process we are engaged in which is an orderly one. And there will be plenty of time for those kinds of questions.

I'll leave the minister here. You can answer for yourself...

(Rumsfeld departs)

Q: Minister Scharping, [in German].

Scharping: [in German].

16

Developing Revolutionary Technology Requires Patience

Address by Lt. Gen. Ronald T. Kadish, USAF
Director, Ballistic Missile Defense Organization
At the Military Appreciation Banquet
Hosted by the Greater Fairbanks Chamber of Commerce, Alaska
Friday, March 2, 2001

Thank you, Senator Stevens, for that generous introduction. Chairman Burns, Mayor Boyles, distinguished guests at the head table, and most particularly distinguished awardees, ladies and gentlemen. I am deeply honored to be with you here this evening, and I particularly want to thank you, Senator Stevens, for extending the invitation. It's also a special pleasure to be part of this annual celebration of the military in your community.

To you, our awardees, I offer my sincere congratulations. The roll call of your achievements makes me proud. Not just everyone in this room, but also our nation, is grateful for your service and your professionalism. Well done.

And I am equally as proud of the spouses here tonight. I understand the sacrifices you've had to make — I've gotten a few reminders of them myself over the years. It's not easy to pull up your roots and lay them down again each time your family receives another set of orders. We couldn't do our jobs half as well if we didn't have your backing, and we are grateful. Yours is a crucial role, too often under-appreciated. Thank you.

I'm the Director of the Ballistic Missile Defense Organization. I'm responsible for missile defense programs, the budget for which runs about $4 billion a year. The organization has about 500 employees working to turn technology into functioning systems.

I am here tonight to talk to you about ballistic missile defense. There's a lot about it that is misunderstood.

Let me take you back to September 8, 1944, when residents of London sat down to dinner. The quiet of that autumn evening was suddenly shattered by a terrific explosion that shook their world. Sixteen seconds later, just 15 miles to the northeast, a second German V-2 exploded in the village of Epping. The era of ballistic missiles had begun, and the world was changed forever.

Over the next eight months, the Germans rained some 3000 V-2 rockets on allied targets, mostly London and Antwerp, killing over 5,000 people and terrorizing hundreds of thousands more. According to Winston Churchill, "[They] imposed ... a burden perhaps even heavier than the air raids of 1940–1941. Suspense and strain were more prolonged. Dawn brought no relief, and cloud no comfort. ... The blind impersonal nature of the missile made the individual on the ground feel hopeless." Perhaps he put it best with his words: "The Angel of Death is abroad in the land, only you can't always hear the flutter of its wings."

During World War II, the only effective defenses were to attack the V-2 factories and launching sites or to occupy the territory from which they could be launched. That fact hasn't changed in 50 years for the United States — today we still have no defense against ballistic missiles after they've been launched.

The current movie, "Thirteen Days," a recount of the 1963 Cuban missile crisis, is a reminder to a whole new generation of Americans how close this country came to nuclear war. I'm not in the habit of plugging movies, but I recommend it to those who have not seen it.

Nuclear war, the unthinkable, almost happened. Former Secretary of Defense McNamara, a principal at the time and an advisor to this film project, certainly believes so. Thirty years later, the Russians told McNamara that Fidel Castro and Che Guevara had urged the Soviets to launch their missiles at the United States despite the fact that America's overwhelming power was just 90 miles away. Castro was not deterred and was willing to sacrifice his country and "die beautifully" in the process. Anastas Mikoyan, the Soviet Vice-Premier at the time — and happily more in control of the missiles than either Fidel or Che

— said, "We see your willingness to die beautifully, but we don't believe it's worth dying beautifully for."

The Soviets were deterred. Castro was not. The missiles were removed from Cuba.

While deterrence has worked in the standoff between the superpowers, this exchange emphasizes the fragility of deterrence in today's more complex world, and it raises questions today about relying solely on deterrence as a final measure of security.

Now let's fast forward to the Gulf War, just ten years ago. Televised images of Israeli citizens donning gas masks in anticipation of Scud raids illustrate just how well Saddam Hussein learned the lessons of the V-2. Who can forget the 28 US service men and women killed when an Iraqi Scud hit their barracks outside Dhahran, well behind the front lines?

What you may not remember is the very close call we had at El Jubayl, an important Saudi offloading and staging port within the range of Iraqi Scuds. A Scud missile landed just off the pier, narrowly missing an amphibious assault ship, the USS Tarawa, along with two tankers carrying aviation fuel, a cargo ship, a Polish hospital ship and a U.S. Army barge. The pier itself was crammed with ammunition and fuel trucks.

As in World War II, to counter these attacks, a major portion of coalition aviation assets was consumed attempting to locate and destroy the launchers and support facilities.

The lessons here seem pretty clear from a warfighting perspective, even without weapons of mass destruction ... Ballistic missiles inflict major disruption on military operations on the front lines and behind. And they create great anxiety among civilian populations who happen to be within range — ballistic missiles are indeed a terror weapon.

Now let's consider the current debate about missile defense. Recalling what former Senator Sam Nunn said more than a decade ago, "We ought to do something unusual in Washington. We ought to let the facts speak for themselves."

Just what are the key facts?

Fact One: The missile threat our nation faces today is far different than the one we faced two or three decades ago. Yes, Russia still has the capability to launch a massive attack on the United States, but the likelihood of that happening has receded dramatically. Similarly, China has a limited but escalating ICBM inventory. What is particularly worrisome, however, is the worldwide proliferation of ballistic missiles of all ranges, and of programs to develop weapons of mass destruction.

When the ABM Treaty was signed in 1972, there were only nine nations that had a ballistic missile capability. Today, almost three decades later, over 30 nations have such capability. Unfortunately, a number of these may pose a threat to the United States, to our allies, or to our troops overseas.

In spite of our counter-proliferation policies, our efforts have merely slowed, not stopped, this proliferation. Some nations have played a catalytic role in pushing these technologies, but the fact of the matter is that over the past 50 years the world's knowledge of missiles and weapons has blossomed. What used to be on the shelves of a few select scientific libraries is now on the Internet, available to just about all who want it. What remains, of course, are the actual engineering challenges, the business of manufacturing and production, yet slowly but surely these are being overcome.

In laying out this picture of the threat our nation faces, I'm reminded of the observation of the Marquis of Salisbury: "If you believe the doctors, nothing is wholesome; if you believe the theologians, nothing is innocent; if you believe the soldiers, nothing is safe." To extend this to the context of missile defense, let me go two further: If you believe our missile defense critics, nothing will work. If you believe passionate advocates, we can do it tomorrow.

The truth is to be found somewhere between these two extremes.

Fact Two: Intercepting a ballistic missile in space is a tough technical and management challenge — tough science and tough engineering — and has been ever since ballistic missiles were invented. But it is not impossible. We are now on the threshold of acquiring and deploying missile defenses, not just conducting research. We are, in fact, crossing over from rhetoric to reality, from scientific theory to engineering fact to deployed systems.

The first systems we will deploy provide close-in defense to intercept a short-range missile in its terminal phase. These include the Army's PAC-3, expected to be operational later this year. It is a greatly improved version of the Patriot missile that gained such notoriety in the Gulf. A few years later, we expect to deploy the Navy Area system that builds on existing fleet air defense capability. Both these systems are limited to defending a relatively small area.

These systems will be followed by the Army's THAAD and Navy Theater Wide systems later in the decade. These will both reach out farther back along the ballistic missile's incoming trajectory and so defend a wider region.

There's one inflexible rule about missile defense — the later you detect and intercept an enemy missile, the closer it will be when you destroy it, and the smaller the area you can defend. Conversely, the earlier you can detect, decide, and act, the farther away it will be when you destroy it, and the greater the area you can defend. In this business, farther is better; it gives you enough time to gain a chance for a second or third shot if you miss.

The National Missile Defense (NMD) system we've been working on destroys missile warheads in midcourse, the longest time of flight for a trajectory. Because it can reach so far out, it has the potential of defending a much larger area — in this case, the United States. To do this we employ space-based and ground-based sensors, (the eyes, if you will, to see the launch and track the flight). We have a battle management system that interprets the information from the sensors, verifies if the missile is hostile, and determines the best point for intercept. Then, under human direction, it launches the interceptor, which we call a kinetic energy kill vehicle.

Currently we have a small, 120 pound kill vehicle with its own guidance and sensing system. Once lifted into space and pointed in the right direction, on its final leg, it can steer itself into the target and obliterate the warhead by violent impact. That collision occurs at speeds of about 15,000 miles an hour or more, so there's not much left of the target reentry vehicle at those speeds.

This is called hit-to-kill — hitting a bullet with a bullet. Traditional explosives don't work well in space, and the nuclear tipped interceptors on which we relied 25 years ago — and on which the Russians still rely — have major political and operational drawbacks.

We've achieved success with hit-to-kill not once, but seven times out of the last ten attempts in the past two years, with three different systems. Nevertheless, the development road for missile defense has been bumpy. Despite the successes, we still haven't achieved the degree of reliability we need. Each of the major programs is behind schedule. Our NMD program, for example, has had one hit followed by two well-publicized failures in our three intercept flight tests so far.

I relearned a basic truth in missile defense: that success occurs in private and failure in full view. That they were well publicized is an understatement. Despite our high profile failures, we have made significant progress in developing this system.

So, to restate the second fact: This is rocket science, and it is difficult, but not impossible. Seven hundred years ago, the current wisdom held that sailors who ventured too far from land would fall off the edge of the Earth. Columbus proved them wrong. Seventy years ago, naysayers were saying that rockets wouldn't work in space because there was no air to push against. Robert Goddard proved them wrong. Seven years ago, critics were still saying we couldn't hit a missile in space. We've done it. Now they say, "OK, you can hit it. But it will be fooled by decoys and countermeasures, so you shouldn't build it."

That leads to Fact Three: You need patience to bring about revolutionary technology. Testing, by its nature, lends itself both to failures and to the successes that rise from their ashes. Wernher von Braun, who served as the project leader for the German V-2 program and later pioneered America's space and missile program, experienced many failures. He named these setbacks "successful failures" because he and his teams learned so much from them — a feature about high tech development our critics tend to forget.

Do they remember that the Atlas ICBM program experienced 12 failures in its 2½-year flight-testing history; that the Minuteman-1 ICBM program suffered 10 failures in a 3½ year testing program; and that the Corona program, for our country's first operational reconnaissance satellite, survived 13 failures and mishaps before Discoverer 14 was orbited and its film recovered?

Yet through it all, patience by our leadership was essential — then and now — despite frustrations resulting from these technical difficulties. I'm talking about national leadership here, the kind of support and patience shown by Senator Stevens, who has championed the cause of missile defense. And I'm talking about the local level support and leadership represented here in this room. This is leadership through vision and patience, the kind that pushed earlier programs through their trials to success.

Our test program follows a deliberate step-by-step approach that builds on simulations, ground testing, and risk reduction flights that don't involve an intercept attempt.

As you listen to the debate unfold, remember these facts. The threat is different today than ten or twenty years ago. In their book on the "V" weapons, Impact, Benjamin King and Timothy Kutta said it best:

> . . .the technology [of the 'V' weapons] is readily available to those who want it. The Scud is only one descendant of 'V' weapons. Today, there are literally thousands of them across the world. We live in their shadow and they will not go away.

Missile defense is rocket science. We are on the threshold of solving the tough issues of defending against those ballistic missiles. We still have some stiff challenges ahead of us, but we are making remarkable progress. And while we have exceptionally talented and dedicated people working the demanding technical issues, we can't be successful without your patience and support.

My congratulations again to our awardees this evening, and congratulations to the military community in Fairbanks for having such wonderful neighbors.

17

US Missile Defense Director Cites Progress, Challenges

(The following article by Lieutenant General Ronald Kadish, director of the Ballistic Missile Defense Organization (BMDO), is adapted from a speech he made to the Greater Fairbanks Chamber of Commerce in Alaska on March 2.)

As the Director of the Ballistic Missile Defense Organization, I'm responsible for missile defense programs, the budget for which runs about $4 billion ($4,000 million) a year. The organization has about 500 employees working to turn technology into functioning systems.

I want to talk about ballistic missile defense. There's a lot about it that is misunderstood.

Let me take you back to September 8, 1944, when residents of London sat down to dinner. The quiet of that autumn evening was suddenly shattered by a terrific explosion that shook their world. Sixteen seconds later, just 15 miles to the northeast, a second German V-2 exploded in the village of Epping. The era of ballistic missiles had begun, and the world was changed forever.

Over the next eight months, the Germans rained some 3,000 V-2 rockets on allied targets, mostly London and Antwerp, killing over 5,000 people and terrorizing hundreds of thousands more. According to Winston Churchill, "[They] imposed ... a burden perhaps even heavier than the air raids of 1940–1941. Suspense and strain were more prolonged. Dawn brought no relief, and cloud no comfort. ... The blind impersonal nature of the missile made the individual on the ground feel hopeless."

Perhaps he put it best with his words: "The Angel of Death is abroad in the land, only you can't always hear the flutter of its wings."

During World War II, the only effective defenses were to attack the V-2 factories and launching sites or to occupy the territory from which they could be launched. That fact hasn't changed in 50 years for the United States—today we still have no defense against ballistic missiles after they've been launched.

The current movie, "Thirteen Days," a recount of the 1963 Cuban missile crisis, is a reminder to a whole new generation of Americans how close this country came to nuclear war.

Nuclear war, the unthinkable, almost happened. Former Secretary of Defense (Robert) McNamara, a principal at the time and an advisor to this film project, certainly believes so. Thirty years later, the Russians told McNamara that Fidel Castro and Che Guevara had urged the Soviets to launch their missiles at the United States despite the fact that America's overwhelming power was just 90 miles away. Castro was not deterred and was willing to sacrifice his country and "die beautifully" in the process. Anastas Mikoyan, the Soviet Vice-Premier at the time—and happily more in control of the missiles than either Fidel or Che—said, "We see your willingness to die beautifully, but we don't believe it's worth dying beautifully for."

The Soviets were deterred. Castro was not. The missiles were removed from Cuba.

While deterrence has worked in the standoff between the superpowers, this exchange emphasizes the fragility of deterrence in today's more complex world, and it raises questions today about relying solely on deterrence as a final measure of security.

Now let's fast forward to the Gulf War, just 10 years ago. Televised images of Israeli citizens donning gas masks in anticipation of Scud raids illustrate just how well Saddam Hussein learned the lessons of the V-2. Who can forget the 28 U.S. service men and women killed when an Iraqi Scud hit their barracks outside Dhahran, well behind the front lines?

What you may not remember is the very close call we had at El Jubayl, an important Saudi offloading and staging port within the range of Iraqi Scuds. A Scud missile landed just off the pier, narrowly missing an amphibious assault ship, the USS

Tarawa, along with two tankers carrying aviation fuel, a cargo ship, a Polish hospital ship and a U.S. Army barge. The pier itself was crammed with ammunition and fuel trucks.

As in World War II, to counter these attacks, a major portion of coalition aviation assets was consumed attempting to locate and destroy the launchers and support facilities.

The lessons here seem pretty clear from a warfighting perspective, even without weapons of mass destruction. Ballistic missiles inflict major disruption on military operations on the front lines and behind. And they create great anxiety among civilian populations who happen to be within range—ballistic missiles are indeed a terror weapon.

Now let's consider the current debate about missile defense. Recalling what former Senator Sam Nunn said more than a decade ago, "We ought to do something unusual in Washington. We ought to let the facts speak for themselves."

Just what are the key facts?

Fact One: The missile threat our nation faces today is far different than the one we faced two or three decades ago. Yes, Russia still has the capability to launch a massive attack on the United States, but the likelihood of that happening has receded dramatically. Similarly, China has a limited but escalating ICBM (Intercontinental Ballistic Missile) inventory. What is particularly worrisome, however, is the worldwide proliferation of ballistic missiles of all ranges, and of programs to develop weapons of mass destruction.

When the ABM (Anti-Ballistic Missile) Treaty was signed in 1972, there were only nine nations that had a ballistic missile capability. Today, almost three decades later, over 30 nations have such capability. Unfortunately, a number of these may pose a threat to the United States, to our allies, or to our troops overseas.

In spite of our counter-proliferation policies, our efforts have merely slowed, not stopped, this proliferation. Some nations have played a catalytic role in pushing these technologies, but the fact of the matter is that over the past 50 years the world's knowledge of missiles and weapons has blossomed. What used to be on the shelves of a few select scientific libraries is now on the Internet, available to just about all who want it. What remains, of course, are the actual engineering challenges, the business of manufacturing and production, yet slowly but surely these are being overcome.

In laying out this picture of the threat our nation faces, I'm reminded of the observation of the Marquis of Salisbury: "If you believe the doctors, nothing is wholesome; if you believe the theologians, nothing is innocent; if you believe the soldiers, nothing is safe." To extend this to the context of missile defense, let me go two further: If you believe our missile defense critics, nothing will work. If you believe passionate advocates, we can do it tomorrow.

The truth is to be found somewhere between these two extremes.

Fact Two: Intercepting a ballistic missile in space is a tough technical and management challenge—tough science and tough engineering—and has been ever since ballistic missiles were invented. But it is not impossible. We are now on the threshold of acquiring and deploying missile defenses, not just conducting research. We are, in fact, crossing over from rhetoric to reality, from scientific theory to engineering fact to deployed systems. The first systems we will deploy provide close-in defense to intercept a short-range missile in its terminal phase. These include the Army's PAC-3 (Patriot Advanced Capability 3), expected to be operational later this year. It is a greatly improved version of the Patriot missile that gained such notoriety in the Gulf. A few years later, we expect to deploy the Navy Area system that builds on existing fleet air defense capability. Both these systems are limited to defending a relatively small area.

These systems will be followed by the Army's THAAD (Theater High Altitude Area Defense System) and Navy Theater Wide systems later in the decade. These will both reach out farther back along the ballistic missile's incoming trajectory and so defend a wider region. There's one inflexible rule about missile defense—the later you detect and intercept an enemy missile, the closer it will be when you destroy it, and the smaller the area you can defend. Conversely, the earlier you can detect, decide, and act, the farther away it will be when you destroy it, and the greater the area you can defend. In this business, farther is better; it gives you enough time to gain a chance for a second or third shot if you miss.

The National Missile Defense (NMD) system we've been working on destroys missile warheads in midcourse, the longest time of flight for a trajectory. Because it can reach so far out, it has the potential of defending a much larger area—in this case, the United States. To do this we employ space-based and ground-based sensors, (the eyes, if you will, to see the launch and track the flight). We have a battle management system that interprets the information from the sensors, verifies if the missile is hostile, and determines the best point for intercept. Then, under human direction, it launches the interceptor, which we call a kinetic energy kill vehicle.

Currently we have a small, 120 pound kill vehicle with its own guidance and sensing system. Once lifted into space and pointed in the right direction, on its final leg, it can steer itself into the target and obliterate the warhead by violent impact. That collision occurs at speeds of about 15,000 miles an hour or more, so there's not much left of the target reentry vehicle at those speeds.

This is called hit-to-kill—hitting a bullet with a bullet. Traditional explosives don't work well in space, and the nuclear tipped interceptors on which we relied 25 years ago—and on which the Russians still rely—have major political and operational drawbacks.

We've achieved success with hit-to-kill not once, but seven times out of the last 10 attempts in the past two years, with three different systems. Nevertheless, the development road for missile defense has been bumpy. Despite the successes, we still haven't achieved the degree of reliability we need. Each of the major programs is behind schedule. Our NMD program, for example, has had one hit followed by two well-publicized failures in our three intercept flight tests so far.

I relearned a basic truth in missile defense: that success occurs in private and failure in full view. That they were well publicized is an understatement. Despite our high profile failures, we have made significant progress in developing this system.

So, to restate the second fact: This is rocket science, and it is difficult, but not impossible. Seven hundred years ago, the current wisdom held that sailors who ventured too far from land would fall off the edge of the Earth. Columbus proved them wrong. Seventy years ago, naysayers were saying that rockets wouldn't work in space because there was no air to push against. Robert Goddard proved them wrong. Seven years ago, critics were still saying we couldn't hit a missile in space. We've done it. Now they say, "OK, you can hit it. But it will be fooled by decoys and countermeasures, so you shouldn't build it."

That leads to Fact Three: You need patience to bring about revolutionary technology. Testing, by its nature, lends itself both to failures and to the successes that rise from their ashes. Wernher von Braun, who served as the project leader for the German V-2 program and later pioneered America's space and missile program, experienced many failures. He named these setbacks "successful failures" because he and his teams learned so much from them—a feature about high tech development our critics tend to forget.

Do they remember that the Atlas ICBM program experienced 12 failures in its 2.5-year flight-testing history; that the Minuteman-1 ICBM program suffered 10 failures in a 3.5-year testing program; and that the Corona program, for our country's first operational reconnaissance satellite, survived 13 failures and mishaps before Discoverer 14 was orbited and its film recovered?

Yet through it all, patience by our leadership was essential—then and now—despite frustrations resulting from these technical difficulties. I'm talking about national leadership here, the kind of support and patience shown by Senator Stevens, who has championed the cause of missile defense. And I'm talking about the local level support and leadership represented here in this room. This is leadership through vision and patience, the kind that pushed earlier programs through their trials to success.

Our test program follows a deliberate step-by-step approach that builds on simulations, ground testing, and risk reduction flights that don't involve an intercept attempt.

As you listen to the debate unfold, remember these facts. The threat is different today than 10 or 20 years ago. In their book on the "V" weapons, Impact, Benjamin King and Timothy Kutta said it best:

". . .the technology [of the 'V' weapons] is readily available to those who want it. The Scud is only one descendant of 'V' weapons. Today, there are literally thousands of them across the world. We live in their shadow and they will not go away."

Missile defense is rocket science. We are on the threshold of solving the tough issues of defending against those ballistic missiles. We still have some stiff challenges ahead of us, but we are making remarkable progress.

18

Missile Defense Flight Test Scheduled for Summer 2001

Pentagon spokesman Rear Admiral Craig Quigley says the missile defense system will conduct an integrated flight test this year but it will once again use the Minuteman booster, not the three-stage Boeing developmental booster.

Speaking March 27 at the regular Pentagon briefing, Quigley said the next intercept test, Test 6, patterned after one that failed last July, will take place in early to mid-summer, and the new Boeing booster will be used in Test 7.

"The one we've been using for the integrated flight test so far is a Minuteman booster basically. It's a two-stage booster... It launches the systems you need to test in outer space," Quigley said.

The spokesman said that Integrated Flight Test 6 "is a near duplicate of last July's test, using just about identical components in every facet of the shot. When last July's shot failed to deploy the decoys appropriately, failed to get the separation of the kill vehicle from the booster, these were much more simplistic things. It just goes to show the incredible complexity of the overall system, I believe, from start to finish."

Asked about the delay in testing, he said "We're going to try to get it right as best we can and double check everything along the way. If we insure a higher chance of success by delaying a test a couple of weeks that has no impact on the program itself, and you get much more and better quality test data points by this marginal delay, that's a good investment." A test shot costs approximately $100 million, he said.

As to the reasons for a new booster, he said that a ground-based system such as the presently proposed missile defense system needs a three-stage booster "for the speed and the range. You obviously want to interdict any incoming missile as far away from U.S. territory as you can and as quickly as you can, and you simply don't get the speed and the range from a two-stage booster that you would from a three-stage booster."

The Defense Department's original plan, he said, was to run a series of three developmental booster tests. "What we're going to do now is have a Pathfinder test, do everything up to but short of actual launch, and do one of those, followed by two live firing tests. And then we'll see what the live firing tests have given us."

Quigley said the Defense Department hopes to conduct the first of the two live shots by late summer, and the second later in the year.

Following is the Pentagon transcript:

Presenter: Rear Adm. Craig R. Quigley
Tuesday, March 27, 2001
1:30 p.m. EST
DoD News Briefing

Quigley: Good afternoon, ladies and gentlemen. I have two announcements this afternoon.

Deputy Secretary of Defense Paul Wolfowitz will deliver brief remarks this evening at the Metropolitan Washington United Service Organizations' 18th annual awards dinner. The dinner will be held at the Ritz Carlton in Pentagon City, beginning at 7:15 p.m., with Dr Wolfowitz's remarks starting at 9:25 p.m. No press availability is planned for the event, but it is open to press coverage, if you wish to attend.

And second, we have three bluetoppers today covering three additional follow-up reports from the office of the special assistant for Gulf War illnesses. The reports concern the results of Gulf War coalition bombing of two different sites and an updated paper providing insights of the Fox tactical vehicle capabilities.

And with that, I'll take your questions. Charlie—

Q: Is Wolfowitz's speech, prepared remarks, going to be available?

Quigley: Eventually, yes.

Q: But if he's got a speech at 9:00 tonight, why can't—

Quigley: Well, I won't have them tonight, Pat. I'm sorry.

Q: Why not?

Quigley: He makes extensive changes to them. I mean, I've only seen him do a couple of speeches so far, but he makes extensive changes to them up until the time he walks up to the podium.

Q: So you're going to give it as delivered, then, huh?

Quigley: Right. Mm-hmm.

Yes, sir?

Q: Can you update us on the two crashes? There's one in Scotland, one in—

Quigley: I can, yes. The subject is the F-15 accident. A body and wreckage from one of the two F-15s reported missing yesterday was located today near the peak of a mountain in the Scottish Highlands. The body has not yet been identified.

The other aircraft and pilot have not yet been found and are listed as "whereabouts unknown" at this point. The search continues.

SAR (search and rescue) efforts were launched by the U.K. Ministry of Defense from RAF Kinloss in Scotland, and they had the lead on the search and rescue efforts. This involves approximately 200 Royal Air Force rescue personnel, police, civilian volunteers, and three different types of aircraft for air searches.

The rescue effort is severely hampered by terrible weather in the area where we continue to look—snow, 50-mile-an-hour winds, a very rugged topography. With the snow and the wind, there are whiteout conditions there. And the weather forecast, unfortunately, predicts that those sorts of conditions will remain there for the next 24 to 48 hours.

Our sincere appreciation goes out to the Royal Air Force search and rescue folks who have helped us get this far. And when it is safe to continue the search, they'll continue to do so.

Q: What was the weather like yesterday at the time of the crash?

Quigley: The weather was good yesterday, but a front came in overnight, I think, Ivan, and today it's awful.

Q: So there is no searching today?

Quigley: I'm sorry?

Q: No searching today because of the weather?

Quigley: No, the actual—the wreckage was spotted early today. And it's a front that has moved in as the day progressed; it didn't start off terrible today, but it is now the conditions that I described. So they were able to find the single crash site and get there to the point where they have recovered the remains of one of the pilots. We don't know which it is yet; they just have not been identified.

Q: Will they be able to do that work today, though, to get to the crash site?

Quigley: I don't think so, because not only is it—it's 7:30 in the evening there, but you're also considerably north, Pam, and you've got your daylight hours shortened anyway by your northern position. So I think it's pretty well dark, and with the whiteout and the weather conditions, I think they've called it quits for today.

Q: Can you define "good" for yesterday? What was the ceiling and visibility? And what they were doing? There's some conflict here. Air Force is now saying low-level training. But as we were saying here, the C model would not normally do that kind of training because that particular model of the 15 is used for CAP or high-altitude flying.

Quigley: Well, I don't have the specifics to the first part of your question, Ivan, other than having the weather described yesterday as being "good" with clear air mass, but I don't have ceilings and wind velocity and things of that sort. But it was described as "good." (One witness reported a snow storm in the area and a low ceiling.)

But the F-15C single-seater principal mission is, indeed, air to air, but it also has an air-to-ground mission. (Correction: The F-15C has no air-to-ground mission. F-15C pilots have a low altitude currency requirement and must be able to perform air-to-air employment functions while at low altitude.)

And the training that they were on was to use a Scottish range for low-level training. So they took off from Lakenheath—just for a quick timeline: the two aircraft took off from Lakenheath at about 12:30 in the afternoon, local time. And at 1:15, the RAF base in Scotland reported that they had lost radar contact. So that's 45 minutes after takeoff from Lakenheath.

Now, the planes were due back at about 2:20 local time for about a two-hour training hop. And then about an hour later, at 3:30, then they formally declared the aircraft overdue and started the search procedures at that point.

Q: Do you know what kind of ordnance, if any—was this a live-fire training exercise?

Quigley: No, there was no live ordnance on board. But each aircraft carried a single captive-carry Sidewinder, air-to-air, short-range infrared homing. This is no warhead, no rocket booster, but the seeker will—it is functional and it allows the pilot to practice engagements and get a very good feel for realism, but without a rocket motor or warhead. And that was the only ordnance on each of their planes.

Q: Were they playing in opposition to each other, or were they playing wing man? Do you know what they were doing?

Quigley: I don't have those details, John.

Q: How are they using the Scottish range then?

Quigley: That is a low-level range—low-level training. And why they particularly had one practice air-to-air missile on their wings, I don't know that yet.

Q: And they had no other coordinates—

Quigley: No.

Q: I mean no—

Quigley: No air-to-ground type of ordnance, no, no.

Yes.

Q: Actually, you said that they had recovered remains. Did you mean that? Have they actually recovered remains now?

Quigley: Yes.

Q: If I could just clarify that with you?

Quigley: Yes.

Q: So, was it a British search and rescue team that landed? Do we know who landed?

Quigley: Yes, it was.

Q: And the remains have actually been brought down off of the mountain?

Quigley: Yes.

Quigley: When you say recovered—

Quigley: That is my understanding, Chris, yes, that they've been brought down the mountain. Now where they are right now I do not know—where the remains are.

Q: Another subject—

Quigley: Any other F-15—Ivan?

Q: German crash—

Q: Well, no, but you said, "the package." Can you refer to the Army\German crash too? Anything else we know about that?

Quigley: No, nothing more as of today. I was about eight miles on a final approach into the field. Two passengers—two people—two crew members on board, both warrant officers, both were killed in the accident, but the Army has just started the accident investigation there.

Q: How is the weather there?

Quigley: I don't have that, John.

Q: Is there a—

Quigley: From the video that I have seen, it looks to be fairly decent. I saw the smoke coming up from the crash site.

Q: Is there any concern in the building about what appears to be this rash of accidents of all different types? And is Rumsfeld considering doing anything other than just watching it happen?

Quigley: Well, you're always terribly affected by the loss of life in any sort of an aircraft accident. But you have such a disparity of types of aircraft here, different parts of the world doing different missions under different circumstances. It's hard to discern any common thread that would tie all of these together.

So other than a concern, as you always would, for the loss of life, there doesn't seem to be a common cause here. They're not all the same type of airplane, they're not all in the same part of the world, they're not all doing the same sort of mission. It's very diverse. And the overall safety record for the year so far seems to be quite good, but there has been, in the numbers of accidents that we've had so far, a very high loss of life.

Q: Someone has suggested that if training was being slightly cut back, or funds for training, one of the first places it would begin to show would be in accidents. Is that a valid assumption?

Quigley: I think you'd see that in readiness reporting before you would see it in actual manifestation of accidents; where you call upon squadron commanding officers to be sensitive to the readiness and the flying hour program preparedness of their flight crews, and if they weren't meeting the marks and getting the requisite number of hours and the diversity of types of training and things of that sort, that should show up in their readiness reporting, and that has not, so far. Ultimately you could, perhaps, come to that conclusion, John, but that would not be the first thing I would think you would see.

Pam?

Q: More on that line, laymen looking at the Pentagon or at the military in general would say, "Well, it might not be all the same planes that are crashing," and indeed you had, you know, a sub accident and the training range accident in Kuwait, "but maybe the underlying common thread is the military personnel, and is the readiness of the troops." How would you address that? Do we have enough information to be able to make those links in—

Quigley: I don't think we do, not that I have seen. A lot of the instances recently have not yet been—I mean the investigations, the courts of inquiry and what have you, have not come to their conclusion as to the cause of the accidents that we've seen here recently. Some have. Some have. But not all, and you're hard-pressed to compare the findings of one with works-in-progress, if you will, on other types.

Q: Speaking of court of inquiry—

Q: (Inaudible.)

Q: Can I just—

Q: We're on the same subject?

Q: The same subject, yeah. If you compare—we're about, what, 40 per cent through the fiscal year, or something like that, if you—

Quigley: Mm, yeah. (Off mike.)

Q: Something like that. If you pro-rate that and look at the Class A rate of accidents, where are we as compared to last year, for instance?

Quigley: Well, I have year-to-date figures, and let me just go through those real quickly. We are half-way through the fiscal year, as of a couple of days from now, the end of March. This is Class A mishap rate per 100,000 flying hours. The Army is about 1.75; the Navy is about 0.99; Air Force, 1.06; and Marine Corps, 1.91.

Q: Does that include—

Quigley: So that's half-way through the fiscal year. Sorry.

Q: Does that include yesterday's accident?

Quigley: Does not include yesterday's accident. You count it differently, also, Pam. If the investigation into yesterday, where you had two F-15s involved, if there was no evidence of some sort of a collision between the two airplanes, you would count that as two events. If there was a collision, you would count that as a single event. So, since we don't know that yet, we just hold that in abeyance for now. There's a total of 38 people have lost their lives in these accidents over the course of the year. And again, that does not yet count the F-15 from yesterday, F-15s from yesterday.

Q: Does it count the Guardrail?

Quigley: Guardrail?

Q: The Army (inaudible)?

Quigley: Yes, I think so, but—yes, it did incorporate those, but not the F-15s.

Q: I suppose we could do the math, but what is the overall rate and what are the comparables for last fiscal year?

Quigley: Well, let me do the second one first, if I could. Army for last fiscal year was .96; Navy was 1.75; Air Force, 1.04; and Marine Corps, 2.63. And again, that's for fiscal year 2000, okay? And I believe I have a total DoD-wide rate at this point of 1.22. And that compares to a year ago of 1.23 overall. So we're right there on an average rate. But you have had a fairly high loss of life at the halfway point of this fiscal year, with 38 deaths. All of last year, for instance, was 58 deaths, so you're slightly ahead of that rate. We hope we don't keep up the pace.

Q: Is there an increase in accidents—in short, is there an increase in accidents or is there not?

Quigley: No, it looks as if the overall figures are right in line with where we were for the end of fiscal 2000. It's just that they have come in a tightly packed bunch, Chris, I think, that have been—and resulting in a high loss of life. The Sherpa accident coming from Florida to Virginia a few weeks ago with the Air National Guard Red Horse unit, that was a lot of people in a single accident, 21 people in a single accident. And so you've had your numbers come up in big chunks during the course of each of these accidents during the course of the year.

Q: Just parenthetic. You mentioned court of inquiry. I'm just curious, is this accidental. Any word yet as to when the court is going to make a determination or recommendation to—(inaudible)?

Quigley: No, I do not have that.

Q: Do you know, in the bombing range accident in Kuwait, what progress they are making there, who the folks have actually interviewed in terms of—

Quigley: They have interviewed some of the injured, if they're fit to be interviewed, John. And CENTCOM says as of yesterday that they're making good progress with their goal of having a report to General Franks by mid-April.

Q: I take it what you're saying here, Craig, is there's no intent now to call any kind of stand-down, 24 hours or otherwise—

Quigley: No, sir.

Q:—to stand back and look at training.

Quigley: No. Again, if you could—if you could pull a common cause here, Charlie, you might come to a different answer, but you can't. It's widely divergent circumstances in each and every case.

Yes, sir.

Q: Next week, India's foreign minister and defense minister will be here in the building. And any idea what is their mission here, meeting with the Secretary of defense? And also, does that include CTBT (comprehensive test ban treaty) or any future U.S.-India defense deals?

Quigley: I'm sorry. I have not gotten a read-out on the anticipated topics of discussion yet.

Q: And just to follow that, Pakistan's military commanders have offered—the military regime—to sign CTBT with the United States. Have you received any official or unofficial word or what is the Defense Department's views on that?

Quigley: I understand the question. I don't know the answer. Let's see if we can take that and find out an answer for that.

Otto.

Q: Back on the readiness issue, several of the CINCs have testified on the Hill today and last week, and they've all begun to—they all cited readiness concerns. CINCPAC Admiral Blair today said that his air force—the Navy and Marine fliers in the Pacific will run out of money—flying money my August if they don't get a reprogramming or a supplemental. You know, what's the status of—are we still waiting for the review before we decide whether there's going to be additional money this fiscal year?

Quigley: Yeah, you know, again, we're half-way through the fiscal year, and I think the Secretary's very much aware of that, and has heard the reports from the unified commanders as well as the service chiefs. And when he feels that the time is right with some clarity of need for dollar amounts and specific purposes, he will not hesitate to go forward to the President asking for a supplemental, if that's what he thinks is necessary.

Q: When will he be finished with is top-to-bottom review? Any target date, yet?

Quigley: He has not—he has not stated a date, although it will be kind of a rolling result, Ivan. Some will be—some of the efforts will be done earlier than others, particularly if you need to have—if you need to be impacted by the fiscal year '02 budget. If it is something that does not need money in fiscal year '02, you could perhaps wait. And some of the efforts will also call for follow-on work that could take several more months, depending on the issue and the level of analysis that you should do in order to come to a good, clear—so it will be a shifting, moving date that they will come to fruition, although he's not let himself be pinned down on any dates.

Q: You're saying this kind of rolling effect based on money, reading you correctly, one then would assume that the weapon systems issues will be pretty close to the top, the big ticket items: F-22s, DD-21, Joint Strike Fighters.

Quigley: He is very clear on the fact that programmatic specifics will follow the strategy, in that order. And I've seen a lot of pieces that have been written in recent weeks that are very quick to jump to the programmatics. And Secretary Rumsfeld is not there. He has had no specific recommendations on programmatics made to him at all, let alone to the President. So he is very focused on getting the strategy piece right and what our nation's military needs to have, what its mission should be as we enter the first part of the 21st century, and then, as an absolutely required follow-on, but in that order, to go to the programmatics about what sorts of equipment we would need for our nation's military to carry out its mission.

Q: But one—I mean, again, when you get down to the strategy, if you see the strategy does not call for the use of aircraft carriers or carrier battle groups, it then becomes pretty clear that his intent is to either phase out the carriers or not build new ones, I mean they hinge together, don't they?

Quigley: But I don't think he's going to treat it—on the strategy piece, it needs to be a total piece, in the sense you need to have an understanding across the board of what our nation's capabilities need to be in the military area. He needs to be satisfied with it, and then he needs to take that to the President and get his concurrence in that. Then, and only then, when the strategy piece is done completely, will you go to the programmatics of how to carry out that strategy.

Chris?

Q: Craig, there's an interesting piece in the *New York Times* about emerging policy differences between this building and the State Department. For instance—

Quigley: I read that.

Q: Did you read it? Do you have any comment on it? And I have a follow-up question.

Quigley: I was amazed, to be honest with you. I just know things differently. My perception of that whole circumstance is very different from the writer's. This is a team, a national security team that speaks together on the phone in a planned manner once a day—in the morning, at 7:15. A more typical day has all of them speaking about three times a day. They have lunch once a week at a roundtable. It's hosted here one week by Secretary Rumsfeld, over at State by Secretary Powell the next week, and what have you. And these are folks that are constantly in touch with each other and working through issues together as a team. I just—the tone of the article is such that there's some sort of a bitter, very unpleasant, very divisive sort of a relationship amongst them. And I just don't see it. I don't see—

Q: But there are—there are disagreements on policy. And whether they're bitter or not bitter—

Quigley: You're always going to see opinions—I don't think the President would want it any other way than to hear different points of view if there are different points of view. But how this team works together is really something to see.

Q: Well, would you like to correct any of the positions given in the article, or are the positions as expressed correct?

Quigley: I would do neither. Their advice is provided privately to the President.

Q: Given that true, too, that this is the traditional resting place of the doves. I mean, the hawks are at the State Department. Isn't that—don't you actually have that confused—

Quigley: I don't know if I'd characterize it that way, either.

Q: Well, I mean, over the years we are very reluctant to use military power at this end. Very happy to use it over at the State Department.

Quigley: I think the leadership in DoD is always taking a look at each circumstance and treating it for the unique circumstance that it is and trying not to use a one-size-fits-all approach.

Q: I think of Chairman Powell's opposition to the Gulf War. Now maybe he's changed his mind; he's over on the other side of the road.

Quigley: I don't know. I'll let Secretary Powell speak for himself on that.

Q: So would you say that there aren't major policy—I mean, you're talking, sir, about style of interaction, but are you saying that there aren't major policy differences, and is that because this building doesn't have a policy on many things yet—(laughter)—or because they agree with the State Department on everything?

Quigley: I would say that you see the national security team working very closely together to present their views to the President on a wide variety of topics. Where their opinions differ, they will clearly state that to the President, but they try very hard to make sure that everybody understands everybody else's positions and the rationale for that, so that the President can get a cogent, comprehensive set of recommendations where he understands, if there are differing views, what are the elements that took that person to take that view, that they think are the significant issues that make them think that way. I mean, you would ask for nothing less, I think, from your team.

Yes?

Q: On the review, is the idea that it's going to complete the strategy, roll out the strategy, and then do the recs, or will you push through everything and then you roll it out as a package?

Quigley: No, you'll have different parts being publicly released at different times. The strategy is going to be right up near the top, certainly before any programmatics. If there are other issues that don't have programmatics attached to them, necessarily, then you can move those to the right and make them later, because you don't need to have them impacted by dollars as part of the '02 budget.

Q: And do you have an idea where we are in the budget planning, sending a detailed budget over to the Hill?

Quigley: No, I don't have that date, either.

Tony?

Q: Yesterday there was a published report saying that Rumsfeld had received a list of, like, 30 programs that could be whacked to save $3 billion a year, approximately. How does that square with your notion that there's been no programmatic recommendations? Was the report inaccurate, or did it mischaracterize the so-called list?

Quigley: I think what you're looking at now is a variety of stories that are coming out, taking pieces of work that are going on in the various reviews that are under way, and perhaps coming to some faulty conclusions as to—based on what they see.

If I read that story yesterday correctly, to me, it is a pretty good description of all of our significant acquisition programs. And if I was trying to understand where the money is in our future acquisition plans, that would be the list that I would ask to see. I don't think I would predict as to what I would then cut from that line, or do I—or from that list. Do I draw a line and everything below the line goes? I just—we're just not to that point yet.

But if you're trying to understand where we have significant acquisition investments in the future, then that list of programs is where the money is—the significant tac (tactical) air programs, the shipbuilding. You don't care about the smaller programs, because they can't make a difference. But I need to understand where the big-ticket items are. That's what that list looked like to me.

Q: (Off mike)—was that it was that this is where we are, and where we're going over the next five or six years, dollar-wise.

Quigley: Right. Right.

Q: In other words, everything is on the table is what you're talking about. This is what—

Quigley: Absolutely. But today—stop the music, okay?—

where are our acquisition dollars for the most part, and where are the big acquisition programs, where there are many billions of dollars in the years ahead.

Alex?

Q: Craig, you mentioned that there had been no programmatic recommendations made to the Secretary, so that he couldn't make any yet to the President.

Quigley: Right.

Q: Has he received specific strategic recommendations yet?

Quigley: Not if it buys equipment.

Q: No.

Quigley: No.

Q: You know, where we are in the world, and the Defense Department has to prepare its—

Quigley: Well, on the strategy piece, that is further along, certainly, than of the programmatic pieces that goes. And when he met with the President last Wednesday, he gave to the President a quick look at the initial findings of his work in that area and also in quality of life. And this—it was kind of, "Mr President, this is where we are at the moment. This is not done but it's kind of how we're dividing up the work, if you will. And here is the work we have come up with so far on both the strategy piece and the quality of life."

Q: Has he scheduled any—or has he had any subsequent meetings with the President or scheduled any, particularly—

Quigley: No, not that I'm aware of—not that I'm aware of. There will be more though, Alex. I mean, there will be—this will be an iterative process over a period of time.

Q: Is it then safe to say at this moment that the emphasis is shifting to the Pacific Rim and the Far East, away from Europe and Eastern Europe?

Quigley: We have to stay tuned on that one, Ivan.

Q: Last week you talked about the Secretary divesting himself of firms in which he may have defense contracts by the end of next month. Has he recused himself during this review from firms in which he continues to have an investment in, relating to their programs? And which programs has he recused himself from?

Quigley: I'm not aware of the Department having made any major acquisition decisions in the last two months.

Q: Well, they have ongoing contracts with the Defense Department—firms that he has investments in. He's recused—he's divesting those eventually. My question is, as he makes this review over the fate of these firms, is he recusing himself from any specific firms?

Quigley: I'm not aware of his involvement in any contract having been signed by the Defense Department since he has come into office.

Q: No, these are firms he has investments in, or as a—you know, might even have a little more significant role than investments.

Quigley: There are contracting officers, Pat, at every level of the Defense Department, depending on the scope of the contract. And there are—

Q: But they can't hold—they can't have defense—they can't have investments in the defense contractors.

Quigley: But I'm a contracting officer at a local installation and I need more paper for my administration department. That's a contract that's going to be let locally, negotiated locally, and those are not decisions that the Secretary of Defense has any part of.

Q: Well, he had a—he had several million dollars in General Dynamics when he was nominated. Has he gotten rid of that General Dynamics stock or is he recusing himself of decisions involving General Dynamics?

Quigley: I don't know as if he's made any decisions regarding General Dynamics, in the example that you've just cited.

Q: Well, I think a number—there are several major programs.

Quigley: Well, I—he would be scrupulous to avoid even the perception of any conflict of interest, and—

Q: (Off mike)—he's recused himself?

Quigley: He has not recused himself from a process that he's not been a part of.

Ivan.

Q: Just on general terms along this line, if someone comes in who has, you know, far-ranging investments and the bottom falls out of the market, which it has, does the United States government still force that person to take those heavy losses and sell immediately—

Quigley: Yes.

Q:—or is there some way they could put them in limbo or, you know—

Quigley: There are a variety of things you can do, but ultimately you need to divest yourself of the interests in those firms. And you are a victim of the market going up or down, and if the market goes down, your losses are greater, if the market goes up, you have more buyers for your equities.

Q: In a case like Rumsfeld, you could be talking about several millions or many millions of dollars, perhaps.

Quigley: Well, and a lot of his holdings are very complicated—limited partnerships, and the like. Where you or I might want to sell or buy some mutual funds tomorrow, we could do it that day, if you're the direct owner of equities in a firm. But if it's a limited partnership, it's a much more complicated structural arrangement to divest yourself of that, and you must find a buyer. So now I must seek a buyer on a good day is a complicated process, but if you combine that complication with a declining market, it's just that much more difficult. But it does not excuse the individual from the ultimate divestiture.

Yes, ma'am?

Q: Yes, on training, the USS Enterprise Battle Group is scheduled to be deployed to the Mediterranean and Persian Gulf sometime the end of April. Has a final decision been made if that battle group is going to use the inner range in Vieques?

Quigley: No.

Q: Congressman Curt Weldon has been in to the Secretary proposing Saint Kitts and Nevis as alternatives to Vieques. Are they really seriously being considered as alternative sites for training for the Atlantic Fleet?

Quigley: Well, the Secretary has received the congressman's letter and a response is being prepared, but I don't think he has responded to him directly, yet.

Q: Okay, but is his proposal—or the Congressman's proposal under serious consideration by the department in the search for alternative training to Vieques?

Quigley: I think that the answer to the letter will show that we have considered his suggestion and will answer the suggestion specifically.

Q: The March 9th report that was due to the President on how the Navy was going to conduct its training through May 1st, 2003, has that been finally submitted to the White House?

Quigley: No, it has not. They know it's not there yet. We've told them that it's late. We are trying to determine a more comprehensive way ahead on Vieques. That long-range training schedule will be a part of that and trying to incorporate that as part of a larger package on the way ahead to Vieques.

Q: Could you elaborate a little more what you mean by a more comprehensive package on Vieques?

Quigley: Well, the report that was called for was simply a listing of the training requirements for battle groups and amphibious ready groups through 2003. That's a pretty simplistic package to put together. But the issue is much more complex. We're trying to be able to come to a solution to the training needs not only of the Enterprise battle group that you mentioned earlier, but downstream training needs as well as part of a comprehensive program on the way ahead on Vieques involving land transfers, money, use of the range, how often, with what ordnance, under what conditions. It's very complex. It took a year to come up with the original agreement. It's taking a while longer than we would have liked probably to prepare what we are working on right now and will ultimately more forward as a proposal.

Q: Do you consider that this existing agreement is still valid or in place?

Quigley: That is our working assumption. That's a starting point, yes.

Q: In Vieques, there has been this group of citizens, I believe (inaudible number) individuals who have signed petitions to have Vieques secede from Puerto Rico. They had meetings in Congress last week. Some of these people are being actually harassed by other anti-Navy sympathizers in Vieques. They claim that they're being, you know, physically attacked and under surveillance by the anti-Navy groups. Is the department concerned about security on the range—on the range and for those people in Vieques who might support the Navy's stance?

Quigley: Well we would always be concerned about security on the range. But I would think it would be incumbent upon the civil law enforcement officials within Puerto Rico if any citizen of the commonwealth feels threatened for whatever reason.

Dale, you had—

Q: (Inaudible.)

Q: Yeah, just to follow this for a second. Is part of this review also involve the status of other military facilities in Puerto Rico? Or is that being discussed as part of—

Quigley: Not that I'm aware of, no. Not that I'm aware of. It's really—that really isn't the issue.

Q: Can I have one more, sir?

Quigley: Well.

Q: Is there any update today from the German MoD that the U.S. military in Europe hold training on foot and mouth disease, I think tomorrow?

Quigley: Tomorrow's the day. Now I asked that very question before coming out here this afternoon. And as of yet, the Germans have not—at least not shared with us or any of the other allies that would use some of those ranges. So we'll have wait and see until tomorrow.

Q: And we've made no formal proposal on mitigation measures yet for military training?

Quigley: Well, you're kind of—nobody expects this to be over real quick. So the impact of the long haul is not yet very clearly known at all.

In the near term, it doesn't have a major impact. There are exceptions for the things that really matter. Units preparing to go to KFOR can continue the training. Units that have a contiguous training area can continue training. The German government has granted waivers for other items.

So right now, today, the impact is not great. What the longer term impact will be is anybody's guess. What time frame are we talking about? And we'll just have to wait and see and see where that takes us. The longer the time, of course, the greater the impact, and we may very well have to design some work-arounds in the weeks or months ahead, depending on the time frame.

Tony?

Q: I want to shift gears from foot and mouth to missile defense a second. Can you give us a—up-to-date on the testing schedules here? BMDO last week confirmed that the first Boeing booster test is not going to happen next month, but delayed till about August or September at the earliest. How concerned is the Pentagon about that delay rippling throughout the rest of the program for the next couple of years?

Quigley: Well, you're always concerned anytime you have a delay in any developmental program because of the downstream effects of that delay. You try in each and every case to mitigate the effect as best you can. In this case, our original plan had been to have a series of three developmental booster tests. What we're going to do now is have a—we're calling it a pathfinder test, and that is to do everything up to and—but short of actual launch of the new booster. So you get the handling training, you get the launch procedures training, and you get everything but the launch, and do one of those, followed by two live firing tests. And then we'll see what the live firing tests have given us.

So the mitigation in this case is to design this pathfinder idea to try to get some training benefit. But it will have an impact on the program; we just don't know how much.

Q: From the podium, can you explain a little bit why it's important to test this new booster, and why can't the U.S. just go along with the one that's been used in the prior three tests?

Quigley: Well, the one we've been using for the integrated flight test so far is a Minuteman booster, basically, but it's a two-stage booster. It will do at this stage of the development of the program itself. It gets your kill vehicle in the air, it launches the systems that you need to test in outer space. But our assessment for the long-term need, for a ground-based system, now, is that you need a three-stage booster for the speed and the range. You obviously want to interdict any incoming missiles as far away from United States territory as you can and as quickly as you can. And you simply don't get the speed or range from a two-stage booster that you would from a three-stage booster. So the long-term goal remains the development of that three-stage booster.

Q: It's crucial to make sure these tests stay on target to—

Quigley: As close as we can. As close as we can.

Q: Does this mean the next hit-to-kill test is likely to be next year instead of this year?

Quigley: No. We'll have an integrated flight test this year, but it will use the Minuteman booster, not the Boeing developmental booster. It was never planned for that either, but we had hoped that integrated flight test seven might be able to use the new booster, and we will not make that.

Q: When do you expect that?

Q: When is flight test seven scheduled for now?

Quigley: I don't know. I don't know. We hope to have the first of the live shots of the three—of the pathfinder and then two live shots, hope to have the first of those by late summer.

Q: For the record, can you compare when, under the original schedule, the first Boeing booster was supposed to launch a warhead, versus what the current schedule is on IF-7, IFT-7?

Quigley: Sure. Yes. I don't know that off the top of my head, but we can get that. (The test was originally scheduled for March 2000.)

Q: For the record for folks.

Quigley: Mm-hm.

Q: Are both those live flight tests following the pathfinder test to take place this year?

Quigley: The first is late summer, and I think the second is later this year, I believe, but I don't have a date on that. But I believe so, yes.

Q: Can I just follow up on that?

Quigley: Sure.

Q: The next intercept attempt—which I thought was six, not seven, actually.

Quigley: The next one is six. We had hoped for the first of the new boosters to actually fly on seven. So six was always going to be the Minuteman.

Q: Right. When is six?

Quigley: I think that's like midsummer, early to midsummer. I don't have an exact date.

Q: That also is moving to the right. Is that because of the review, or what?

Quigley: I think what you're going to see in integrated flight test six is a near duplicate of last July's test, using just about identical components in every facet of the shot.

Q: Why does it take so long to get there?

Quigley: We're going to want to make sure that—you know, when last July's shot failed to deploy the decoys appropriately, failed to get the separation of the kill vehicle from the booster, these were much more simplistic things than—It just goes to show the incredible complexity of the overall system, I believe, from start to finish. We're going to want to make darn sure, as best we can, that we check and double-check every system and subsystem before the test is actually—These are expensive. These are about $100 million for a test shot. We're going to try to get it right as best we can, and double-check everything along the way.

Q: Isn't the point of testing to kind of just go out and do stuff? I mean—

Quigley: Sure, but that should never be done in a lackadaisical manner. If we can ensure a higher chance of success by delaying a test a couple of weeks that has no overall impact on the program itself, and you get much more and much better quality test data points by that marginal delay, that's a good investment.

Q: So should we expect future tests also to have delays of up to 12 months between each other?

Quigley: Depends on what you find in each of the succeeding flight tests. If you have components that are developed and they proceed very smartly along their development path with no glitches noted, you can anticipate sticking to a schedule, but if there are snags along the way—and the new booster would be an example of that—you're going to have to adapt your testing program to reflect the reality of the snags that you've developed along the way.

Yes—

Q: Do you have comments on the published report that—on the Chinese missile program? And also, last week's CIA report that China is still exporting missiles to Iraq, Iran, Libya and Pakistan?

Quigley: I'll let CIA talk about their report, but we're very much aware of the Chinese ongoing modernization of China's military, and that would include weapons systems that are arrayed along the coast facing Taiwan. By the same token, it all depends on how China would use its modernized military in the years and decadesto come. It could be a force of stability there in that region, or it could be a source of instability and, obviously, we hope it's the former.

Q: Any threat to the U.S. security, to U.S. national security, from Chinese stepping up the military missile defense—

Quigley: Well, it's always something that we watch very carefully, but I think, at this point, no.

Q: Thank you, Craig.

Quigley: You're welcome.

19

Under Secretary of State-Designate John Bolton on Arms Control

President Bush's nominee to be Under Secretary of State for Arms Control and International Security Affairs, John Bolton, told the Senate Foreign Relations Committee March 29 that he considers "sound, verifiable arms control agreements and energetic non-proliferation strategies" to be "critical elements of American foreign policy."

Appearing at his confirmation hearing, Bolton pointed to administration goals to reduce the U.S. nuclear arsenal, support South Korea's efforts to engage its neighbor to the north, and build effective missile defenses that will protect not only all 50 American states from rogue missile attack or accidental missile launches, but also U.S. allies and military forces deployed overseas. He indicated that the United States will engage both Russia and China on the subject of missile defense.

He also said the administration will not ask Congress, during its current session, to ratify the Comprehensive Test Ban Treaty (CTBT), and he called for Russia to end sales of destabilizing weapons to nations such as Iran.

Following is the text of Bolton's statement as prepared for delivery:

Statement of John R. Bolton
Before the Senate Foreign Relations Committee
March 29, 2001

Mr Chairman, and members of the Committee, it is a great honor to appear before you today as President Bush's nominee to be Under Secretary of State for Arms Control and International Security. This is the third time I have appeared before this Committee as a nominee, and my fourth Senate hearing as such (the other being before another Committee well known to Senator Biden). I am deeply indebted to the President and to Secretary of State Powell for proposing me for this position, and, if confirmed, I will strive mightily to justify the confidence in me they have shown.

I believe it is just as important to have the trust and confidence of Congress in carrying out my prospective responsibilities. In my earlier Executive Branch positions, I have attempted to be fully available to Members and staff in both Houses, on both sides of the aisle, equally for informal consultations or for hearings. I found, in responding to Committee questions for this hearing, that I testified before Congress 25 times during the four years I served as Assistant Secretary for International Organization Affairs. I wouldn't be at all surprised if that pace were exceeded should you confirm me for the Under Secretary position. Especially given the Senate's central and explicit Constitutional role in the treaty-making process, I am committed to developing the closest possible working relationship with you and your staffs. This is something I believe in strongly not simply from a practical political perspective, but also from years of studying and working on separation-of-powers issues.

Just last month (February) in Norfolk, the President spoke of today's security environment: "the grave threat from nuclear, biological, and chemical weapons has not gone away with the Cold War. It has evolved into many separate threats, some of them harder to see and harder to answer. And the adversaries seeking these tools of terror are less predictable, more diverse. With advanced technology, we must confront the threats that come on a missile. With shared intelligence and enforcement, we must confront the threats that come in a shipping container or in a suitcase."

Accordingly, the President has ordered broad reviews of national security policy including our approach to deterrence, arms reductions, and missile defense. Each is an element of an overall posture designed to meet emerging challenges. I personally consider that sound, verifiable arms control agreements and energetic non-proliferation strategies can and should be critical elements of American foreign policy. Such policies are most efficacious when they receive broad, bipartisan support from Congress after vigorous international advocacy and tenacious negotiation by the Executive Branch. Let me discuss briefly some of the important directions that President Bush and Secretary Powell have already outlined, and that I hope to have the opportunity to implement.

President Bush has already made clear his high priority to reduce nuclear weapons in ways consistent with our national security. As a candidate, he said that it "should be possible to reduce the number of American nuclear weapons significantly further than what has been agreed to under START (Strategic Arms Reduction Treaty) II." The President restated this objective in February, when he reemphasized his commitment "commensurate with our ability to keep the peace, to reduce our nuclear arsenal on our own." We would, of course, also urge Russia to reduce its nuclear forces, welcoming such actions as positive steps.

On the non-proliferation front, there is much to be done. On the Korean peninsula, the administration fully supports South Korea's efforts to engage the North. Secretary Powell has made clear that with regard to the 1994 Agreed Framework, the U.S. will "abide by its commitments," but at the same time, "we will review some concerns that exist." These include concerns over whether the verification provisions are adequate to the "kinds of verification and monitoring in which we're interested." North Korea, Secretary Powell has already noted, is "a dictatorial regime" that is "essentially led by one person. The whole country looks to this one person for direction." So we need to engage with "clear-eyed realism about the nature of that regime."

As the U.S. considers new agreements, for example to curtail North Korea's missile programs, we will also insist on strong verification as a sine qua non for any agreement. As the Secretary said last January, "we also have to make sure that in any deal we might get, it is absolutely verifiable, we can monitor it, and only then can we be assured that it is something that we should take to the Senate or to the American people or to the Congress in general and say, this is a good deal for America."

On missile defense, President Bush's position is clear: we will "build effective missile defenses, based on the best available options, at the earliest possible date. Missile defense must be designed to protect all 50 states — and our friends and allies and deployed forces overseas — from missile attacks by rogue nations, or accidental launches." As Secretary Powell said, "we see missile defense as part of an overall strategic framework; it stands with our strategic offensive weapons, it stands with our arms control discussions and negotiations, and it stands with our non-proliferation efforts."

The administration will engage with our allies to explain why, in the Secretary's words, "deterrence is enhanced if (an adversary) also knows that if he was able to launch a missile at us, we have the capacity of intercepting that missile and knocking it down." And we will engage with China and Russia. As the Secretary has stated, "we will let the Chinese and the Russians know that it is not directed at them but at other nations that we have less confidence in their ability to act in rational ways."

Should our missile defense plans and the ABM (Anti-Ballistic Missile) Treaty come into conflict, President Bush has already said that he "will offer Russia the necessary amendments ... so as to make our deployment of effective missile defenses consistent with the treaty." After all, as Secretary Powell has said, "the Treaty needs to be modified or eliminated or changed in some rather fundamental way." We hope to persuade the Russians to move beyond the ABM Treaty, but this will not happen overnight. As Secretary Powell has noted, we still "have a lot of conversations to have with the Russians" over this. If confirmed, I will do my part to try to bring these conversations to a successful outcome.

On the CTBT, Secretary Powell has stated, "we will not be asking for the Congress to ratify the Comprehensive Test Ban Treaty in this session. We are mindful of the work that was done by President Clinton's Special Advisor General (John) Shalikashvili. We will examine that work closely. But we believe that there are still flaws with the Treaty as it was voted down in 1999. Nonetheless, we will continue to examine the elements of that Treaty as part of our overall strategic review." The Secretary stated further that President Bush "has indicated he has no intention of resuming testing as part of our efforts. We do not see any need for such testing in the foreseeable future."

Multilateral diplomacy and managing international organizations play an increasing role in arms control, and several existing problems require attention. For example, the Organization for the Prohibition of Chemical Weapons (OPCW), is experiencing a series of financial and management difficulties that threaten the very integrity of the Chemical Weapons Convention. If confirmed, I would, as a priority work, closely with Congress and like-minded countries to try to resolve these issues and help the OPCW play its role in helping to ensure a world free of chemical weapons.

Russia and China are key to preserving international stability. With Russia, we will discuss our missile defense plans and their proposals for regional defenses, which were noteworthy for recognizing the nature of the threat, and the willingness to work with us on it. So we take that as an encouraging sign, so long as Russia understands that we will not allow others to dictate our agenda. Moreover, we must encourage Russia to get on with reform, including stopping the proliferation of missile and nuclear technology, and ending sales of destabilizing weapons to nations such as Iran. This is critically important.

China, of course, poses unique challenges. As the Secretary said so well, "A strategic partner China is not, but neither is China our inevitable and implacable foe." We will engage with China on missile defense. But also critically important, the November 2000 missile non-proliferation arrangement commits China not to assist other countries in developing nuclear-capable missiles in any way, and to put in place comprehensive missile-related export controls. While Chinese performance on exports has improved recently, we nonetheless have reservations about some of their practices. The administration will watch closely to be sure that China is meeting its commitments.

On Taiwan, Secretary Powell has stressed: "Let all who doubt, from whatever perspective, be assured of one solid truth: We expect and demand a peaceful settlement, one acceptable to people on both sides of the Taiwan Strait." As he said, "we will provide for the defense needs of Taiwan in accordance with the Taiwan Relations Act."

Mr Chairman, as I said at the outset, it is a great honor to have received the President's nomination for Under Secretary of State, and I am truly grateful for the possibility of once again serving our nation. Thank you for the opportunity to make these brief remarks, and I would now be happy to respond to the Committee's questions.

20

Deputy CIA Director Examines Challenges Posed by North Korea

The deputy director of U.S. central intelligence says current conditions in North Korea "hold the potential for both engagement and confrontation."

John McLaughlin told participants in a conference sponsored by Texas A&M University that while North Korea was once a metaphor for some of the most extreme aspects of the Cold War, it is today a metaphor "for the most challenging aspects of the new world that has come in its wake."

He told the audience April 17 that North Korea's challenge to the United States and its allies "has grown in complexity and peril." It is driven, McLaughlin said, by a traditional conventional threat and by a newer threat of weapons of mass destruction as well as by the humanitarian challenge driven by economic decline.

Conventionally, he said North Korean artillery "could rain havoc down on Seoul" and the North Korean military has the largest pool of special forces in the world.

On the proliferation side, McLaughlin said North Korea "continues to aggressively market its ballistic missiles, equipment and technology" to places such as Iran and Pakistan "where they have the potential to alter geopolitical and military calculations in important ways throughout the Middle East and South Asia." This activity, he said, "has accelerated the pace at which other countries acquire and refine potential delivery systems for weapons of mass destruction." Kim Chong-il knows that proliferation "is something we want to stop," he added.

The official also noted that although nuclear activity has been frozen by the 1994 Agreed Framework between the United States and North Korea, all of North Korea's plutonium has not been accounted for.

"Even as the North challenges the world in one small but lethal field of modern (conventional) technology," McLaughlin said, "it presents another challenge as old as life itself: malnutrition and starvation." While Kim Chong-il's diplomatic opening represents "tactical flexibility," he said "we have yet to see any comparable movement away from the legacy of Kim Il-song and all that it represents. Real change will not come until that happens."

The United States must work the problem of North Korea in a fluid environment, according to McLaughlin. In East Asia, he said, the United States is "still often called on to be partner, protector, or honest broker." At the same time, the only global superpower, he said, is seen "as a nation whose interests and priorities do not always coincide with the other major actors in the region."

If a crisis arises in the North, McLaughlin concluded, "its solution will fall to the nations of East Asia and the United States. We will, together, have the chance to resolve it in concert, not conflict. It is a chance none of us can afford to miss."

Following is the text of McLauglin's remarks as delivered:

Remarks by Deputy Director of Central Intelligence John E. McLaughlin
Texas A&M Conference
"North Korea: Engagement or Confrontation"
17 April 2001

You've given me a tough job tonight. The Conference organizers asked if I would come and discuss the issue of the North Korean threat. In some ways, this is easy. It has after all been a high priority for the Intelligence Community for years, and you have been discussing aspects of it all day long. In another sense, though, it is a challenging assignment, because so many of the factors that defined the classic threat are changing-and changing in a region that is not just very fluid but which also must find its place in a world vastly different from the one that gave birth to the North Korean regime.

What perspective do I bring to this? Like so many of you, I have been to Korea, I have been to the DMZ (DeMilitarized Zone), and I have had to think about the problem a lot. But to be fair, I would not call myself an expert in the class of so many in this room. The perspective I bring is that of an intelligence officer whose personal career has centered more on assessing change in areas such as the former Soviet Union and Central Europe—areas where totalitarian regimes experienced transformation in dramatically different circumstances. I also bring the perspective of an intelligence officer charged with gauging the relative weight of various challenges and opportunities for U.S. interests across the globe. By any standard, events on the Korean peninsula must rank high on that scale.

The title of your Conference centers on a question: engagement or confrontation? We all know the second very well. Confrontation has been a virtual constant in U.S. relations with North Korea for more than half a century. The far newer phenomenon is engagement—cautious, tentative, guarded, halting-apply the adjective of your choice.

Engagement or confrontation? Ultimately, they describe policy options. It is, of course, not the mission of U.S. Intelligence to prescribe policy, and I would not presume to do so this evening. But, on our best days, we do hope to inform policy.

That said, let me say explicitly that no one should comb through these remarks for clues about the future direction of U.S. policy on Korea. These are personal reflections on one of the most complex and significant issues of our time.

When it comes to North Korea, conditions there clearly hold the potential for both engagement and confrontation. For a state like the North—often reflexively hostile to the outside world, yet in need of it as never before-engagement and the potential for confrontation can coexist—and are likely to co-exist—even in the best of scenarios.

The Nature of the Challenge

What are the elements of the problem? For the United States, North Korea is—first and foremost—a challenge. It was throughout the Cold War, and it is so now. In fact, it could be said that North Korea was a metaphor for some of the most extreme aspects of the Cold War and is today a metaphor for the most challenging aspects of the new world that has come in its wake.

Let's look back for a moment and then talk about how the picture has changed. As you all know, the armistice of July 1953 created on the Korean peninsula a long pattern of tense standoff, punctuated by occasional crisis. For U.S. Intelligence, North Korea became—as much as anything—an order-of-battle problem. Count the troops. Count the tanks. Count the guns. Add up the capabilities. Estimate their intentions. I know I'm making this sound easier and simpler than it was, but my point is that we were dealing with a much less fluid picture back then.

Like everyone else, we knew the regime was brutal within its borders and a menace beyond. Its commando raids into South Korea and its assassination attempts against successive South Korean presidents—including the 1983 bombing in Rangoon that killed 21 people—were clear windows into the minds and morals of North Korean leaders.

And yet, North Korea's status as a client of the Soviet Union and China—a prickly client, to be sure—did impose constraints on its behavior. With the end of the Cold War and the scaling back of the subsidies that went with it, those constraints began to erode. Today, it may be a fragile regime, but it is one that operates with fewer constraints on its behavior and often outside international norms. And, as I implied earlier, it operates in a world where the reference points—technological, geopolitical, economic, military—are themselves in flux.

In short order, the challenge that North Korea poses to us and our allies has grown in complexity and peril. Its traditional feature—the conventional threat we examined this afternoon-remains in place. And—as we saw in September, 1996 and June, 1999—the North has found it hard to abandon tactics like commando incursions and naval confrontations-even when they fail miserably.

But added into this mix is an increased threat from weapons of mass destruction and the humanitarian challenge we could face, given the increased stress that poverty and economic decline must be creating in the North.

The Conventional Threat

Let's talk for a minute about the conventional military picture. I reveal no secret when I say that on the battlefield North Korea cannot defeat the South and the United States. But it could inflict tremendous damage in a losing cause.

The North Korean military, like all but the most elite of North Korean society, has suffered the effects of the country's economic implosion. It does not exercise often or well. Its equipment is aging. Its military production is scant. But it is large, and most of it is forward deployed.

Its artillery could rain havoc down on Seoul, a mere 30 miles from the DMZ. It has the biggest pool of special forces in the world-not the best, as we have seen, but with enough punch to sow panic and destruction.

These are capabilities. The intention to use them is a very different matter, and this has been debated thoroughly for years. The case can be made that it would be foolish for the North to use these capabilities. And the case can be made that it would be foolish to make that assumption. But, the bottom line is that like any military commander, we in the intelligence profession can ill-afford to ignore capabilities.

In fact, I can tell you that we tend to make our mistakes not when we convince ourselves that a foreign group or leader might do something, but when we convince ourselves that they will not.

Here is a short passage from one of our intelligence assessments: "...an invasion of South Korea is unlikely unless North Korean forces can develop a clear-cut superiority over the increasingly efficient South Korean army." That judgment came out on the 13th of January, 1950. It had a fairly short shelf life.

No matter what we think the North Korean leadership might do with its military, it is a linchpin of their state. They take it very seriously. And so must we as the ally of South Korea and its democracy, and as a nation with 37,000 of its own troops serving, working, and living among 45-million friends in what could one day be harm's way.

That holds true whether we believe the North sees its armed forces as a mark of prestige, a constituency to be satisfied, a tool that might bring respect, or even one that might bring conquest. The military has priority on whatever resources the North has. This is stated policy, the so-called "military first" policy. But it is hardly the whole story.

...and the Unconventional Ones

Were Kim Chong-il and his lieutenants simply sitting atop a large collection of conventional forces, they would still be a grave concern. But it would be one whose destructive power and geographic reach the United States and South Korea have together understood and managed for decades.

As real as the conventional threat may be, North Korea's challenge to regional and global security is magnified by two other factors I've already mentioned.

First, the North's pursuit of weapons of mass destruction and long-range missiles, and its readiness—even eagerness—to become missile salesman to the world. And second, the economic and humanitarian disaster that has afflicted the people of the North—a catastrophe whose effects will endure for generations, no matter how the Korean situation finally plays out.

Weapons of Terror

Looking first at those advanced weapons: as we all know, it was not a brigade of tanks or division of infantry that riveted our attention and concern on the Korean peninsula early in the last decade. It was the nuclear plant at Yongbyon.

The Agreed Framework has frozen activity there. But we still cannot account for all of North Korea's plutonium. And—with an opaque regime in which the practice of denial and deception is embedded in national strategy—we still cannot say for sure that nuclear weapons-related work is not going on somewhere else.

Indeed, the North probably has one or two nuclear bombs—and it may also have biological weapons alongside its chemical ones.

Regarding missiles, the outlines of the North's program are far less mysterious, for the leadership sees the No Dong and Taepo Dong as tools of public diplomacy as well as national defense.

It has so far held to its missile launch moratorium and it has signaled its interest in negotiating a missile deal with us.

At the same time, the North's proliferation activities remain robust—for a profit and for a purpose: To keep our attention, to underline their greatest source of leverage, and to remind us of what it is they are willing to haggle over.

North Korea continues to aggressively market its ballistic missiles, equipment, and technology. We find the No Dong and its variants in places like Iran and Pakistan, where they have the potential to alter geopolitical and military calculations in important ways throughout the Middle East and South Asia.

In short, the North has accelerated the pace at which other countries acquire and refine potential delivery systems for weapons of mass destruction.

The flight of a Taepo Dong over Japan more than two years ago added a new and worrisome dimension to the North's own definitions of deterrence and power projection. And it is busy at work on new models that could reach the United States itself with nuclear-sized payloads.

The Humanitarian Challenge

Turning to the second factor I mentioned: even as the North challenges the world in one small but lethal field of modern technology, it presents another challenge as old as life itself: malnutrition and starvation.

A combination of natural calamity and human mismanagement may have claimed up to a million lives in the 1990s. Even today, the North's sputtering economy remains unable to provide remotely sufficient food or work for its people.

Even with the charity of other nations, malnutrition is widespread. Without this charity, famine would be epidemic. Many North Koreans must simply fend for themselves, seemingly forgotten by a system that nonetheless demands their obedience. Some just flee.

As for the others, their dire poverty is captured in a single picture—one that I am sure many of you in this room have seen. It is a satellite photo of the Korean peninsula at night. North China and South Korea are a blaze of lights. North Korea is totally dark outside the single dot that is Pyongyang. The fishing fleets in the Sea of Japan give off far more light than does all of North Korea.

No one who looks at that photograph should forget that

there are some 23 million human beings struggling in that darkness.

North Korea's Leadership: Tactical Flexibility

And what of the small group in that dot of light, the small group that commands North Korea. It was rich ground for analysis this morning.

And we, too, see changes—some encouraging, some not.

No matter what you make of Kim Chong-il's diplomatic opening, it does at least reflect a tactical flexibility. His words and actions are well worth weighing and watching. We have all seen the signposts.

His behavior at the North-South summit. His dispatch of Vice Marshal Cho to Washington and his reception of American diplomats in Pyongyang. His acceptance of foreign aid and foreign aid workers. His efforts to attract foreign money to his investment enclaves. His small adjustments to the domestic economy.

But the key is whether any of these steps signal the start of a process. For in and of themselves, they have yet to bring real improvement to the North. Yet they do suggest the leadership there knows it must do something to better conditions in the country—for its own survival, if nothing else.

Kim's trips to China in January of this year and May of last year are also significant. But so is the fact that China's economic reform was made possible in large part by the passing of Mao and the de-emphasis of major portions of his legacy. In North Korea, we have yet to see any comparable movement away from the legacy of Kim Il-song and all that it represents. Real change will not come until that happens.

...Risky Strategy

So far in Pyongyang, the son has held fast to the father's legacy, including the goal of Northern preeminence in a reunified Korea.

It is easy to caricature Kim Chong-il—either as a simple tyrant blind to his dilemma or as a technocratic champion of sweeping change. But the extreme views of him tend to be the product of bias, ignorance, or wishful thinking. The reality is more complex.

At home, he has shown his hard side—through his purges

of the elite, his light regard for the suffering of ordinary Koreans, and the swift destruction of any expression of popular discontent. Abroad, he has shown his pragmatic side—through his willingness to engage old enemies and his skilled brinkmanship as he does so.

Like his father, he has been shrewd enough to make bad behavior the keystone of his foreign policy. He knows that proliferation is something we want to stop. Thus, Kim Chong-il has tried to drum up outside assistance by trading off international concerns about his missile programs and sales. He has—more subtly, of course—done much the same thing with foreign fears of renewed famine and the chaos that could accompany any unraveling of his regime.

These are the wild cards he adds to strengthen what would otherwise be a deuce-high hand. This is his leverage with the world. Along the way, he will seek to exploit any daylight he can find between the United States, South Korea, Japan, the European Union, or anyone else who might be inclined to offer him economic help. And from his perspective, it makes good sense.

Decisive to the success of this strategy is the projection of a credible threat. And here—as we know—the North has its bases covered. But, like any policy founded on threats, it comes with the built-in possibility of accident or miscalculation-by those who conduct it, or by those who react to it.

The Nature of the Regime

Before I can say anything about the future of the North Korean regime—and its challenge—a few words are in order about what makes it tick today.

It is a peculiar creation. The leaden, bureaucratic Marxism we saw falter in the late 20th Century—with its gray Central Committees and half-forgotten Central European ideology—is an imperfect guide to North Korea and offers few reliable analogies for how the North Korean regime might some day experience transformation.

The transformation of the Central European countries at the beginning of the last decade was eased by at least three things not present in the North Korean equation: extensive exposure to and penetration by the outside world (East Germany is the best example); economies already on the road to privatization (Hungary was the extreme case); and the presence of dissident movements powerful enough in a country like Poland to represent an effective parallel society.

Instead of these cushioning factors, in North Korea, the command economy, central planning, and other familiar features introduced there long ago by the Soviets exist alongside something else. A single story makes the point. A foreign visitor asked a North Korean what he thought of Kim Il-song. "He is God," came the answer. Then a tougher one. "What do you think of Kim Chong-il?" The Korean thought a moment, looked around, and replied: "He is 70 per cent God."

Those answers might be very different were the North Korean outside the country. But they do say something about the tone and tenor of the regime on the inside.

Now I'm sure there are subtleties and complexities about the regime that we can neither discern nor appreciate. But that aside, the key is that power continues to reside with Kim Chong-il and the cluster of relatives and allies who run the military, the security forces, and the rest of the state and party apparatus.

No matter how you view them, it is evident they rule a state that is simultaneously impoverished and addicted to living beyond its means. They preach the values of self-reliance, but they rely on foreign aid. The priorities they set and enforce have delivered a huge army, a broken economy, widespread hunger, and a challenge for all of us.

...and Its Future

Because totalitarian elites tend to mask their own policy deliberations and drive opposition underground, the health and stability of their regimes are notoriously difficult for outsiders to gauge. North Korea is no exception. Predictions of its collapse have come and gone, and I will not venture one here now.

But I will say the North faces tough choices. Kim Chong-il probably recognizes the obvious truth that the economic competition with the South is lost. And he has seen for himself the economic gains brought by reform in China.

Yet he also knows the security risks involved and he knows the fates of other leaders who fell victim to change they could not control. He may have seen images of Gorbachev in retirement. Of Honecker in exile. Of a startled Ceausescu on his palace balcony the day the crowd stopped cheering.

At this point, Kim Chong-il may have a toe in the river of change. And he is moving just as we would expect him to: Slowly, carefully, with plenty of room to bargain, maneuver, or pull back.

After a decade of deprivation, the real story may be the durability of the North—a grim testament to the power of a people's ability to endure hardship.

Clearly, the North is under serious stress and it is likely to remain so. But frankly, no one can be confident about when, how, or even whether that stress might achieve critical mass and lead to fracture.

That formulation may not be intellectually satisfying. But I hope you will agree that it is intellectually honest.

The Regional Context

As the situation in the North unfolds, there is a final element of change we must consider: The regional context, which—like so many other things we have talked about today—was reshaped by the close of the Cold War.

Russia and China are each redefining their power, their influence, and their reach, and their relationship with each other. Japan is focused on ending its long economic recession and has heightened security concerns in the aftermath of Pyongyang's missile tests. And South Korea has emerged as a vibrant society with a strong democracy and the world's twelfth largest economy—a stark contrast to the stagnation in North Korea, whose economy barely registers on the charts.

And East Asia as a whole is looking anew at the United States, now the only global superpower. In that capacity, we are still often called on to be partner, protector, or honest broker. But we are also seen as a nation whose interests and priorities do not always coincide with the other major actors in the region.

It is in this fluid environment that the United States must work the problem of North Korea. We find in the immediate neighborhood friends and allies like South Korea and Japan, and others, like Russia and China, whose interests may converge less frequently with ours but who nonetheless share with us a common, significant stake in the ultimate destiny of North

Korea. No one will benefit from prolonged instability. There are the cost of reconstruction—whenever the time comes to tally it up—will demand the resources of more than one country.

If we ever face a crisis in the North, its solution will fall to the nations of East Asia and the United States. We will together have the chance to resolve it in concert, not conflict. It is a chance none of us can afford to miss.

Conclusion

Intelligence officers like to say that change typically brings uncertainty, and that uncertainty raises the odds of surprise. With so much change in and around the Korean peninsula, that old truth certainly applies. But none of us should be surprised by the prominence of North Korea as a challenge for policymakers and intelligence analysts.

In a very real sense, it is one of the inevitable issues of American foreign policy. Inevitable because—no matter what level of engagement we may want —the North seems sure to engage us. It could be across a table. It could be with the consequences of its negative behavior or its own instability. Or it could be some combination of them all.

What is clear—as this Conference demonstrates—is the complexity, gravity, and importance of the North Korean issue and its very certain role as a signpost for the future of East Asia.

Thank you very much.

21

Missile Defense will not Decouple U.S. and Allies, Official Says

Deputy Assistant Secretary of State for Strategic Affairs Lucas Fischer says missile defense "must be capable of protecting allies, friends, and deployed forces overseas as well as the United States," and must provide protection against accidental and unauthorized missile launches.

"We must be ready to reexamine the role of systems for direct defense against missile attack," Fischer said. He added that developing and acquiring a defense against a small number of missiles "would be a substantial additional factor dissuading states from seeking, or increasing, such a missile delivery capability."

Addressing an April 25 conference on missile defense sponsored by the Danish Parliament's Foreign Policy Committee, Fischer said the presence of missile defenses contributes to the prospect that a potential hostile attack "will be frustrated." The ability to complicate "a prospective opponent's calculation of success," he said, adds to uncertainty and weakens confidence that an attack will succeed. That is why "missile defenses must play a central role in today's deterrence posture," he said.

The missile defenses that the Bush administration intends to pursue "will be designed to engage and destroy a limited number of missiles of increasing range and sophistication, which are capable of delivering weapons of mass destruction and are being developed or sought by rogue states," Fischer said. The purpose of defenses, he added, is also to start to diminish what has been an "almost exclusive reliance on offensive weapons for deterrence."

Fischer emphasized that deploying missile defenses "will not 'de-couple' the U.S. from its friends and allies." The United States, he said, "is not interested in deploying defenses that would separate us from our friends and allies." Instead, he said, deploying defenses against coercion and attack by a limited arsenal of ICBMs (intercontinental ballistic missiles) from rogue states will increase the ability of the United States "to fulfill its security commitments in regional conflicts."

The official said the United States views missile defense as "a necessary element of deterrence and an opportunity for a collective approach to enhancing security for all."

On the subject of Russia's proposal for theater defenses, Fischer said, "the Russian concept would not provide for the area defense of North America or Europe," and, therefore, cannot be substituted for the concept proposed by Washington.

On the 1972 Anti-Ballistic Missile Treaty, he said it "will have to be replaced, eliminated, or changed in a fundamental way" because it prevents the development and deployment of a missile defense system.

Following is the text of Fischer's remarks as prepared for delivery and made available in Washington:

U.S. Deputy Assistant Secretary of State for Strategic Affairs Lucas Fischer
Before the Danish Parliament
Foreign Policy Committee Conference on NMD—Implications for the Global Order
Copenhagen, April 25, 2001
Remarks as Prepared for Delivery

Ladies and Gentlemen:

It is a privilege for me to be able to return for another visit to Copenhagen, and I am very honored to have been invited to speak at this important conference on missile defense. Its sponsorship by the Danish Parliament's Foreign Policy Committee demonstrates the seriousness with which this issue is being considered in Denmark, and this gives the United States an additional and important opportunity to present its views in a public and multinational forum.

Ensuring security has always relied on a mix of

complementary elements. That mix has always, for example, included diplomacy and political alliances and, further, national defense efforts and military alliances to bind these efforts together. With the advent of nuclear weapons and other weapons of mass destruction, the consequences of war grew even more terrible, and the use of nuclear deterrence to prevent war became a necessary further element in both national and alliance efforts to achieve security. Yet those developments in turn underlined the importance of classic diplomacy and its modern corollary—efforts through arms control and confidence-building to reduce instabilities and increase predictability and mutual understanding.

"Deterrence" has been a shorthand description of that more complicated situation, and its central element has been an assured capability to mount a devastating nuclear response to attack. Now, we stand 10 years after the Cold War's end, and we face clear evidence that the proliferation, and indigenous development, of weapons of mass destruction and their means of delivery pose the growing prospect of the threat of their use not only on a regional but on a global basis. It is therefore more than time to review our policy and reassess the range of threats to national and Alliance security and consider the right balance of tools to protect it.

There is no doubt that a retaliatory capability must still be a vital component of deterrence, and of our overall security posture. But the changes I've alluded to—that the Cold War is over and that our opponents in that odd relationship are no longer opponents, and that a new set of states with different ambitions and security calculations are exploiting the limits of our nonproliferation efforts—mean that the exact role of that component, and its specific implications for forces and policy, need reexamination. They mean, moreover, that we cannot continue to assume that deterrence will always succeed—any more than we can assume that nonproliferation will always succeed—and we must be ready to reexamine the role of systems for direct defense against missile attack.

Let me, therefore, state my theses.

- First, while technical accidents can perhaps always happen, a continued, stable security relationship of the United States and its allies with Russia faces far fewer dangers than that with its Soviet predecessor of 20 years ago. At that time, we all spent much effort considering how deterrence might lose stability, how in extreme circumstances rational states might feel obliged to make extreme choices. Those speculations were perhaps justified by the importance of avoiding such an event; but the watersheds of the INF (Intermediate-range Nuclear Forces) and START (Strategic Arms Reduction) treaties, CFE (Conventional Armed Forces in Europe), the reunification of Germany, the end of the Warsaw Pact, and NATO's reaching out to Russia underline that we live in a different world. The implications of this wholly beneficial development need to be thought through and reflected in the strategic force programs of each side.

- Second, while offensive retaliatory deterrence is an essential part of a sensible response to WMD and missile delivery threats—just as are continued and intensified efforts to prevent proliferation of such systems and their technology—we cannot expect it always to be sufficient.
- Therefore developing and acquiring a defense against small missile forces would be a substantial additional factor dissuading states from seeking, or increasing, such a missile delivery capability; a further reason, if such capabilities have been obtained, not to threaten their use; and, if these fail and a missile is launched — a means to intercept and thereby defeat it.

Let me expand on the particular concerns that underlie those latter points.

We are confronted with a more diverse, less predictable and more risk-prone group of states armed with or seeking weapons of mass destruction and increasingly longer-range ballistic missiles to deliver them.

These states are pursuing weapons of mass destruction and missile capabilities as tools of coercion and blackmail to achieve their objectives within their regions of interest. They also see these weapons as usable military instruments against their neighbors and as coercive tools of diplomacy, whose threatened use could deter the United States and our allies from coming to the assistance of friends in regions of vital interest. These weapons are sought as a means to counter our conventional forces and to break the cohesion of our alliances and coalitions. We need to ask what would have happened in 1991 or 1999 if Iraq or Yugoslavia had possessed ballistic missiles with chemical and biological warheads of sufficient range to reach the U.S. or our allies? A recent U.S. Intelligence Community estimate found that during the next 15 years the United States will likely face an ICBM threat from North Korea, probably from Iran, and possibly from Iraq. And well before that we can expect Iran, and perhaps Iraq, to have acquired capabilities to strike much of NATO Europe.

We have concluded that the prospect of weapons of mass destruction actually being used is greater than during the Cold War. As I stated earlier, deterring these new threats is different from the deterrence of the past, which is why for the deterrence of new and growing contemporary threats, both offenses and defenses are required.

Ballistic missile defenses contribute to deterrence of these threats by holding out the prospect that such a potential aggressor's attack will be frustrated, and by complicating a prospective opponent's calculation of success, adding to his uncertainty and weakening his confidence. Thus, missile defenses must play a central role in today's deterrence posture. We must also keep in mind that some potential threats, such as accidental or unauthorized launches of ballistic missiles, are, by their very nature, inherently undeterrable. For such contingencies as well, missile defenses provide an element of insurance that is in addition to their deterrent value.

- Therefore, our response to these new threats should incorporate combinations of offensive and defensive capabilities, as well as all the other elements of diplomacy, nonproliferation efforts, alliance frameworks, and effective tactical forces.

As you know, President Bush has stated that we will deploy missile defenses, based on the best options, at the earliest possible date. And he has also stated that these defenses must be capable of protecting not only the United States and our deployed forces, but also our friends and allies.

Our consideration of missile defense policy is taking place within a strategic framework that includes our present and future offensive force requirements and measures to strengthen our nonproliferation efforts.

The President and the Secretaries of State and Defense believe that the United States has a unique opportunity to think boldly in reviewing all aspects of American defense policy, strategy, and programs. Our approach is to identify key challenges to American security and to establish the broad principles guiding our strategy.

To formulate more detailed policies on these issues, President Bush has initiated a major and multifaceted national security strategy review. In addition to nuclear offense and defense matters, other elements of the administration's overall defense review include studies of conventional forces, acquisition reform, financial management, quality of life issues, and intelligence and space.

The key elements that we are thinking about in the area of deterrence strategy and requirements are as follows:

First, we are reviewing the conceptual framework for deterrence in light of contemporary and future threats.

Second, we are reexamining our nuclear weapons force requirements. U.S. policy is to achieve a credible deterrent with the lowest number of nuclear weapons consistent with our present and future national security needs and our Alliance commitments. Moving to lower numbers could involve proven arms control tools, innovative unilateral initiatives, or some combination. We will seek to persuade Russia to join us in future offensive reductions, but we are prepared to lead by example.

As long as nuclear weapons remain one of the pillars of deterrence, these weapons must be safe, secure, reliable, and effective. The level of forces we will in the end retain will be conditioned upon a number of factors, not least of which is the fact of proliferation of weapons of mass destruction and ballistic missile technology.

Third, we aim to develop recommendations on ballistic missile defenses consistent with our policy to develop and deploy, at the earliest possible date, effective defenses drawing on the best technologies available. We seek to identify and assess the spectrum of ballistic missile defense capabilities that can contribute to U.S. security and that of our allies. These defenses will be designed to engage and destroy a limited number of missiles of increasing range and sophistication, which are capable of delivering weapons of mass destruction and are being developed or sought by rogue states. It is important to emphasize that they will be capable of countering only limited attacks, not large ones. These defenses must be capable of protecting allies, friends, and deployed forces overseas as well as the United States, and must also be capable of protecting against accidental and unauthorized missile launches.

The purpose of defenses is also to start diminishing our almost exclusive reliance on offensive weapons for deterrence. This is important to our effort, as Secretary of State Powell has said, "to make the world a safer place with fewer nuclear weapons and with the ones that remain having less currency." We are committed to creating a new strategic framework, one defined by lower levels of nuclear weapons and a greater role for missile defense.

The President and Secretaries Powell and Rumsfeld are committed to substantive and meaningful consultations with our allies. As that review proceeds and in order to formulate sound decisions, we value and want allied input.

As all of you are aware we have some diplomatic challenges to work through regarding Russia, China, and the Anti-Ballistic Missile (ABM) Treaty.

Russia and China have expressed their strong opposition to our missile defense plans. The President has said that we will address Russian concerns about the impact of our defenses on their deterrent. Our defenses will be designed to deter and defend against limited attacks from rogue states, not against a large attack.

As for the fate of the ABM Treaty, it is hard to argue that this 1972 treaty meets the needs of today's strategic framework. In fact, the opposite is true. The ABM Treaty in its current form prohibits us from developing and deploying effective missile defenses against rogue missile threats. We will deploy defenses as soon as possible; therefore, we believe that the ABM Treaty will have to be replaced, eliminated, or changed in a fundamental way.

We must remember that Russia, too, faces a threat from the proliferation of ballistic missiles and weapons of mass destruction. Indeed, we believe that Russia's proposal on theater defenses for Europe demonstrates a recognition of this threat. The Russian proposal envisions a cooperative effort with Europe for point defenses of deployed European and Russian forces. It is important to note that the Russian concept would not provide for the area defense of North America or Europe. In view of this, the Russian proposal can not be a substitute for the missile defense concept articulated by President Bush and his national security team. We are, however, studying Russia's ideas carefully at NATO and will respond collectively as an alliance.

We will continue to work to persuade Russia that deployment of effective missile defenses does not threaten the Russian deterrent.

We are also ready to have a serious discussion with China and to listen to its views. This point was made to Vice Premier Qian during his recent U.S. visit. The Vice Premier reiterated China's interest in a dialogue on missile defense as soon as possible. We intend to engage in such a dialogue in the future.

Of course, a key part of any discussion we have with Moscow and Beijing will continue to be their roles and responsibilities with respect to the emerging missile threats from rogue states such as Iran, Iraq, and North Korea.

Perhaps the harshest criticism of missile defense is the suggestion that an "invulnerable" United States will seek to act unilaterally without regard for the concerns and priorities of its friends and allies. I want to emphasize that missile defenses will not "de-couple" the U.S. from its friends and allies. The U.S. is not interested in deploying defenses that would separate us from our friends and allies. The principle of shared risk is not in doubt or open to question. Indeed, protections from coercion and attack by a limited arsenal of ICBMs from rogue states will increase the U.S. ability to fulfill its security commitments in regional conflicts. We see missile defense as a necessary element of deterrence and an opportunity for a collective approach to enhancing security for all. As President Bush has said "America's development of missile defenses is a search for security, not a search for advantage."

And so I hope that I have conveyed to you what underpins the U.S. view of missile defense and of the wider threats and trends in the world that we believe require all of us to move in this direction.

Thank you for giving me the opportunity to begin this conference, and I will be happy to respond to your questions.

22

Excepts: House Members Debate Bush Missile Defense Plan

Reps. Weldon, Skelton, Abercrombie, Sparatt May 1, Remarks (4310)

Several lawmakers serving on committees, subcommittees, and caucuses related to military issues debated the merits and shortcomings of President Bush's proposed missile defense system May 1 in the House of Representatives.

Representatives Curt Weldon (Republican of Pennsylvania), the chairman of the House Armed Services subcommittee on Military Readiness, told fellow lawmakers that "what the President is going to offer is a layers approach, much like we have advocated, where we deploy those quickest possible technologies that are proven and tested to give us some short-term capability."

"It is about time that we begin deploying technologies that can assist us," said Weldon, the founder and co-chairman of the Congressional Missile Defense Caucus.

Missile defense "is for Americans, for Europeans, for Russians, and for all peace-loving people on the face of the Earth," the Pennsylvania lawmaker continued.

Presenting a perspective from the Democratic Party, Representatives Ike Skelton of Missouri, the ranking minority member on the House Armed Services Committee, told fellow lawmakers that he does not oppose missile defense but believes, "as with any aspect of national security, that our expenditure should be proportional to the threat posed."

Reducing the missile threat "should be a cooperative undertaking involving the United States, nations that wish us well, and nations that do not," the Missouri Democrat said.

Every missile not built "is one we do not have to defend against," he said.

Developing U.S. policy on missile defense should be a cooperative process within the government as well, Skelton said.

"I hope the President will work with Congress in that effort," he said. "This is an area where I can assure the President that bipartisanship is possible."

Representative Neil Abercrombie (Democrat of Hawaii) said it was "imperative" that Congress "assess the role of missile defense policy in the overall context of national security and economic stability."

Abercrombie, a member of the House Armed Services Committee, pointed to the availability of advanced technologies and "the ambivalent attitudes toward non-proliferation agreements" by Russia, China, and North Korea.

Those three countries "have well-armed missiles capable of striking parts or all of the United States, and other nations, such as Iran, may possess similar technology in the not too distant future," he said.

While these dangers have led some to call for new strategies to meet the threat, Abercrombie said, the United States should be wary of "strategic decisions that might antagonize our international competitors and/or partners, leading them to adopt a posture even more belligerent in nature."

Abercrombie, who is the ranking Democrat on the House subcommittee on Military Personnel, also urged that the threat to America "be viewed holistically."

It should be viewed "with an eye receptive to the benefits of negotiation, diplomacy, and arms reduction possibilities, mindful of adversarial intent," he said, noting that the possibility of a threat "does not necessarily deem it likely."

Consideration of missile defense systems "must not acquire a 21st century Maginot Line Mentality," Abercrombie said.

Representative John Spratt (Democrat of South Carolina), a member of the House Armed Services Committee, said he thought missile defense was worth pursuing, adding that "if it works, I think it is worth deploying."

But, he cautioned, "we have not proved that it works, not yet. In fact, after spending more than $60 billion on missile defense, we have learned as much about its limits as about its potential."

Every form of defense that has been explored "at great expense has been found to be an Achilles heel of one sort or another," Spratt said.

According to Spratt, boost-phase interceptors can be thwarted by fast-burn boosters or ablative covers; space-based systems move in fixed orbits and can easily be targeted and taken out; and sea-based systems are constrained by the finite amount of space available on a limited number of ships.

Ground-based, mid-course interceptors are "our clear first choice," Spratt said. However, he added, even this strategy has its shortcomings, as "the problem of discriminating warheads from decoys and chaff is a daunting problem that is a long way from being resolved."

Spratt said that through programs like Nunn-Lugar and the Cooperative Threat Reduction Program the United States has helped to "deactivate so far 5,288 Russian warheads, 419 long-range missiles, and 367 silos."

These numbers, "what we have accomplished under these cooperative programs, dwarf the number of warheads that even the most robust NMD (National Missile Defense) system could have handled or could have stopped," he said.

Spratt urged President Bush to consider carefully the effect his proposed missile defense system could have upon these programs.

"We do not want to diminish that effort and leave ourselves less secure rather than more secure," the South Carolina Democrat said. "That is why I plead to the President not just for the statement of policy, but also for balance and also ask him to make a bipartisan effort founded on consensus and not just on the unilateral position that his administration is pursuing."

Following are excerpts from the May 1 Congressional Record:

(begin excerpts)

SUPPORTING THE PRESIDENT'S MISSILE DEFENSE INITIATIVE
House of Representatives
May 01, 2001

Mr WELDON of Pennsylvania. Madam Speaker, I rise in support of the President's announced speech to move forward with missile defense for this country.

It is outrageous to me, and it should be to our colleagues, Madam Speaker, that 10 years after 28 young Americans came home in body bags from Desert Storm, that we still do not have a highly effective theater missile defense system to protect our troops.

We have made some progress. We have pushed the PAC3 system, to the extent now where it is about to be deployed. We have made progress on the THAAD program, having had successful intercepts three times. We have had success in our Navy areawide program.

The Israelis have had success with the Arrow program. We are now moving together with them on the theater high energy laser program, which offers promising potential for us. We are working with the Europeans, particularly the Germans and Italians on the Medium Extended Area Defense System, or MEADs.

We are making progress, but we still have not had the success that we need. I am convinced that part of that is because for the past 8 years we had no consensus and leadership from the White House pushing this country on military defense as John Kennedy challenged America to land on the moon in 1960, and 9 years later we did it.

Madam Speaker, all of that is changing today, as the highest elected official in our country comes out solidly in favor of missile defense as a resource for defending our people.

Now, some would say, well, why do we worry about missiles when a terrorist can take a truck bomb and do the same thing? Well, we are concerned about terrorists activities. In fact, that is why in our committee we have plussed up funding for work — related to chemical and biological terrorism significantly over the past several years; but the fact is the weapon of choice by Saddam Hussein to kill 28 young Americans was not a truck bomb. It was, in fact, a low-complexity SCUD missile that sent those young Americans, half of them from my State, back home in body bags to be buried by their families.

Some say we cannot rush to judgment on national missile defense, and I can tell my colleagues what the President is going to offer is a layers approach, much like we have advocated, where we deploy those quickest possible technologies that are proven and tested to give us some short-term capability.

I say it is about the time that we begin deploying technologies that can assist us. Some of our colleagues will say, wait a minute, the Russians will be backed into a corner. I say that is hogwash. Yes, the Russians do not trust us today.

Madam Speaker, I would say if I were a Russian today, I would not trust America either on missile defense, because three times in the last 10 years, we have publicly rebuked Russia on cooperation of missile defense. The first was after Boris Yeltsin in 1992 accepted George Bush's challenge to work together, and we began the Ross-Mamedov between our State Department and the Russian Ministry of Foreign Affairs.

In 1993, when Bill Clinton came into office, he abruptly canceled those talks. That sent a signal to Russia, we do not want you involved. The second time was in 1996, when the only cooperative missile defense program between this country and Russia, the Ramos project, was canceled by the Clinton administration.

It was only because CARL LEVIN, people like the gentleman from Missouri (Mr SKELTON) the gentleman from Hawaii (Mr ABERCROMBIE), and the gentleman from South Carolina (Mr SPRATT) went to war with the White House that we were able to reinvigorate the Ramos program and keep it alive, but the signal was sent to Russia we do not want to work with you.

The third example was in 1997, at a time almost everyone says that ABM treaty needed to be flexible. The administration sent its negotiators to Geneva to negotiate two outrageous protects that would actually tigthen up the ABM treaty. One would create demarcation between theater and national missile defense artificial differentiation, the other would be multilateralization of the treaty.

The administration knew that neither the House or the Senate, especially the Senate would ratify those protocols, but they convinced the Russians that that was our position. Even though the Constitution requires the administration to submit those kinds of changes to the Senate for their advice and the consent for 3 years, the administration never did that, because they knew the Senate would not ratify them.

The Russians for the third time were tricked in their mind,

tricked into believing that America really was serious about cooperating with them.

When the Duma included those two protocols, the part of START II ratification last spring, all of a sudden our Senate said no way are we now going to pass START II, because the Duma did what the administration did not do. They attached the protocols to the ABM treaty, as additions to the START II treaty, something that we would never accept in the country.

It is no wonder the Russians do not trust us. If I were in Russia today, I would not trust America's intentions in missile defense either. It is time to get beyond that. We can, in fact, rebuilt a trust that we have lost and get the Russians know that missile defense is not about backing them into a corner.

Missile defense is for Americans, for Europeans, for Russians, and for all peace-loving people on the face of the Earth.

MISSILE DEFENSE
House of Representatives
May 01, 2001

Mr Skelton. Madam Speaker, it is no secret that missile defense is perhaps one of the most significant national security issues facing the House this year. How our country decides to pursue reducing that specific threat affects how much we will be able to spend on other aspects of defense, how we will deal with our friends and allies, and how America participates in shaping the world.

I do not oppose missile defense. Neither do many Democrats. But I believe, as with any aspect of national security, that our expenditure should be proportional to the threat posed.

My friend, the gentleman from Hawaii (Mr Abercrombie), has laid out some very sound principles by which I believe we should proceed in considering our system, and that is a significant one.

Reducing the missile threat should be a cooperative undertaking involving the United States that wish us well, and nations that do not. Every missile not built is one we do not have to defend against.

Developing our policy should also be a cooperative process, Madam Speaker. I hope the President will work with Congress in that effort. This is an area where I can assure the President that a bipartisanship is possible.

I look forward to hearing from the expert, the gentleman from South Carolina (Mr SPRATT), and I also compliment the gentleman from Hawaii (Mr Abercrombie on his seminal work in this area. I thank him for that.

Let me speak first about the threat as it involves military intelligence. Missile defense, if nothing else, is at the terminal end of military operations. Its use represents a failure to deter, and perhaps, more to the point, a missed opportunity to have assessed accurately intentions and activity of a potential enemy.

There is no substitute, and I will repeat it, there is no substitute for comprehensive intelligence-gathering and analysis if the preventative value of missile defense is to be maximized.

Now, there are several points that should be brought out that can be termed as principles on missile defense. The deployment of missile defense systems to protect our country and its interests is a decision that should be considered in the following context.

First, missile defense investment must be measured in relation to other military requirements.

Missile defense must counter a credible threat.

Missile defense will require an integrated, fully-funded military and intelligence effort, and I will repeat, that reliability and timely intelligence is critical to the success of any missile defense system.

Missile defense must be proven to work through rigorous, realistic testing prior to any final deployment decisions. In other words, it has to work.

Missile defense must improve overall United States national security. This is fundamentally a question as to whether deployment defenses will encourage opponents to deploy counter-offenses, encouraging in the process a global missile proliferation race.

Missile defense must be deployed with an understanding that those benefiting from its protection will share in its costs. That is, if the benefits of a missile defense system are extended to share with American allies in Europe or elsewhere, equitable burden-sharing arrangements need to be made.

Finally, deployment of missile defense will be debated in relation to the provisions of the antiballistic missile defense system.

Madam Speaker, the whole issue of missile defense will be a serious issue this year. The President is making a statement regarding that later today. It is an area where bipartisanship is needed. It is an area that I feel very certain that bipartisanship will happen, but we need to be thorough and not rush to judgement and do something that is wrong or inaccurate, or something that does not work or meets the threats that are obviously apparent.

Again, let me commend our friend, the gentleman from Hawaii (Mr ABERCROMBIE), on his efforts. I looked forward to hearing our friend, the gentleman from South Carolina (Mr SPRATT), who has done a great deal of work in this area.

UNITED STATES MISSILE DEFENSE

House of Representatives

May 01, 2001

Mr. Abercrombie. Madam Speaker, with the President making his remarks today on missile defense, I think we need to recognize unprecedented political challenges loom on the strategic horizon. Current U.S. defense force planning is set within an atmosphere of great uncertainty. Historic rivals of the United States, such as the Soviet Union and Eastern Bloc nations, have either disintegrated altogether or lost much of their competitive influence.

Regional state actors, particularly on the Asian continent, show signs of future ascendancy on the world political stage. Other nation states, some exhibiting anti-U.S. bent, continue to challenge American allies and interests around the world, even as U.S. peacekeeping and peacemaking commitments evolve.

The very definition of American interests is in transition as varied threats emerge in the post-Cold War world . . .

The availability of advanced technologies has also reached a significant level of concern as Russia, China, and North Korea, continue to exhibit ambivalent attitudes towards nonproliferation agreements.

The 2001 Reports of the Secretary of Defense to the President and the Congress notes the spread of materials with potential applications to nuclear, biological, and chemical weapons, and highlights the proliferation of advanced long-range delivery systems.

Another study, the Quadrennial Defense Review 2001 Working Group by the National University laments, and I quote, "Given the diffusion of advanced military technologies and the proliferation of weapons of mass destruction, one could envision an adversary armed with longer-range missiles and cruise missiles, weapons of mass destruction, advanced integrated air defense systems, and/or sophisticated anti-ship mines and missiles by 2010, if not sooner. . . ."

Set within this context, U.S. strategists are challenged with questions about nuclear strategy and force posture, arms control regimes, and missile defense modernization options. Missile proliferation has introduced an immediate threat to American uniformed personnel stationed abroad, and brought to the fore the prospect of ballistic missile attack on the United States as a real possibility within the next 5 to 7 years.

China, Russia and North Korea each have well-armed missiles capable of striking parts or all of the United States, and other nations, such as Iran, may possess similar technology in the not too distant future.

This new setting has led some to call for a new strategic synthesis and a doctrinal requirements to, in the words of Michael Krepon, and I quote, "reduce the dangers from missiles and weapons of mass destruction in the uncertain period ahead."

Still, the view of the threat from abroad should not create a threat from within. An effort must be made to avoid strategic decisions that might antagonize our international competitors and/or partners, leading them to adopt a posture even more belligerent in nature. Krepon suggests, and I quote, "The net effect of missile deployments should be to reinforce reductions in nuclear forces, reassure allies, support nonproliferation partners, and reduce the salience of missiles and weapons of mass destruction."

Thus, the threat to America should be viewed holistically. It should be viewed with an eye receptive to the benefits of negotiation, diplomacy, and arms reduction possibilities, mindful of adversarial intent. The possibility of a threat does not necessarily deem it likely. Whereas missile threats to the United States and allies indeed exist and are likely to increase, other threats also remain. America, therefore, should invest in a force structure commensurate with likely threats. Above all, consideration of missile defense systems must not acquire a 21st century Maginot Line mentality.

Calls for nonpartisanship respecting an issue are generally rhetorical and strategic in nature as regards their political origin. Missile doctrine made manifest in congressional policy, however, cries out for just that approach. No other defense posture is as pregnant with controversy and potential for bitter political conflict. The costs of commitment alone set off warning bells throughout the budget spectrum. Discussion can rapidly descend into confrontation and accusation if we do not pledge to bring serious, sober consideration and resolution to the table. What is needed presently is the equivalent of a congressional deep breath.

We need to remember the various missile launch scenarios are abstract evaluations and the solutions promulgated in response are visions, for the most part, still on paper and in the mind's eye.

Missiles, offensive or defensive, are at best a technological answer to a military question, not a diplomatic answer to a question of negotiation. International diplomacy and national policy remain an art, not a science. Science is fixed and immutable in its consequence, while art, as Andy Warhol said, is what one can get away with.

Congress must guard against allowing missile defense systems becoming the policy, allowing the technology, in effect, to develop its own psychology. There is gradually being created in the United States a burgeoning military and corporate apparatus dependent in large measure on missile defense to rationalize its existence.

It is imperative, therefore, that the Congress assess the role of missile defense policy in the overall context of national security and economic stability. The issues are real. The responsibility is ours.

NATIONAL MISSILE DEFENSE

House of Representatives
May 01, 2001

Mr Spratt. Madam Speaker, President Bush will outline today his plan for national missile defense. I reserve judgment until I hear the speech, but I have been following SDI and NMD,

National Missile Defense, for years; and I have a few thoughts of mine that I want to share with the House, for whatever they may be worth.

I think National Missile Defense, NMD, is worth pursuing, and if it works, I think it is worth deploying. But we have not proved that it works, not yet. In fact, after spending more than $ 60 billion on missile defense, we have learned as much about its limits as about its potential. Every form of defense we have explored at great expense has been found to be an Achilles heel of one sort or another. Boost-phase interceptors can be thwarted by fast-burn boosters or ablative covers. Space-based systems, whether they are lasers or kinetic interceptors move in fixed orbits and can easily be targeted and taken out. Sea based systems are constrained by an obvious factor the finite space availability on ships available.

We for now settle on ground-based, mid-course interceptors, which I consider to be our clear first choice, the right way to go, but I will be first to tell you that the problem of discriminating warheads from decoys and chaff is a daunting problem that is a long way from being resolved.

We have spent 18 years and $ 60 billion since Mr Reagan made his speech; and if we have learned anything, it is that missile defense is not likely to render nuclear weapons impotent and obsolete. It may enhance deterrence, I believe it will; but it is not likely to replace deterrence.

There is, however, a threat, a threat of an unauthorized or accidental attack, a threat of a rogue attack, existing and emerging, and I think it would be wise to have a missile defense system to meet that threat. But we have to recognize, we have to be realistic and recognize that a rogue or unauthorized attack can well come in an unconventional manner and probably will, rather than by missile with the sender's signature written all over it, and that threat, the threat of nuclear weapons in the hands of parties undeterred by our ability to strike back, is a very real threat best opted at its source.

If we strike ahead to defiantly on our own abrogate the ABM treaty and deploy any defense systems that we want to deploy, we may very well jeopardize the arms control measures that make us secure and make ourself less secure rather than more.

Now, I think that ground-based interceptors are the first

right step. We build the SBIRs–Low system anyway. We are working on a technology here with ground-based interceptors that are complementary to the technology we use for theater missile defense systems. Everybody agrees that is a need we need to develop; and it will be proved to be useful, I think, to have a system on the ground which can be tested continually and improved incrementally.

But having said that, having said that, I want to say, I do not think we should be so zealous to deploy any system that we deploy a substandard system that has not been tested and tested rigorously or else we will find ourselves on a rush to failure.

Finally, I think we need to be realistic. We are soon going to get a defense budget from the Pentagon. We are told it could be to $ 200 billion to $ 300 billion to $ 400 billion more than the $ 2 trillion we have already provided in the FYDP for the next 6 years. We need to be realistic about not only the acquisition costs but the life cycle costs of a ballistic missile system.

I do not think NMD deserves a trump card in our budget. It is time, I think, that we in the Congress and elsewhere in the government stopped treating BMD, ballistic missile defense, as a political totem. That is what it has become, a political totem like no other weapon system we have ever seen.

It is time for us to start treating this just as any other weapon system. It does not need cheerleaders. It does not need pallbearers, what BMD, what NMD need is candor. It needs to be held to the same standards of feasibility, cost effectiveness as every other weapon system we buy and deploy.

If we are going to sell this system to others, our allies, our adversaries, our former adversaries, to Russia, we need to have unity or some cohesion among ourselves, bipartisan unity.

I think if we stay within these bounds, we can build that kind of bipartisan consensus. We should never lose sight of this fundamental fact. We have got a rough, rocky relationship with the Russians right now, but we are making progress. While we can work with Russia, we should work with Russia to secure their missile systems, to secure their nuclear and fissile materials. And bear this in mind, a critical point, through programs like Nunn-Lugar and the Cooperative Threat Reduction Program, we have helped to deactivate so far 5,288 Russian warheads, 419 long-range missiles, and 367 silos. These numbers, what we have accomplished under these cooperative programs, dwarf the number of warheads that even the most robust NMD system could have handled or could have stopped.

We have only begun in that effort. We do not want to diminish that effort and leave ourselves less secure rather than more secure, that is why I plead to the President not just for the statement of policy, but also for balance and also ask him to make a bipartisan effort founded on consensus and not just on the unilateral position that his administration is pursuing.

23

Excepts: Rep. Weldon Outlines Rationale for Missile Defense

May 2 Speech Calls Bush Plan "Asymmetric Deterrence") (6610)

America is "totally vulnerable" to a missile attack, according to Representative Curt Weldon (Republican of Pennsylvania).

"If an accidental launch occurred of one missile from Russia, from North Korea, which we know now has the long-range capability, or from China, we have no capability to respond," Weldon said in a May 2 speech in the House of Representatives.

"Working together for peaceful protection of our friends, our allies and our neighbors, is the solution of the 21st century. That is what George Bush outlined for us yesterday" in his missile defense plan, said Weldon, a member of both the House Armed Services Committee and the House Select Committee on U.S. National Security and Military/Commercial Concerns with the People's Republic of China.

The President "is on the right track," Weldon said, "He did not say we have all the answers, because we do not, but he did say, together, there is nothing we cannot accomplish."

Weldon, who is chairman of the House subcommittee on Military Readiness, said that the United States is pursuing a missile defense system much like the one Russia already has.

"The first reason we need missile defense is to protect us against an accidental or deliberate launch," said Weldon, the founder and co-chairman of the Congressional Missile Defense Caucus.

Weldon reminded his colleagues that the Central Intelligence Agency (CIA) has documented that North Korea test-launched a three-stage Taepo Dong II rocket in August of 1998.

"It did not complete its line of flight, but the CIA estimated if it had, it would have been able to reach American soil, the

West Coast of California, parts of Alaska and parts of Hawaii," Weldon said.

The missile defense system proposed by President Bush is one that would only "give us the ability to defend against small number of missiles, an accidental launch or a deliberate launch of perhaps 1 to 10 missiles, that we could defend against," he said.

Such a system, Weldon added, "does not destabilize our relationship with Russia because Russia knows full well that they could launch hundreds of missiles at America and very easily overcome the kind of system that President Bush is talking about."

President Bush has proposed a new dynamic, the Pennsylvania lawmaker said.

"I call it asymmetric deterrence, and that means that we continue to negotiate with our allies and friends and countries like Russia, and we continue to rely on deterrence as the ultimate threat to an attack on our homeland, but we now begin to allow missile defense systems," said Weldon, a member of the Republican Policy Committee.

"The fact is that Russia believes in missile defense, as does America. They believe in deterrence, as does America. The Soviet Union developed the only operational ABM system around Moscow. That system has been upgraded four times, and it still exists today," said Weldon, who is the founder and chairman of the Congressional U.S.—former Soviet Union Energy Caucus.

"When I travel to Mowcow and meet with my Russian friends and we talk about missile defense, I candidly ask them, If you really believe in deterrence alone, take down your ABM system. Be as vulnerable as America is, and have no system and rely on deterrence," he related.

"They look at me and smile and laugh and say, 'You know we will never do that'," Weldon said.

The Russians "believe in missile defense," Weldon said. "They have aggressive and very capable theater missile defense systems. They have the SA–10, the SA–12, the S–300, the S–400."

In fact, he continued, "Russia's systems are comparable to systems that we are building. So it is not a case of America pursuing missile defense and embarrassing Russia because they do not have any systems; they have some of the best systems in the world available today."

Weldon, who also sits on the House Science Committee, said he was convinced that Russia's leaders "can and will understand that America's intent on missile defense is not to create an arms race."

"The Russians believe in missile defense because they know the threats are real," Weldom said.

"We believe in missile defense because the threats are real," he said.

Following are excerpts of Weldon's May 2 speech from the Congressional Record:
(begin excerpts)

DEFENSE OF AMERICA'S HOMELAND
House of Representatives
May 02, 2001

Mr Weldon of Pennsylvania. Madam Speaker, I rise tonight to focus on an issue that is dominating the front page of every newspaper in America today and that is the defense of America's homeland. President Bush gave a major speech yesterday where he outlined a commitment to pursuit of a national missile defense and provide a protection for this Nation....

I will talk about the objections that are being raised by some; why we need this kind of capability; what the current system capability is that we are developing. And I am going to respond to criticisms that this will start a new arms race....

Madam Speaker, my real topic tonight is to focus on the missile defense speech that President Bush presented yesterday at the National Defense University. He said that we need to change the basic parameters which we live under and deal with in our relations with Russia and other countries relative to the ABM Treaty. The ABM Treaty, which was negotiated in 1972, allows both the United States and the former Soviet Union to rely on deterrence so that neither country would attack the other for fear of retaliation.

In addition, that treaty says that each country can have one missile defense system, one ABM system. The Russians chose to deploy such a system around Moscow, which protects about

75 percent of their population. America chose not to pursue any system, because it was politically impossible in America to choose one city over another and leave the rest of America vulnerable.

Today, Madam Speaker, America is totally vulnerable. If an accidental launch occurred of one missile from Russia, from North Korea, which we know now has the long-range capability, or from China, we have no capability to respond.

Now, is that such a far-fetched idea or notion?

Well, Madam Speaker, let me document for our colleagues what occurred in January of 1995. As we know, the Russians have hundreds of missile launchers, all of which can reach any city in America within 25 minutes, and all of which have nuclear warheads on top of them.

Now, there is a very sophisticated command and control system on those missiles, as there are on our missiles; but a significant number of Russia's missiles are on mobile launchers. They are called SS–25s. If my colleagues saw a photograph of one, it would look like it is on the back of a tractor-trailer truck. But that missile, even though it can be transported any place over an open road area, can travel the necessary distance to hit any city in America and devastate that city. Each of those SS–25s are controlled locally, even though they have to have the command authorization of the central Russian Government.

Let us look at what happened in January of 1995. Norway was going to launch a rocket into the atmosphere to sample weather conditions. So Norway contacted Russia and told the Russian Government not to worry when we launch this three-stage rocket; it is simply for us to gather more information about weather conditions affecting our country. Now, because Russia's military has been in a state of disarray, they have not been able to invest and reinvest in improving their conventional alert systems and their intelligence collection systems. So that when Norway launched that three-stage rocket, the Russian intelligence agencies misread it as an attack from an American nuclear submarine.

Boris Yeltsin acknowledged the week after that incident that Russia had, in fact, for one of only three times that we know of, put their entire offensive ICBM system on alert, which meant, Madam Speaker, that Russia was within 15 minutes of launching an ICBM with a nuclear warhead against an American city.... With 7 minutes, left Boris Yeltsin overruled them and called off the response against an American city.

Now, Madam Speaker, for just one moment let us imagine that one of those missiles is accidentally launched, which are preprogrammed to hit a certain spot in America, and all of their missiles are preprogrammed, as ours are preprogrammed. What if that occurred and what if President Putin then realized Russia had made a grave mistake; that they accidentally allowed, either because of a lack of control of a command unit, who may have gotten the launch codes, or because of some other glitch, Russia accidentally launched one missile against America? What would the phone conversation be like between President Putin and President Bush?

Well, it might go something like this: "President Bush, I am sorry to tell you we have made a tragic mistake. We have accidentally launched a missile against one of your cities. We did not mean to do it, but our command and control system failed." What would be President Bush's response? Would he then call a national press conference and tell the people of that target city that they have 25 minutes to move? Because, Madam Speaker, we have no defense today against a ballistic missile launch against America. We have no defense system in place.

For the past 6 years, Madam Speaker, I have chaired the research and development committee for national security. I have been on the security committee for 15 years. So I work these issues. The possibility of an accidental launch is not very high, but it does exist.

And the fact is that today America has no defense against such a launch. There is no system we can put into space, there is no plane we can send up that can shoot down an incoming ICBM at the speed it would be travelling.

The same thing occurred in 1991 when in Desert Storm Saddam Hussein decided that he wanted to harm American soldiers. He could have put a bomb on a truck, and he could have had it driven into Saudi Arabia where our troops were headquartered. But he did not do that. Saddam Hussein chose the weapon of choice, a low-complexity Scud missile with a conventional bomb on top of it and fired that missile into an American barracks in Saudi Arabia. We could not defend against that missile, much like we cannot defend against a missile that would be launched against an American city.

As a result of the launch of that Scud missile by Saddam Hussein, 28 Americans came home in body bags because we let them down. America had no system in place to defend against that kind of a missile attack, even in a small area the distance between Iraq and Saudi Arabia.

The sad part, Madam Speaker, is that 9, 10 years later we still do not have a highly effective system for missile defense to protect our troops and allies and our Nation. . . .

So the first reason we need missile defense is to protect us against an accidental or deliberate launch. The CIA has now documented that North Korea, an unstable nation, in August of 1998 test-launched a three-stage Taepo Dong II rocket that traversed into the atmosphere. It did not complete its line of flight, but the CIA estimated if it had, it would have been able to reach American soil, the West Coast of California, parts of Alaska and parts of Hawaii.

That allowed that CIA to say publicly that North Korea has the ability to launch from its soil a long-range, three-stage missile that could deliver a light payload against an American city. That missile might not be very accurate, they might aim for Los Angeles and hit San Francisco, but if you are a resident of San Francisco, it does not matter where they aimed.

The point is, North Korea has a capability that they never had. Unlike when the ABM Treaty was developed, you only had two major countries with this kind of ability, the Soviet Union and the United States, and we could respectfully agree that neither would attempt to attack the other for fear of retaliation. Also, when the Soviet Union was in fact a coherent country prior to 1992 before the breakup, the Soviet military was well-paid and well-fed. They had discipline. They were well-respected in Russia. Today, there are severe internal problems and stability problems within the Russian military.

Therefore, because of those problems, there is a greater likelihood of a problem potentially occurring, as there is with the possibility of North Korea or China threatening a launch against the U.S.

Madam Speaker, it is not just whether or not they would launch a missile against us, because the opponents of missile defense will say, wait a minute. Does anybody really believe that North Korea is going to fire a missile against the United States? We would wipe them out. We would wipe China out. That is not the issue, Madam Speaker.

The problem is that we now know North Korea has the capability. We also know that North Korea is developing a nuclear weapon, if they do not already have one, which could be placed on a missile.

Let us take a scenario for a moment. Let us suppose that North Korea would invade South Korea, which they have talked about off and on for years. The U.S. would, because of our relationship, probably come to the aid of South Korea. And what if North Korea's leadership then, and they have certainly indicated unstable decision-making processes in the past, suppose they said to America, If you do not pull your troops out of South Korea, we are going to launch our long-range missile at one of your cities.

Now, unlike in the past, we know North Korea has that kind of very rudimentary capability. Do we then attack North Korea preemptively? Do we wipe out any capability they might have? Do we bomb their cities?

Madam Speaker, we cannot allow a rogue state to have the potential for causing problems in the decision-making process of our President and command officers because of the potential for a launch, illogical launch as it might be, against our sovereign Nation or our allies.

The idea of a missile defense system under George Bush is not what Ronald Reagan proposed, and there will be some in this country who say, there goes George Bush trying to restart the Cold War, trying to bring back Star Wars, or the Strategic Defense Initiative. That is not what President Bush was talking about yesterday. No one is proposing that we attempt to build a shield over America that could stop Russia if they wanted to attack us with all of their missiles. . . . We are only talking about a limited capability, a system that would give us the ability to defend against a small number of missiles, an accidental launch or a deliberate launch of perhaps 1 to 10 missiles, that we could defend against. This does not destabilize our relationship with Russia because Russia knows full well that they could launch hundreds of missiles at America and very easily overcome the kind of system that President Bush is talking about.

For these reasons, Madam Speaker, it is important that America provide a defense for our people.

The interesting thing is that some of the opponents of missile defense have consistently opposed all research in this area. And I would say to our colleagues, as I did several years ago when we voted on H.R. 4, my missile defense bill in the House, and we pulled more democrats with us than President Clinton did, 103 Democrats voted in favor of H.R. 4, 102 Democrats voted against it and all but two Republicans voted in favor of that bill, giving us a veto-proof margin. Our goal is to give us the capability that every nation in the world is now pursuing. . . .

We do want to cooperate with our allies. This is not just about protecting Amerca. . . .

The goal that President Bush laid out for the world in that we need to change the dimension. It should no longer be a policy of mutually assured destruction.

Now, to me as a teacher, it is outrageous that we would base our foreign policy with Russia on mutually assured destruction. You attack us, we will annihilate you. We attack you, you will annihilate us. That is a crazy way to have a world order, especially when you have other nations that are not in any way, shape or form anywhere near as reliable as the Soviet Union was during the Cold War, and we did not have the instability that we now have inside of Russia with the problems, internal with their military and the command and control and alerting problems that they have in reading what is happening in terms of rocket launches around the world.

So for all of these reasons, President Bush proposed a new dynamic. I call it asymmetric deterrence, and that means that we continue to negotiate with our allies and friends and countries like Russia, and we continue to rely on deterrence as the ultimate threat to an attack on our homeland, but we now begin to allow missile defence systems.

Now, the question is, why would America pursue missile defense, it is only going to back Russia into a corner. That is not true. The fact is that Russia believes in missile defense, as does America. They believe in deterrence, as does America. The Soviet

Union developed the only operational ABM system around Moscow. That system has been upgraded four times, and it still exists today.

When I have been in negotiations with Russian friends, and I have gone to Russia 23 teams, I speak the language, I formed and I chair the Interparliamentary Commission with the Russia Duma and the Federation Council. When I travel to Moscow and meet with my Russian friends and we talk about missile defense, I candidly ask them, If you really believe in deterrence alone, take down your ABM system. Be as vulnerable as America is, and have no system and rely on deterrence.

They look at me and smile and laugh and say, You know we will never do that.

The point is that the Russians believe in missile defense. They have aggressive and very capable theater missile defense systems. They have the SA–10, the SA–12, the S–300, the S–400 . . . .

In fact, Russia's systems are comparable to systems that we are building. So it is not a case of America pursuing missile defense and embarrassing Russia because they do not have any systems; they have some of the best systems in the world available today.

Why then, Madam Speaker, would Russia not trust us? Why then would the Russian leader publicly express his concerns about the President's speech? Why would Russian leaders and European leaders express concern about moving forward with missile defense?

Let me say this, Madam Speaker. If I were a Russian today and if I had witnessed what the Clinton administration did in terms of cooperation with Russia, I would not trust America in the area of missile defense either.

Let me give you the reasons why I say that, Madam Speaker. We have sent mixed signals to Russia for the past 10 years. The first one came in 1993. In 1992, Boris Yeltsin challenged George Bush, Sr to work together on missile defense, to have Russian scientists and American scientists cooperate and explore ways that we could work together. George Bush, Sr accepted that challenge. The two Presidents of the two countries involved the Ministry of Foreign Affairs in Russia with the State Department in the U.S. . . .

In 1993, when Bill Clinton and Al Gore came into office, they had opposed missile defense. Without consulting with the Russian government, they abruptly canceled the Ross-Mamedov talks. We sent the first signal to the Russians that we do not want to cooperate with you on missile defense. We do not want to be your partner in looking at ways to change the dynamic of our relationship.

The second signal was sent to the Russians in 1996 and 1997. We had in fact funded one joint program between our Defense Department and the Russian defense department in the missile defense area called Ramos. Ramos was designed to build two satellites, one controlled by Russia, one controlled by the U.S., identical in operation, so that each country would get the same identical information when a rocket was launched someplace on the surface of the Earth, so we would have the same alert mechanism. It also was designed to build trust between our countries in the area of missile defense. . . . In 1996 and 1997 with no advance notice to the Russians nor to the Congress, the Clinton administration decided to cancel the Ramos program. When the Russians found out about this, they were livid. I got three phone calls and faxes and e-mails at my office from senior Russian leaders. . . .

I then went over to the Senate and enlisted the support of Democrat Senator Carl LEVIN who agreed with me as the top Democrat on the Armed Services Committee in the Senate. He and I worked vigilantly with our colleagues, and we overturned the administration's decision. The program is still funded today. But the damage was done. Because for the second time, the Clinton administration told the Russians, "We do not want to cooperate with you."

The third time occurred in 1997. At a time when most people in the world and in this country were acknowledging that the ABM treaty had outlived its usefulness because we were no longer in a bipolar world with two countries, the Soviet Union and America. We now had other countries with long-range missile capability, China and North Korea and Iran moving in that direction. At a time when most in this country were saying, let us provide some flexibility in the way this treaty is being interpreted, what did the Clinton administration do? They sent our U.S. negotiators to Geneva where we were in ongoing discussions with the Russians over the ABM treaty.

Instead of trying to find ways to make the ABM treaty flexible, the Clinton administration was negotiating a tightening up of the ABM treaty, contrary to the thought of almost everyone in this country. I for the life of me could not understand what the Clinton administration was doing. When I read about these discussions with the Russians, I heard about this plan to multilateralize the treaty, bring other countries in, even though they did not have long-range missiles, and I heard about this artificial demarcation, differentiating between theater and national missile defense, Madam Speaker, I did something that no other Member of Congress did.

I went to Geneva. I got the approval of our State Department, and we set up a negotiating session. The chief U.S. negotiator was on my side, Stanley Rivales and the chief Russian negotiator was sitting across from me, General Koltunov. We talked for 2½ hours about the administration's negotiations for these two ideas of tightening up the ABM treaty. So I inquired of General Koltunov, "General, why do you in Russia want to bring more countries in as signatories to the ABM treaty?" Only two nations were the original signatories, the Soviet Union and the U.S. Why did you pic-three former Soviet states, Kazakhstan, Belarus and Ukraine, to become equal partners to the U.S. and Russia? That will make it more difficult to amend the treaty. And none of those three countries have long range missiles. They have all been returned to Russia after the breakup of the Soviet Union.

General Koltunov looked at me and he said, "Congressman Weldon, you are asking that question of the wrong person. We didnot propose to multilateralize the treaty. The person sitting next to you did."

Meaning that our government was trying to push the Russian government into expanding the treaty to include three former Soviet states. Why would you do that especially when none of those three countries had long-range missiles, unless your purpose was to make the ABM treaty more difficult to modify?

The second question dealt with demarcation. I could not understand how we could negotiate with the Russians an artificial differentiation between a theater missile defense system for a given area and a national missile defense with longer range. So I said to the chief Russian negotiator, General Koltunov, "General, explain to me, how did you arrive at these numbers of interceptor speed and range?". . . .

General Koltunov told me, after thinking for a few moments, "Well, Congressman, there were serious negotiations between our scientists and your scientists, and they arrived at these numbers." But he did not give me any justification. Well, I was not satisfied. I came back to the United States. We concluded those negotiations in Geneva. President Clinton sent the signal to Russia that America was supportive of tightening up the ABM treaty. So the Russians again for the third time took us at our word. But the Clinton administration knew, Madam Speaker, they could not get either of those two changes to the treaty through the U.S. Senate, even though the U.S. Constitution requires any substantive change to any treaty to be submitted to the Senate for advice and consent.

For 3 years, from 1997 to the year 2000, actually to the year 2001 because that is today, until the end of the Clinton administration, the administration failed to submit either of those changes to the ABM treaty to the Senate as required by our Constitution so the Senate could debate them . . . So for 3 years, the Russians had been convinced by Clinton that we were supportive of tightening up the ABM treaty, even though the administration knew the Senate and the American people would not support those changes.

Last May, when the Russian Duma was considering ratification of the START II treaty, a treaty which our Senate had already passed years ago, the Clinton administration, I am convinced, convinced the Russian leadership to have the Duma add those two changes to the ABM treaty onto the back of the START II treaty. Why would they do that? Because they knew the START II treaty had already been ratified by the Senate and because they knew they could not get those two ABM changes through the Senate, so they said if the Russians add them on, then the Senate will have to accept them when the treaty comes back to us for re-ratification. So when the state Duma in Russia ratified the START II treaty last spring, they added those two Geneva protocols on the START II treaty, it then came back to the U.S., and what did our Senate say? "No way are we going to pass the START II treaty."

So the Russians for the third time saw America going back on what they thought was our word. Three times in 8 years we sent mixed signals to Russia about missile defense. It is no wonder that the Russians do not understand what America's real intentions are in terms of missile defense. Now, they understand my intentions, because I have a good solid relationship with them. They know that I want us to be involved with Russia. The Russians know that we want to be partners with them. We want to find common ground . . . .

I took several Members of Congress from both parties along. We went to Moscow before the vote here so that we could reassure the Russians that our intent in moving forward in missile defense was not to back the Russians into a corner. We did not see Russia as the enemy. We were not doing this to try to create an advantage over Russia. And that we wanted to work together with Russia.

Madam Speaker, I am convinced through my contact with Russian leaders that they can and will understand that America's intent on missile defense is not to create an arms race. The Russians believe in missile defense because they know the threats are real. We believe in missile defense because the threats are real . . . .

Madam Speaker, with the Russian leaders that I work with, people like Dr Yevghenie Velakof who heads up the Kurchatov Institute understand what we are trying to accomplish. In fact, Dr Velakof and I coauthored an op-ed 3 years ago that was entitled *From Mutually Assured Destruction to Mutually Assured Protection*. Dr Velakof understands what George Bush is trying to do. When Russians understand that we are serious and want them involved and that we are not playing games, they will cooperate with us . . . .

That is why the Russians are concerned about missile defense. It is not because of the system. It is because of an inconsistent, incoherent, roller coaster foreign policy where three times in 8 years we sent mixed signals to Moscow on missile defense . . . .

In fact, our goal is to work with Russia; it is to work NATO; it is to work with Ukraine; it is to work with Canada; with the European countries to develop something we have not had before, an ability to shoot down offensive missiles.

Mr Speaker, over 70 nations today in the world have missiles that they control. Countries like Iran, Iraq, Syria, Libya, India, Pakistan, North Korea and a whole host of other countries all have missiles. Some have conventional weapons on them. Some have the potential to put a chemical or a biological agent on them, but they all have missiles and they all have launchers.

Mr Speaker, today in the world over 22 nations can build missiles and are building them, and they are selling them to other nations. Missiles are out of control. We did not expect this threat to come from unstable nations for another 15 to 20 years, but over the past 10 years we have lost control of proliferation. Because of Russia's instability and because of China's lack of compliance, Russia and China have allowed technology to flow to unstable nations which then have given those nations abilities in missile technology that we did not think they would have for at least 15 years.

Let me talk about that for a moment, Mr Speaker, because that has a direct bearing on why President Bush yesterday said we have to have missile defense now, because the threats are here today. Iran now has a Shahab III system they are working on. The Shabab IV and V, which are medium-range missile systems, can kill tons of people all throughout Europe and can hit Israel directly. We know Iraq has missiles. We know all these countries have missiles.

How did they get this technology, Mr Speaker? Unfortunately, because of America's lack of enforcement of arms control agreements.

Two years ago, I asked the Congressional Research Service, an independent, bipartisan research arm of the Library of Congress, it is not to partisan, all of our colleagues use it, I asked them to do a study for me of how many instances of arms control violations had occurred in the 1990s. I put that report in the Congressional Record last year.

The answer is that up until 1998, we had evidence that Russia and China had illegally transferred technology, much of it missile technology, to unstable nations in violation of arms control agreements 38 times; 20 times by the Chinese, 18 times by the Russians. The arms control agreements are supposed to have sanctions applied when we catch other countries in violation. Much like if we catch an American company illegally selling technology to a foreign nation that they should noting selling to, we arrest their officers. We fine them and, if necessary, we put them in jail. Thirty-eight times we caught the Russians and Chinese illegally giving technology to our enemies. Only two times out of 38 did we impose the required sanctions when we caught the Chinese transferring M–11 missiles to Pakistan, when we caught the Chinese transferring ring magnets for their nuclear program to Pakistan. The other 36 times we turned our head. . . .

These devices have Soviet markings on them. These devices were clipped off of SSN–19 long-range Soviet missiles. These devices used to be in missiles in Russian submarines aimed at U.S. cities, but because of treaties, when Russia discarded these old missiles they were supposed to destroy these, but they did not do it. We caught the Russians three times transferring not one set of these devices, but over 100 set of these devices to Iraq.

What would Iraq want with them? Iraq would want them to put in their missiles like the one they sent into Desert Storm that killed 28 young Americans to make missile more accurate. We allowed the technology to flow, and we did nothing about it.

Here is the evidence, Mr Speaker. I cannot say where I got them, but I can say agencies of our government have over 100 sets of these devices. And let me say, my guess is there are probably thousands of these devices that were illegally sent from Russian entities to Iraq and Iran . . . .

The biggest challenge for President Bush is rebuilding the trust of the Russian people and its leadership that America wants to be a stable trading partner with Russia. We will not tolerate proliferation. We will not tolerate giving foreign unstable nations illegal technology, but we want Russia to succeed. We want to help them create a mortgage program for their people, which is my number one priority. We want to help their defense industry get back on its feet and produce other products. We want to engage their military with our military. We want to help them solve the problem of nuclear contamination in the Arctic, a big issue for the Russians. We want to help Russia succeed and become a trading partner of the U.S.

Missile defense is not the reason that Russia is concerned, it is the lack of trust and confidence in what America really wants that has the Russian leadership and the Russian people concerned.

Mr Speaker, we need to move forward with missile defense in cooperation with the Russians and the rest of the peace-loving people in the world. I cannot, for the life of me, as a teacher, understand how those in this country still want to rely on offensive weapons to kill each other, as opposed to defensive weapons to protect our people. That does not make sense to me.

We can achieve what President Bush wants.

Now, it is a tough task, because you are talking about hitting a bullet with a bullet, stopping a projectile in the atmosphere that is moving very quickly, and stopping it with another bullet. And you cannot hit that projectile when it is on the way down or it will rain terror on the people in that country, in this case our people . . . .

We need technology, as President Bush rightly outlined, to hit the missile in the ascent phase, as it is on the way up. It is called boost-phase intercept. The reason why that is important is, you knock that missile who on the way up, and the only people harmed are the people who launched the missile against someone else.

What President Bush is saying is, we need to develop a new capability, using technology with our allies, to give us that kind of protection; and he has proposed for the first time in the last 10 years that he will use the bully pulpit to move the technology forward.

Are we prepared today? No. There still is additional testing. Have we had success? Absolutely. Out of 31 attempts, we have been successful in over half of them. Our THAAD program has had intercepts, successful ones. Our PAC–3 program has had five successful intercepts. Our National Missile Defense program has had one successful intercept. We know the technology is achievable. It is an engineering problem to integrate the systems, and that is the challenge that we have to help the President overcome.

I am convinced, Mr Speaker, that those of our colleagues in this body and the other body who supported missile defense last year and the year before will again come back and support President Bush. This is not a partisan issue. The battle for missile defense in America was not a Republican battle; it was won by a bipartisan effort with Democrats and Republicans coming together, understanding that threats were emerging quicker than we thought they would emerge.

We need to work together to give the President the kind of support he has outlined in his vision for a new world order, one where we focus cooperative efforts together. The Europeans can cooperate with us, as they are already doing. In fact, I am hoping right now to establish a meeting, an unofficial meeting, in one of the Arab countries, where I will plan to invite the Israelis and the Russians to sit down and have a conversation about how we can jointly pursue missile defense cooperation in the Middle East, with Jews and allies working together, with Americans and Russians . . . .

The chairman of the International Affairs Committee for the Russian Duma, Dmitrii Rogozin, will be here, and he and I and others will come together and talk about cooperation. We will then travel to Moscow and we will have a conference in Moscow on missile defense cooperation. We will work together to find common ground, to build confidence among both countries to move forward together.

We need to put away the arguments and the petty wars of the Cold War era. Relying on mutually assured destruction is not the answer. Working together for peaceful protection of our friends, our allies and our neighbors, is the solution of the 21st century. That is what George Bush outlined for us yesterday. He is on the right track. He did not say we have all the answers, because we do not, but he did say, together, there is nothing we cannot accomplish . . . .

There are those who will say, there are a few of them, who will say this is not technologically possible. Mr Speaker, that is hogwash. In fact, to counter those, we have put together a task force of professors. None of the professors we have on this ad hoc committee are working for any contractor. They are all professors.

I am going to be inviting all of my colleagues in Congress to ask those professors, one at a time or as a group, to come into your offices . . . .

They will be available as we begin this debate to counter those who will simply try to use their doctorate titles to convince us that somehow we cannot accomplish this.

I asked the head of the Boeing program in a hearing last year, a fellow by the name of Dr Teller, how difficult it was to achieve the result of missile defense for America and its peoples .... He said managing the Space Station was a tougher challenge than building missile defense.

Together, Republicans and Democrats, allies and our own people, we can create a new world, a safe world, where all of our people can be protected from what happened to those 28 Americans in 1991.

24

Bush Calls for Nuclear Cuts, Missile Defense Development

The United Sates and its allies must find new ways to keep the peace in today's world, in which the major threats come from rogue nations where "terror and blackmail are a way of life," President Bush told a national audience May 1.

One such way, he said, is "a new framework" to include missile defense, developed in consultation with U.S. friends and allies.

Speaking in a televised appearance at the National Defense University in Washington, Bush said today's new world requires "new concepts of deterrence that rely on both offensive and defensive forces."

Emphasizing that Cold War deterrence is no longer enough, the President said that to maintain peace and protect U.S. citizens as well as allies and friends, "we need a new framework that allows us to build missile defense to counter the different threats of today's world. To do so we must move beyond the constraints of the 30-year-old ABM (Anti-Ballistic Missile) Treaty."

He said the Treaty "does not recognize the present or point us to the future. It enshrines the past. No treaty that prevents us from addressing today's threats, that prohibits us from pursuing promising technology to defend ourselves, our friends and our allies, is in our interests or in the interests of world-peace."

Bush said the new framework must encourage "still further cuts in nuclear weapons." Nuclear weapons "still have a vital role to play in our security," he said. However, "we can and will change the size, the composition, the character of our nuclear forces in a way that reflects the reality that the Cold War is over."

The President said that he is committed to achieving a "credible deterrent with the lowest possible number of nuclear weapons consistent with our national security needs, including our obligations to our allies." He said that he will "move quickly" to reduce nuclear forces and the United States "will lead by example, to achieve our interests and the interests for peace in the world."

Bush said that he will dispatch "high level representatives" to allied capitals in Europe, Asia, Australia and Canada "to discuss our common responsibility to create a new framework for security and stability that reflects the world of today."

The delegations, to begin leaving next week [May 6–12], will be headed by Richard Armitage, deputy secretary of state; Paul Wolfowitz, deputy secretary of defense, and Steve Hadley, deputy national security advisor.

He described their mission as "real consultations," part of an on going process to involve his cabinet secretaries and others. "We are not presenting our allies with unilateral decisions already made. We look forward to hearing their views...and to take them into account."

Bush said that he will "reach out to other interested states, including China and Russia," and he hopes that Russia and the United States will work together to develop a new foundation for world peace in the 21st century.

Following is the text of his remarks as delivered:
(begin text)

THE WHITE HOUSE Office of the Press Secretary
May 1, 2001

REMARKS BY THE PRESIDENT TO STUDENTS AND FACULTY AT NATIONAL DEFENSE UNIVERSITY
Fort Lesley J. McNair Washington, D.C.
2:40 P.M. EDT

THE PRESIDENT: Thank you very much, Mr Secretary. I appreciate your being here. I also want to thank Secretary Powell for being here as well. My National Security Advisor, Condi Rice is here, as well as the Vice Chairman of the Joint Chiefs, General Myers. I appreciate Admiral Clark and General Ryan here, for being here as well. But most of all, I want to thank you, Admiral Gaffney, and the students of NDU for having me here today.

For almost 100 years, this campus has served as one of our country's premier centres for learning and thinking about

America's national security. Some of America's finest soldiers have studied here: Dwight Eisenhower and Colin Powell. Some of America's finest statesmen have tought here; George Kennan. Today, you're carrying on this proud tradition forward, continuing to train tomorrow's generals, admirals and other national security thinkers, and continuing to provide the intellectual capital for our nation's strategic vision.

This afternoon, I want us to think back some 30 years to a far different time in a far different world. The United States and the Soviet Union were locked in a hostile rivalry. The Soviet Union was our unquestioned enemy; a highly-armed threat to freedom and democracy. Far more than that wall in Berlin divided us.

Our highest ideal was — and remains — individual liberty. Theirs was the construction of a vast communist empire. Their totalitarian regime held much of Europe captive behind an iron curtain.

We did't trust them, and for good reason. Our deep differences were expressed in a dangerous military confrontation that resulted in thousands of nuclear weapons pointed at each other on hair-trigger alert. Security of both the United States and the Soviet Union was based on a grim premise: that neither side would fire nuclear weapons at each other, because doing so would mean the end of both nations.

We even went so far as to codify this relationship in a 1972 ABM Treaty, based on the doctrine that our very survival would best be insured by leaving both sides completely open and vulnerable to nuclear attack. The threat was real and vivid. The Strategic Air Command had an airborne command post called the Looking Glass, aloft 24 hours a day, ready in case the President ordered our strategic forces to move toward their targets and release their nuclear ordnance.

The Soviet Union had almost 1.5 million troops deep in the heart of Europe, in Poland and Czechoslovakia, Hungary and East Germany. We used our nuclear weapons not just to prevent the Soviet Union from using their nuclear weapons, but also to contain their conventional military forces, to prevent from extending the Iron Curtain into parts of Europe and Asia that were still free.

In that world, few other nations had nuclear weapons and most of those who did were responsible allies, such as Britain and France. We worried about the proliferation of nuclear weapons to other countries, but it was mostly a distant threat, not yet a reality.

Today, the sun comes up on a vastly different world. The Wall is gone, and so is the Soviet Union. Today's Russia is not yesterday's Soviet Union. Its government is no longer Communist. Its president is elected. Today's Russia is not our enemy, but a country in transition with an opportunity to emerge as a great nation, democratic, at peace with itself and its neighbors. The Iron Curtain no longer exists. Poland, Hungry and the Czech Republic are free nations, and they are our allies in NATO, together with a reunited Germany.

Yet, this is still a dangerous world, a less certain, a less predictable one. Most nations have nuclear weapons and still more have nuclear aspirations. Many have chemical and biological weapons. Some already have developed the ballistic missile technology that would allow them to deliver weapons of mass destruction at long distances and at incredible speeds. And a number of these countries are spreading these technologies around the world.

Most troubling of all, the list of these countries includes some of the world's least-responsible states. Unlike the Cold War, today's most urgent threat stems not from thousands of ballistic missiles in the Soviet hands, but from a small number of missiles in the hands of these states, states for whom terror and blackmail are a way of life. They seek weapons of mass destruction to intimidate their neighbors, and to keep the United States and other responsible nations from helping allies and friends in strategic parts of the world.

When Saddam Hussein invaded Kuwait in 1990, the world joined forces to turn him back. But the international community would have faced a very different situation had Hussein been able to blackmail with nuclear weapons. Like Saddam Hussein, some of today's tyrants are gripped by an implacable hatred of the United States of America. They hate our friends, they hate our values, they hate democracy and freedom and individual liberty. Many care little for the lives of their own people. In such a world, Cold War deterrence is no longer enough.

To maintain peace, to protect our own citizens and our own allies and friends, we must seek security based on more than the grim premise that we can destroy those who seek to destroy us. This is an important opportunity for the world to re-think the unthinkable, and to find new ways to keep the peace.

Today's world requires a new policy, a broad strategy of active nonproliferation, counter proliferation and defenses. We must work together with other like-minded nations to deny weapons of terror from those seeking to acquire them. We must work with allies and friends who wish to join with us to defend against the harm they can inflict. And together we must deter anyone who would contemplate their use.

We need new concepts of deterrence that rely on both offensive and defensive forces. Deterrence can no longer be based solely on the threat of nuclear retaliation. Defenses can strengthen deterrence by reducing the incentive for proliferation.

We need a new framework that allows us to build missile defenses to counter the different threats of today's world. To do so, we must move beyond the constraints of the 30 year old ABM Treaty. This treaty does not recognize the present, or point us to the future. It enshrines the past. No treaty that prevents us from addressing today's threats, that prohibits us from pursuing promising technology to defend ourselves, our friends and our allies is in our interests or in the interests of the world peace.

This new framework must encourage still further cuts in nuclear weapons. Nuclear weapons still have a vital role to play in our security and that of our allies. We can, and will, change the size, the composition, the character of our nuclear forces in a way that reflects the reality that the Cold War is over.

I am committed to achieving a credible deterrent with the lowest-possible number of nuclear weapons consistent with our national security needs, including our obligations to our allies. My goal is to move quickly to reduce nuclear forces. The United States will lead by example to achieve our interests and the interests for peace in the world.

Several months ago, I asked Secretary of Defense Rumsfeld to examine all available technologies and basing modes for effective missile defenses that could protect the United States, our deployed forces, our friends and our allies. The Secretary has explored a number of complementary and innovative approaches.

The secretary has identified near-term options that could

allow us to deploy an initial capability against limited threats. In some cases, we can draw on already established technologies that might involve land-based and sea-based capabilities to intercept missiles in mid-course or after they re-enter the atmosphere. We also recognize the substantial advantages of intercepting missiles early in their flight, especially in the boost phase.

The preliminary work has produced some promising options for advanced sensors and interceptors that may provide this capability. If based at sea or on aircraft, such approaches could provide limited, but effective, defenses.

We have more work to do to determine the final form the defenses might take. We will explore all these options further. We recognize the technological difficulties we face and we look forward to the challenge. Our nation will assign the best people to this critical task.

We will evaluate what works and what does not. We know that some approaches will not work. We also know that we will be able to build on our successes. When ready, and working with Congress, we will deploy missile defenses to strengthen global security and stability.

I've made it clear from the very beginning that I would consult closely on the important subject with our friends and allies who are also threatened by missiles and weapons of mass destruction.

Today, I'm announcing the dispatch of high-level representatives to Allied capitals in Europe, Asia, Australlia and Canada to discuss our commom responsibility to create a new framework for security and stability that reflects the world of today. They will begin leaving next week.

The delegations will be headed by three men on this stage; Rich Armitage, Paul Wolfowitz, and Steve Hadley; deputies of the State Department, the Defense Department and the National Security staff. Their trips will be part of an ongoing process of consultation, involving many people and many levels of government, including my Cabinet Secretaries.

These will be real consultations. We are not presenting our friends and allies with unilateral decisions already made. We look forward to hearing their views, the views of our friends, and to take them into account.

We will seek their input on all the issues surrounding the new strategic environment. We'll also need to reach out to other interested states, including China and Russia. Russia and the United States should work together to develop a new foundation for world peace and security in the 21st century. We should leave behind the constraints of an ABM Treaty that perpetuates a relationship based on distrust and mutual vulnerability. This Treaty ignores the fundamental breakthroughs in technology during the last 30 years. It prohibits us from exploring all options for defending against the threats that face us, our allies and other countries.

That's why we should work together to replace this Treaty with a new framework that reflects a clear and clean break from the past, and especially from adversarial legacy of the Cold War. This new cooperative relationship should look to the future, not to the past. It should be reassuring, rather than threatening. It should be premised on openness, mutual confidence and real opportunities for cooperation, including the area of missile defense. It should allow us to share information so that each nation can improve its early warning capability, and its capability to defend its people and territory. And perhaps one day, we can even cooperate in a joint defense.

I want to complete the work of changing our relationship from one based on a nuclear balance of terror, to one based on common responsibilities and common interests. We may have areas of difference with Russia, but we are not and must not be strategic adversaries. Russia and America both face new threats to security. Together, we can address today's threats and pursue today's opportunities. We can explore technologies that have the potential to make us all safer.

This is a time for vision; a time for a new way of thinking; a time for bold leadership. The Looking Glass no longer stands its 24-hour-day vigil. We must all look at the world in a new way, to preserve peace for generations to come.

God bless. (Applause.)

25

Excepts: Deputy Defense Secretary on Reducing Missile Threat

(Wolfowitz off to Europe, Russia for Missile Defense Talks) (3580)

Deputy Secretary of Defense Paul Wolfowitz says the United States has "no interest" in seeing Russia, or for that matter Los Angeles, Chicago, New York or Washington "vulnerable to limited missile attacks."

During a May 4 speech to the American Jewish Committee's 95th annual meeting at the Washington Capitol Hilton, the deputy secretary said the U.S.-Russian relationship should not be based on mutual annihilation, but should be focused, instead, on reducing mutual vulnerabilities.

Wolfowitz made his remarks as he prepared to depart for consultations on missile defense in Paris, Berlin, Warsaw and Moscow. He said he expected "the most difficult pointed discussions we'll have will surely be in Moscow." He travels with Deputy National Security Advisor Stephen Hadley who will also stop, first, in London and Brussels for his own missile defense consultations.

When U.S.-Russian ballistic missile defense talks were held in 1992, Wolfowitz told the audience, the Americans told the Russians that the United States wanted to be in a position in the future to be able to shoot down a missile launched at Russia. It prompted the question: "You mean, you really would be interested in helping to defend Russia?" And Wolfowitz responded, "It seems to me the answer is, obviously, 'yes'."

With the Cold War now long gone, the deputy secretary said, "we need in our relationship with Russia to get the nuclear dimension out of that relationship. We shouldn't be saying that the centerpiece of U.S.-Russian relations is the ability of our two countries to annihilate one another with nuclear weapons."

He also talked about the Middle East and the Persian Gulf and said that hope for peace in the region rests on the liberation of Iraq "from the tyranny of Saddam's regime." The United States favors a change of leadership in Iraq, he said, "that will preserve the territorial integrity of that country" while assuring that the Iraqi government would threaten neither its own people nor the region at large. The U.S. would "like nothing more than to see Saddam go." he added, "and I think in pursuing that goal we are also helping the Iraqi people."

"We must see Saddam without illusion if we are to know how to deal with the dangers that he creates," Wolfowitz said. "We cannot appease him. His appetites cannot be satisfied. There will be no peace in the region and no safety for our friends there—Arabs or Israelis, Kurds or Turkomons—as long as he remains in power."

Following are excerpts of Wolfowitz's remarks as delivered:

(begin excerpts)

American Jewish Committee
Remarks by Deputy Secretary of Defense Paul Wolfowitz, Capitol Hilton, Washington, DC, Friday, May 4, 2001.

Like our predecessors at the beginning of the 20th Century, we live in a period of exceptionally rapid growth and technological progress on a scale and at a pace that are without historical precedent. And we, too, share in the great optimism that the world's economic progress will broaden and deepen and perhaps even accelerate.

Common also to both periods of history has been a great optimism about the prospects for peace. In 1910, Norman Angell's sensational best seller argued that the notion that nations could profit from war was obsolete, indeed as he titled his book, it was The Great Illusion. In his view, economies had become so interdependent that war had been rendered unthinkable.

One of the Angell's disciples, David Starr Jordan, then President of Stanford University, argued that despite the threat of a war in Europe, such a war would never come for, as he concluded, "the bankers will not find the money for such a fight;

the industries will not maintain it; the statesmen cannot. There will be no general war." Unfortunately for him, he made that prescient forecast in 1913. A year later with the assassination of Archduke Franz Ferdinand, the great illusion gave way to the Great War.

In 1938, the year of the Munich Crisis, Hitler's evil intentions compelled him to throw aside caution and embrace outright risk. Reflecting in that same year on the enormous changes he had witnessed since the beginning of the 20th Century, Winston Churchill wrote, "The smooth river with its eddies and ripples along which we sailed at the beginning of the century seems inconceivably remote from . . .the rapids in whose turbulence we are now struggling." In a mere 38 years, the world had been transformed.

Hopefully history will not repeat itself and events of the last century will not be harbingers of our own destiny. But as we try to manage our course along what has so far been the relatively smooth river of this new century, there are issues that we must consider if we are to realize our most optimistic hopes.

Near the top of the list of these issues is the proliferation of dangerous, militarily useful technology. As those who follow events in the Middle East will understand particularly well, some of the world's most irresponsible powers and terrorists are determined to acquire weapons of mass destruction and ballistic missiles to deliver them. Some of them are already within missile range of Israel and our other allies in the region. Others are developing missiles that will bring our allies within range. Some have already used them.

The threat of ballistic missile attack is not something in the remote future, not something uncertain. It is already ten years into our past. When Saddam Hussein was launching terror weapons called Scuds against Israel, I was there with Deputy Secretary of State Lawrence Eagleburger. We saw children walking to school carrying gas masks in gaily decorated boxes—no doubt to try to distract them from the possibility of facing mass destruction. They were awfully young to have to think about the unthinkable.

Ten years ago in the waning days of Desert Storm, a single Scud missile hit a U.S. military barracks in Dhahran and killed 28 of our soldiers and wounded 99. Thirteen of those killed came from a single small town in Pennsylvania called Greensburg. It was the worst single engagement of the Gulf War for the American forces. And yet today, more than ten years later, our capacity to shoot down a Scud missile—the most primitive that we have to worry about—is not much improved.

We are a couple of years away from deployment of the PAC–3 missile, our answer to the Scud. The Isarelis have just recently deployed their response, the Arrow. But for either of us, 10 years is a long time to respond to a threat of that seriousness. We didn't, I might point out, get to the moon in 10 years with that kind of approach.

Not long ago I spoke to the American Turkish Council and I took a bold risk, reciting an old Turkish saying in Turkish, a feat that I won't attempt for you today. I'll do it in English. The saying goes, "bad news comes back, even from Baghdad." Ten years after the Gulf War we're still getting bad news from Baghdad, from the same tyrannical regime. This regime which has meant bad news for so many for so long poses one of today's most pressing obstacles to peace. It has become clear that there is no cost-free or risk-free option in dealing with that regime.

We must see Saddam without illusion if we are to know how to deal with the dangers that he creates. We cannot appear him. His appetites cannot be satisfied. There will be no peace in the region and no safety for our friends there—Arabs or Israelis, Kurds or Turkomons—as long as he remains in power.

But we are not without options, for Saddam has significant vulnerabilities, bearing out Franklin Roosevelt's observation that "dictatorships do not grow out of strong and successful governments, but out of weak ones." Saddam's primary vulnerability is that he is a failure—politically, economically, and militarily. His power rests on fear, like Joseph Stalin's, and because he is feared, he is also hated. Thus, he faces significant potential opposition both outside and inside his own country, and he has failed to exercise control over significant areas of Iraq, particularly in the North.

As Secretary of State Powell has said, "Saddam Hussein is sitting on a failed regime that is not going to be around in a few years' time. The world," Secretary Powell said, "is going to leave him behind and his regime behind as the world marches to new drummers, drummers of democracy and of free enterprise." And let me add to that, it is our obligation to help this forward march in every way that we can. In doing so, we help ourselves.

The demise of the Soviet Union demonstrates how international conflicts are often caused by the character of national regimes, not by any kind of international misunderstanding. The Cold War was caused by the evil regime in the Soviet Union—not by a failure of diplomacy. In a similar way, Slobodan Milosevic and his evil cronies were responsible for the tragedies and suffering in the Balkans over the last decade, whose effects we are still coping with today. The American Jewish Committee worked for years against Milosevic, speaking out forcefully on behalf of his victims, especially the Bosnian Muslims. Without Milosevic's influence and power, that Balkans have a much better chance today to embark on their own forward march.

Today the tyrannical regime in Baghdad is the root cause of the most immediate dangers that we face in the Persian Gulf. Hope for Iraq and hope for peace in the region rests on the liberation of that country from the tyranny of Saddam's regime. In the interest of human rights and global stability, the United States favors a new leadership in Iraq, a humane, inclusive leadership that will preserve the territorial integrity of that country and live at peace without threatening its own people or the region. Again, to quote our Secretary of State, "We believe a change in the regime in Iraq would be in the interests of all concerned."

But so long as regimes of that character exist, we must protect ourselves and our allies and our friends. As President Bush said in a speech at the National Defense University this past Tuesday (May 1), "Today's most urgent threats stem not from thousands of ballistic missiles in Soviet hands, but from a small number of missiles in the hands of the world's least responsible states, states for whom terror and blackmail are a way of life."

This new strategic environment demands new concepts and new forms of deterrence. As the President also said, "Today's world requires a new policy, a broad strategy of active, non-proliferation, counter-proliferation, and defenses. We must work with allies and friends," the President said, "who wish to join with us to defend against the harm they can inflict. And together we must deter any one who would contemplate their use."

In the interest of world peace, it is essential that we build a strong foundation for peace through strong alliances and a strong American military capability. These provide the basis for stability and continued progress. Our military strength is not antithetical to our peaceful ambitions and our peaceful goals. It supports them. We cannot take for granted the allies and friends that we have now. We must continue to build and solidify those relationships and try to win new friends around the world.

President Bush has also made it a national priority to strengthen America's armed forces, to strengthen the bond of trust with the American military. As the President has said, "Peace is not ordained, it is earned by the hard and often dangerous work of our men and women in uniform. They do what is truly noble work. They voluntarily put their lives at risk to defend liberties that we hold dear and the security that we enjoy."

This administration is dedicated to working on behalf of our forces and their families who risk so much and sacrifice so much. We must continue to improve pay and quality of life for our military. We must reexamine the balance among force levels, the number of our commitments and our deployments overseas, and we must give our forces the tools they need and the respect they deserve. We will work for this.

So in this time of great challenge and equally great opportunity, let us take a lesson from Nehemiah, the practical man of action. Today I suppose that if he were heading for high office in government he'd most likely be filling out forms and awaiting confirmation. But, he was a man of action who led the Jews who had returned from Babylon as they rebuilt the walls of Jerusalem. He inspired them to persist in their formidable task, even in the face of threats from their enemies.

The Bible tells us that as they rebuilt the walls of Jerusalem "each did his work with one hand and held a weapon with the other. Every builder while he worked had his sword at his side." In the same way, we must strengthen our alliances and buttress our defenses, even as we work to build a more peaceful world.

As we set about the task of fashioning a safer, more secure world, we must remain vigilant to those who would threaten us and our allies. Working together, we can assure that what lies before us is not a great illusion, but a great peace.

Thank you.

Harold Tanner (President of the American Jewish Committee): Thank you very much, Mr Secretary. Thank you for being here. Paul Wolfowitz has agreed to answer two questions and then he has to leave.

Wolfowitz: If they're not nice questions, I'll only do one.

Question: Mr Secretary, I came in as you were speaking so forgive me if you answered my question in the earlier part of your remarks. But you talked extensively of the threat of Iraq, and yet I didn't hear you talk about sanctions or the administration's new proposed policy on sanctions. I wonder whether you would comment upon both aspects—the existing sanctions and what you propose.

Answer: We're working out the details of the new approach to sanctions that Secretary Powell outlined in his February, I believe it was, trip to the Middle East. But I think the fundamental point of what we're trying to achieve there is to lay a basis through revising the sanctions both to preserve what is important in those sanctions and also to try to establish a clear basis for the other elements of our policy.

When I say a clear basis I'm referring to the fact that Saddam Hussein unfortunately has made great propaganda successes out of the argument that we are only interested in punishing the Iraqi people. I think our strategy has to rest on separating Saddam from the Iraqi people and making it as clear as possible that American actions are aimed at him and at his tyranny, not at the people who suffer under his rule.

Indeed, I think a point that is sometimes missed is that there is, not only around the Arab world, considerable criticism, and that's a mild word, that sanctions are making the Iraqi people suffer. There is a wide recognition that Saddam's tyranny makes the Iraqi people suffer as well. And unfortunately, a suspicion, since it's easy for them to suspect the United States, that somehow that is our intended desire.

As I have tried to make clear in this speech, we would desire nothing more, like nothing more than to see Saddam go, and I think in pursuing that goal we are also helping the Iraqi people. So I see those two things as mutually reinforcing.

Q: Sir, Conrad Rubenstein from Australia, Israel and Jewish Affairs Council. Can I commend you and the administration on the priority you're attaching to missile defense. I think the President's speech the other day was very reassuring and dealt with some of the initial criticisms in terms of the global dimension that it has and the fact that it's really committed to enhancing deterrence and security globally. That's especially important in Asia and obviously in the Middle East and elsewhere, and I'm delighted that you and your colleagues will be going on a mission over the next week or two to convince skeptical elements about the merits of the proposal. I'm just wondering if you could say a word or two more about how you're going to convince the skeptics that this priority is a very important one in view of the dramatic threat that the proliferation of WMD (weapons of mass destruction) really does represent.

A: I didn't plant the question, but I think you for the question, and I'm going to try to make two points, first, using that question as an opportunity to appeal to this audience, which has obviously got a lot of influential opinion makers in it. We as a country have also got to put the Cold War behind us. We had many debates about missile defense in the context of the Cold War—debates that are very interesting to revisit as an academic. Did SDI (Strategic Defense Initiative) break the back of the Soviet Union or were they collapsing anyway? Was it a fantasy on Reagan's part, or was it something that made sense?

The point is, the nature of what we are trying to do with missile defense today is entirely different from a defense against a Soviet Union. And the nature of the threats we're dealing with today are entirely different from the threat posed by the Soviet Union. And third, and most important, we need in our relationship with Russia to get the nuclear dimension out of that relationship. We shouldn't be saying that the centerpiece of U.S.-Russian relations is the ability of our two countries to annihilate one another with nuclear weapons.

As I said to a Russian general who came to visit me the other day, I studied some Russian literature in college; my father who was a mathematician at Cornell made me study Russian because it was the language of science; Russian music is great. I said, Russia is a great country, but not because you have nuclear weapons, and the sooner Russia does what so many former empires have done, building a normal country on a normal basis, the sooner that greatness will be recognized.

And that, I believe, is the framework in which President Bush is approaching not just the issue of missile defense but the issue of reducing our offensive nuclear weapons as well and moving away from threats of mutual annihilation.

The second point—this is in answer to your question now. I'm going to be going with Steve Hadley, Deputy NSC Advisor, on consultations next week in Paris. He'll be in London and Brussels first; I'll join him in Paris and go with him to Paris, Berlin, Warsaw and Moscow. And I anticipate the most difficult pointed discussions we'll have will surely be in Moscow. But this won't be the first time Steve Hadley, as a government official, went to Moscow to talk with Russian officials about missile defense. The first time was in 1992, when he participated with Dennis Ross, who became famous for other things, in what were known as the Ross-Mamedov talks where we began for the first time talking with the new Russian security authorities about what we viewed as a common interest in defense against limited ballistic missile attacks.

There were two points in these discussions that, 10 years later, people who are in the room remember still vividly. The first point, perhaps least surprising, was when we began showing them our projections of how missile capabilities were developed in various countries like North Korea, Iran, and showed them the sort of typical CIA or Pentagon briefing that shows maps with missile arcs of varying ranges, and the Russians pointed out most of these missiles are going to reach us long before they can reach you.

But the most striking point came in a discussion when the American side said we would like to be in a position 10 or 15 years from now where if there were a missile launched at Russia, we would have the capability to shoot that missile down ourselves; and the Russian eyes popped. You mean, you really would be interested in helping to defend Russia? The answer was "yes" and it seems to me the answer is abviously "yes".

We have no interest in seeing Russia vulnerable to limited missile attacks, not do I believe we should tolerate any longer than we have to having Los Angeles or Chicago or New York or Washington, D.C. vulnerable to limited missile attacks. It's not a good thing; it's not a healthy world.

I think instead of making mutual annihilation the basis of our relationship, we ought to look at reducing mutual vulnerabilities. And that is what we hope to be able to persuade the Russians of, and our experience from 10 years ago suggests to me that at least some of them are willing to listen. Thank you for listening to me today.

26

Byliner: Senator Joseph Biden on National Missile Defense

Following is the text of a speech by Senator Joseph Biden [Democrat, Delaware], as prepared for delivery at the Cato Institute on June 27)

National Missile Defense and Strategic Security in the Post-Cold War World

by

Senator Joseph Biden

Good afternoon. It is a special honor to address this symposium. This may be the first gathering to be sponsored by both supporters and opponents of a national missile defense. That is a significant step forward in the national debate on missile defense. It reflects a realization that national security issues are too important to be left to partisan politicking.

As you surely know, I am a skeptic regarding national missile defense. I can understand why such a capability might be desired. I am not at all sure, however, that it is yet feasible. Neither am I convinced that the system proposed by the Pentagon would work satisfactorily, or even that deterrence is so bad.

I will be happy to elaborate on those points when I take your questions. But I suspect that you have been debating them all morning. So let me give you instead some thoughts on the strategic context within which the issue of national missile defense must be considered.

Let's begin with the objective of statecraft. It is not simply to achieve this deployment or to preserve that treaty. Rather, it is to maximize our overall national security. Many issues are so narrow that we can ignore the broader context; we ignore relativity theory when analyzing whether a bridge needs repair. National missile defense is not one of those narrow issues, however; we must consider its place in the strategic context of our time.

I submit that we are at a pivotal point in our strategic relationships with major countries in the world. A decade ago, we began the transition to a post-Cold War international system. That transition continues today. Our strategic weapons policy decisions over the next year or so could determine that transition, for good or for ill.

We have moved from a largely bi-polar world to one in which our military might is effectively unchallenged, although Russia retains the capability to inflict immense damage upon us. Many aspects of strategic arms relationships, however, still remain unsettled:

- What nuclear force levels will the United States and Russia maintain in the coming years?
- Will formal arms control treaties, with their associated benefits of predictability and verification, become a thing of the past?
- Will China continue its strategic doctrine of "minimal deterrence?" Or will it significantly increase the number and accuracy of its missiles or warheads, perhaps deploying MIRVed (Multiple Independently-Targeted Reentry Vehicle) ICBM's (Intercontinental Ballistic Missiles)?
- Will Chinese actions lead India and Russia to increase their forces, perhaps igniting an Asian arms race? Will other countries in East Asia decide to go nuclear?
  — Will non-proliferation be reinforced as a principal objective of the nuclear weapons states, or will they help other countries to develop those weapons and the missiles (or cruise missiles) with which to deliver them?
- Will our allies remain confident of our commitment to their security and accepting of our leadership? Or, for one reason or another, will they seek to

counterbalance us, keep their distance from us, or rely more upon their own military forces?

- Will the countries seen today as potential developers of nuclear weapons and long-range missiles live up to our fears? Or will changes on the Korean peninsula, in Iran, or in the Middle East reduce the current threats and give us more time and more options?

What sort of world will we face in the coming decades, and what role will we play in it? When the Cold War ended, many predicted a "New World Order" in which the great powers would realize their common interests and work together to maintain international stability.

That new world has yet to come about.

A whole series of issues has divided Russia from the United States. Russia's military, economic and political weakness has given us greater freedom of action, but has also made Russia more distrusting of the West. Meanwhile, international and ethnic disputes that had been sublimated in the Cold War have surfaced and bred wars, terrorism and proliferation.

These new instabilities have led supporters of a national missile defense to view the current era as a window of opportunity in which to build a shield against ballistic missile attack, before Russia or China becomes strong enough to block us. Some see missile defense as a hedge against an unstable leader who might not be deterred even by our overwhelming force. Others see it as a means of maintaining our freedom from blackmail if another country were to threaten nuclear retaliation in an effort to keep us from intervening to save an ally from invasion. Still others see it as a shield against a small attack by any country, and eventually as a shield against all attacks, even from Russia.

What I find interesting—and a little frightening—is the unrelieved pessimism that underlies that approach to the world. A decade ago, even conservatives saw hope for "a world transformed." Now that vision has been discarded, and their hope is put instead in better weapons—both offensive and defensive—to maintain U.S. predominance.

I think the conservatives are missing a bet here. The world has yet to be transformed into a really benign place, but there have still been some real advances. I think we still have an opportunity to build a more stable world. On the other hand, I fear that acting upon our worst fears will only make those fears come true.

U.S.-Russian relations are often frustrating, but they are far better than they were in the Cold War. Russia has a NATO relationship. It participates in peace-keeping operations. It has allowed international action on Iraq. It has lowered its strategic nuclear forces and is more than willing to continue that process. It no longer targets its missiles at the United States—which is no safeguard against a future decision to fire them at us, but is a very good safeguard against an accidental attack. And, however much we may question Russia's motives or its sincerity, it has offered to help wean North Korea away from long-range ballistic missiles.

U.S.-Chinese relations are similarly a glass that is either half-full or half-empty. China's impatience regarding Taiwan is a matter of great concern; rash actions there could lead to terrible consequences. China has also contributed significantly and foolishly to the proliferation of long-range missiles and weapons of mass destruction.

At the same time, China—which once argued that every country should develop nuclear weapons—now recognizes the need for nuclear non-proliferation. It has given North Korea good counsel on that. It ratified the Chemical Weapons Convention. It reduced its cooperation with Iran. It did not block international action on Iraq. It is reducing the stranglehold that the People's Liberation Army had on its economy. And it is opening up its economy to the world, which will further erode the grip of the Communist Party upon people's daily lives and their political expectations.

In recent weeks, we have seen possible steps toward a transformed world on the Korean peninsula. Will continued rapprochement with South Korea and with the United States open North Korea to economic reform and lead it to end its long-range missile programs? A safe bet is that it won't happen overnight. But the odds of these good outcomes are better than they have been in more than half a century.

The same is true in the Middle East, where Israel, the Palestinians, and Syria are enmeshed in difficult—but serious—efforts to settle their disputes. Similarly, in Iran, while conservative clerics still view America as the Great Satan, other clerics—with overwhelming popular support—are slowly moving Iran toward a more rational view of the world.

These trends may change. A safer world to come is far from certain. But we would be foolish to ignore these forces, just as we would be foolish to ignore the risks posed by weapons proliferation. We would also be foolish if we were to sacrifice these possibilities through a short-sighted obsession with deploying a national missile defense.

I think that a single-minded push for national missile defense would indeed sacrifice some real opportunities to make the world a safer place:

- If we were to abrogate the ABM (Anti-Ballistic Missile) Treaty, we would sacrifice both the START process and, perhaps, the INF Treaty.
- Russia might then see the world's trouble-makers as its only friends, and undercut the world's non-proliferation regimes.
- If we were to deploy the national missile defense proposed by the Pentagon, China would surely increase its nuclear forces. China is already modernizing its nuclear forces, at least to improve their survivability. Our deployment—even if Russia acceded to it—would lead China to do more.
- If we were to abrogate the ABM Treaty, China, too, might well engage in increased arms proliferation.
- Our allies, as well, would be deeply shaken. Whatever our reasons, they would see our actions as reckless, rather than prudent. This would undermine our influence in the world, even if it were to increase our military freedom of action.
- Finally, the world's trouble-makers would still be tempted to cause us grief, but with renewed support from an aggrieved Russia and China.

And make no mistake: even if we were to achieve a perfect defense against ICBM's, there are other ways to devastate us with weapons of mass destruction. As our Intelligence Community has made clear, those other ways are cheaper, easier, and much harder to track—hence, less likely to lead to prompt retaliation.

Thus, it is not long-range ballistic missiles, but the other delivery systems that raise the real specter of a failure of deterrence. My conservative friends are fond of saying that arms control is dangerous because it distracts us from real threats to our security. I would say, rather, that national missile defense will distract us from those real threats.

I noted at the beginning that the objective of statecraft is to maximize our overall national security. I doubt that deploying the Pentagon's national missile defense will do that. I am certain that abrogating the ABM Treaty will not do that.

Must we give up forever the idea of national missile defense? No. I said that I can understand why such a capability might be desired, and I do. The problem with a national missile defense, however, aside from the fact that it's never as easy to achieve as its supporters claim, is how to deploy it without sacrificing other interests that we value greatly.

One answer, I think, is that the political transformation must precede the strategic one. The end of the Cold War was the beginning of that political transformation, but not the end of it. We must achieve greater comity among the world's nuclear powers before we will be in a position to move safely to strategic missile defense. A premature effort to force strategic defense upon an unwilling world will only sacrifice the halting, but real, transformation that is still under way.

Another answer is that the type of national missile defense is as important as the timing of it. It will be much easier to get other powers to accept joint missile defenses aimed at agreed threats than a U.S. defense that is designed to combat all threats. That is part of the logic behind Dick Garwin's proposal of a land- or sea-based system using boost-phase interceptors.

Russia's recent proposals are also for boost-phase interceptors. Those proposals may not be workable. They would be less useful for us as than for Russia or Western Europe, which are vulnerable to threats from shorter-range missiles than those that we would face. But the Russian proposals are a base upon which we might build a different approach to national missile defense.

We should pursue Russia's proposals very seriously. A cooperative missile defense could knit Russia into a Western defense framework. Indeed, some Russian generals have called for that, despite their distrust of us. This would transform Russia's role in the world. It might just pave the way for a world-wide shift from pure deterrence to an agreed mix of offense and defense.

What we should not do is proceed with deployment of the Pentagon's proposed national missile defense. Even if next month's test should succeed, we all know that too much will remain untested. Even if the system should achieve its projected capabilities, we all know that it will not stop a missile with biological weapon sub-munitions or with sophisticated countermeasures. Even if Russia were finally to make its peace with such a system, the likely price would be a return to Russian MIRVed ICBM's and the risk of an Asian nuclear arms race that would pose further risks of nuclear proliferation.

In recent weeks, supporters of national missile defense and skeptics like me have found ourselves in agreement on the bottom line, although hardly on our reasons for it. Perhaps this symposium should formalize that agreement. If the Council for a Livable World, the Cato Institute, and the National Defense University Foundation were to join in recommending that a deployment decision be postponed, that would be noticed—just as people noticed last week's debate in which Jim Woolsey and Richard Perle had nothing good to say about the Pentagon's system.

For the short run, we can agree on the doctor's approach of "do no harm." That is the message we must send—not just to the President, but also to those conservative Republicans who would accuse the President and the Vice President of being "soft on missile defense." If we really want the President to "do no harm" and to defer a deployment decision, then we must also agree not to use that decision for partisan advantage. That is a real challenge now, but I think we can do it.

27

General Kadish's Senate Testimony on National Missile Defense

Development of the National Missile Defense (NMD) system now being tested by the U.S. military is admittedly "difficult and challenging," but it is by no means "impossible or infeasible," Air Force Lieutenant General Ronald T. Kadish told the Senate Armed Services Committee June 29.

Kadish, director of the Ballistic Missile Defense Organization, testified at a hearing on the limited NMD program which is due to undergo its next major test on July 7. President Clinton is expected to announce his decision regarding deployment of the NMD system later this year.

"I do not share the assessment that what we are attempting to accomplish with our system is in any way impossible," Kadish said, adding that "those who charge that the system cannot be technologically feasible simply do not have all the information they need to make such a conclusion."

"I believe the tests planned over the course of the next five years will continue to build our confidence in our ability to discriminate, to identify target warheads in spite of anticipated countermeasures, and to destroy any incoming warheads using advanced hit-to-kill technology," he said.

Kadish rejected criticism of the testing system devised. "Is it a perfect system? No, but it beats little or no testing at all, which is the problem generally faced by those states that are being given credit by some of our critics for developing unsophisticated countermeasures that are believed by them to be capable of overcoming our planned system," he said.

And he strongly denied accusations that system tests have been rigged to produce favorable results. "I testify here before you today that I would not tolerate, nor would those above me or below me in the Defense Department tolerate, such activity," he declared.

Following is the text of Kadish's remarks as prepared for delivery.

Mr Chairman, Members of the Committee. I am delighted to have the opportunity to testify on the U.S. National Missile Defense program.

Today, I would like to outline for you what we are doing in the program, why we are doing it, and how we are progressing. I also will address the independent assessment that General Welch has just completed. Then I want to amplify my comments on the acquisition approach we are taking and the testing program, and close with some thoughts on the "attacks" the program recently has received.

The impetus behind our program comes from the threat assessment by the Intelligence Community and the bipartisan Rumsfeld Commission. The Director of Central Intelligence testified before Congress earlier this year that, "Over the next 15 years, our cities will face ballistic missile threats from a variety of actors ...." He specifically pointed to North Korea's ability to test its Taepo Dong II missile this year, a missile that "may be capable of delivering a nuclear payload to the United States." Given this capability, the threat of an attack on the United States territory will become increasingly likely during the next few years, a potential for which we must be prepared.

We expect these initial capabilities to include only relatively simple countermeasures. These emerging capabilities and timelines have been significant factors in how we have gone about developing the NMD system and why we picked the approach that we did.

System Description

Let me begin by explaining why we picked the midcourse phase of a ballistic missile's trajectory to execute the intercept. There has been a lot of discussion, including by a number of very distinguished persons, about the potential benefits of a boost-phase system or even a terminal-phase one; but most of the focus has been on the boost phase.

Chart I helps illustrate some of the points associated with intercept options.

In the boost-phase, there are many ways we can approach the problem. We can do it from land, as the Russians have suggested—in other words, a Russian-based (joint U.S./Russian) boost-phase intercept system—or we can do it using either a surface or subsurface sea-based system. In both cases, the ship-based interceptors would have to be launched from a point very close to the booster launch point, i.e., in waters where ships are highly vulnerable; the response would have to be very rapid (the timing for this approach is obviously critical). The first signal we would get would be from a satellite indicating a launch; as soon as it recognizes that there had in fact been a launch.

Of course, an immediate intercept response to this signal assumes that we are very clear it is a hostile ICBM (intercontinental ballistic missile) launch. We do not necessarily want to be shooting down a satellite launcher or a test shot. Clearly, there are some very important command-and-control issues associated with this system and its development. If the launch is validated as hostile, then we could try to intercept with a high-performance interceptor which we do not now have—to get out quickly and shoot down the missile in its boost phase.

Another alternative is a space-based system. Here there is a choice of either a space-based laser system or a space-based interceptor. Of course, were we to use a kinetic energy interceptor from space, it would have to be an extremely high-performance interceptor to reach the missile in its boost phase, or we would have to accept the reality that the intercept would take place during the missile's mid-course phase. As to a space-based laser, as you know, we have the Space-Based Laser (SBL) technology under development. The launch of the first integrated flight experiment for this system is scheduled for the 2012 time period. Development and deployment would stretch considerably beyond that.

So besides the obvious point that each of these systems probably would violate the ABM (Anti-Ballistic Missile) Treaty, we also have rather lengthy development times associated with them. None of these approaches could produce a system in the 2005 time period.

A terminal-phase system would provide defense at the other end of a ballistic missile's trajectory. This approach has some very distinct advantages in terms of being able to sort out decoys. The effect of the earth's atmosphere on the warhead and penetration aids can significantly assist our discrimination capability.

The disadvantage associated with this approach is that we would have to have a very large number of interceptors at many locations because this is a "point defense" system. Defending all 50 states and major metropolitan areas in them with a terminal system would require an extensive number of deployments—a very expensive and probably very contentious concept (since many, less populated areas would remain unprotected). Also, because intercepts would take place virtually overhead, there are some obvious disadvantages regarding nuclear, biological, and chemical warhead fallout.

Each phase has its advantages and disadvantages, including the mid-course phase that we selected.

The big advantage of the mid-course, from a defensive point of view, is that we have relatively more time to react than during the other two phases. We have more time to make decisions, to sort the decoy from the warhead, and to ensure human-in-the-loop control. This extra time also allows us the ability to shoot, and then verify the success of that shot, and then shoot again if necessary, a so-called "shoot-look-shoot" capability. Additionally, multiple shots (simultaneously and/or sequentially) at the target give a higher probability of being able to hit it. And if we were unable to discriminate between, for example, a very sophisticated decoy and a warhead, we would shoot them both down. Multiple shots and a shoot-look-shoot capability can provide for a more robust defense. The longer time period of the mid-course phase allows that.

The downside of the mid-course phase, of course, as so many critics remind us, is that it is quite easy to generate decoys in this phase (since it takes place outside the atmosphere). This poses a major discrimination challenge, one with which we are quite familiar. I will come back to this issue.

Importantly, given the progress we already have made in

the development of technologies for the planned NMD system, if we are to develop a system in the shortest possible time period against a relatively simple offensive system, a midcourse defensive system is the way to go. This is the approach we have chosen. It is an approach that does not rule out later adding either boost or terminal phase complements to the system, should the threat evolution require it and future technology allow it. If the President decides to deploy, we can have an initial capability by 2005. The remainder of my discussion describes the system we could deploy, pending that decision.

Chart 2 shows the basic system elements of the selected NMD system. It begins with the space-based warning system, the system that picks up the fact that a booster has been launched and provides some initial trajectory information. The Defense Support Program (DSP) satellite system is already in place. The DSP has been there for many years to detect launches, and we are planning to replace this constellation with more capable SBIRS (Space-Based Infrared System) High satellites. Six planned Space-Based Infrared System satellites will be inserted into geosynchronous and highly elliptical orbits and will have greater sensitivity and an improved ability to project trajectories.

Once we have the detection, track, and initial impact projection data from the space-based sensors, the information is passed on, through the command and control system, to the Early Warning Radars (EWRs). These are also in place today at a variety of places around the globe. These UHF radars will be upgraded to enhance their current ability to track the targets, providing better information to help us determine where the targets are headed and provide better information for the intercept.

This information is then passed to the X-band Radars—high frequency, short wavelength radars—that can do an excellent job of discrimination. Using these radars, we can begin to sort out the decoys and other objects from the real warhead or warheads. This is the kind of radar planned for deployment on Shemya, an island at the end of the Aleutian Islands (more about this later).

Assuming we knew the missile track and that it was heading toward the United States, we would launch the ground-based interceptors. This interceptor will have two main elements—

the booster and the exoatmospheric kill vehicle. We are now using in our tests a booster that is a surrogate for the final operational booster. The operational booster will be built from a combination of three modified off-the-shelf commercial boosters. We have run into some unexpected technical problems in the modifications, which have had an impact on the schedule, and we are working to resolve these. In the meantime, we will continue to conduct our tests with the surrogate.

Finally, we have the interceptor kill vehicle itself. The EKV is the front end of the National Missile Defense (NMD) Ground Based Interceptor (GBI) missile. It is launched with a three-stage booster. In all integrated flight tests to date, we have used a surrogate booster. Later flight tests will use the operational booster. The booster propels the EKV toward an approximate intercept location so that the EKV can perform terminal maneuvers to impact the target. Once the EKV separates from the booster, it acquires, tracks, and discriminates its target, ultimately maneuvering for a hit-to-kill collision. The EKV weighs about 130 pounds and measures about 51 inches long. It uses a multiple-waveband seeker to acquire, track, and discriminate its target. This seeker consists of infrared and visible light focal plane arrays and a cryogenic cooling system attached to a telescope, supported by processing hardware and software. Onboard guidance and navigation equipment calculates homing maneuvers, and divert propulsion and attitude control system motors make the needed lateral and pointing movements to zero in on a target and destroy it.

Before launch, the EKV receives key information from the Battle Management, Command, Control, and Communications (BMC3) element as to the incoming threat and the predicted position and time of the intercept. The GBI's Command Launch Equipment uses that information to construct a firing solution and launch the interceptor. After launch, the EKV uses an onboard communications system to receive further targeting information from the BMC3 element's In-Flight Interceptor Communications System, or IFICS. This information may include a more precise estimate of the threat's position and speed, as well as additional discrimination data based on radar measurements. The NMD EKV was designed by Raytheon. It has been used in integrated flight tests 2 (sensor fly by only), 3 (intercept), and 4 (near hit).

The key to ensuring that this entire system works together is the battle management system that integrates all the elements, including the multiple sensors, which enhances the system's overall discrimination capability.

Lastly, I should point out that we will later be adding a new Space-Based Infrared System in low earth orbit, the so-called SBIRS-Low, to provide even more effective launch detection and discrimination against later, more sophisticated threats.

Chart 3 provides an illustration of how the NMD system works, the concept of operation showing how the pieces of this complex system fit together. It starts with the detection of the launch of the threat missile by the satellite system. This information is transferred to the large early warning radar that helps predict the envelope within which the target is expected to travel. We can then commit the interceptor, based upon the projected trajectory, since this is basically a ballistic trajectory. The X-band Radar refines that track and does a significant amount of discrimination of decoys from the target reentry vehicle, and passes that information to the interceptor. This radar can also provide data through the battle management system to the interceptor in mid-course for course correction and seeker pointing after the interceptor has been launched. This inflight communications ability will be included for the first time in our next flight test on July 7.

Then the kill vehicle itself, on its own, does the final sorting among the decoys and the target, diverts toward the right target, and does a hit-to-kill, direct intercept. The kinetic energy from this high-speed collision (with closing velocities of approximately 15,000 miles per hour) will literally pulverize the target. In relative terms, these reaction timelines for NMD program operators are very short. In some cases, however, the time allotted to us in the mid-course phase of flight could allow us to get off a second shot against the same target, thereby increasing the probability of an intercept.

Program Schedule

Chart 4 addresses the NMD schedule. One of the key aspects of this program is our intent to upgrade and evolve this system over time. This is an important point. It was our original intent, and it continues to be our intent.

We start off with a single-site system with 20 missiles, a single X-band Radar, multiple EWRs that already are available but will be upgraded, and then the SBIRS-High, which are planned to replace the DSP satellites. This configuration of the system we refer to as the initial "C-1", or Capability 1, system.

As the threat grows in number, the X-Band Radar software can be upgraded and 80 missiles added. We refer to this later system, which we would deploy by 2007, as the "Expanded C-1" system. The SBIRS-Low satellite sensor system would be added later for additional detection and discrimination capability as the threat evolves.

Obviously, with the small size of the system we have here, it is not even remotely a threat to the large quantities of the Russian missile systems. It is clearly intended for the small quantities of missiles that we might expect from the countries of concern.

The important point here is that subsequent enhancements include significant hardware and software upgrades and the addition of a substantial additional discrimination capability. Basic improvements are funded.

Flight Tests

Chart 5 shows the initial system flight tests. There have been four such flights to date. The first two flights were not intended as intercept flights. They were intended to gather data on the EKV's ability to discriminate. There were two such "fly-by" tests, using two different candidate kill vehicles, each built by a different contractor team. This was during a competitive phase, and there were two systems at that time—a Boeing/TRW system and a Raytheon system. Both candidate vehicles were flown. The first test was called 1-A since, on the originally planned flight (#1), although the target missile was launched and flew, the interceptor was incorrectly programmed and did not fly. So we wasted that target, but later reused the interceptor for flight test 1-A.

Both these flights were successful in that they allowed us to make a fair comparison of their relative capabilities. What is particularly important, though, is that they also gathered an enormous amount of data on targets that are even more sophisticated than the ones the so-called "Expanded-C1" system, the 100-interceptor system we could deploy by 2007, is designed to defeat.

When we went to the intercept phase of our flight test program, starting with the third flight, we simplified the target cluster, because our objectives were very different. We wanted to see if the interceptor could operate through to intercept, and to see if the whole system could work together. Some people have said, "You dumbed it down," and I will address this point later. Let me just say now that that was not what we were doing at all. What we were doing on the first two flights was trying to make flight comparisons and to gather a lot of data for later use. When we started the intercepts on flight #3, we wanted to be able to verify our capability against the expected threat.

On this third flight test, IFT-3, the target complex consisted of the warhead bus, a balloon decoy, and a re-entry vehicle. What was interesting about this particular flight, which resulted in a successful intercept, is that the kill vehicle looked first at the decoy, then assessed it as not being the right object, searched for the real target, found it, diverted toward it, and slammed into it, destroying it. In other words, the test demonstrated a basic discrimination ability and an intercept ability. The test was successful.

IFT-4, the fourth flight-test, integrated more of the NMD system elements. This integration showed the transfer of data from radars to command-and-control, and from command-and-control to the booster launch. Everything went well until we got to the last five and a half seconds of the flight. At that point, the infrared seekers on the missile failed to cool down, the target was not picked up properly, and no intercept occurred. A post-flight analysis indicated the cause of the failure was an obstruction in the cooling system. We have taken corrective actions to address the material handling and flight preparation processes and made adjustments to the hardware to ensure that this problem does not reoccur. This failure did not require a major redesign of the EKV.

While we demonstrated integration of the system, we did not demonstrate final intercept. This we will try again with our July 7th test flight, IFT-5. In this test, we will add the one system link not utilized on IFT-4, namely the in-flight communications system to send guidance and final seeker pointing information on the target to the interceptor while in-flight.

Overall NMD Decision and Deployment Schedule

Chart 6 lays out the schedule. To put the planned tests and the decision process into perspective, let me first go through that internal DoD acquisition decision process and relate it to the flight tests.

There are basically four major acquisition decisions to be made.

The first of these, the so-called "Deployment Readiness Review," (which Dr Gansler chairs, and which has all of the senior military and civilian relevant leadership as participants) is scheduled this year. It will assess the technological state of the program and provide a recommendation to the Secretary of Defense. The Secretary will then make a recommendation to the President.

To meet a 2005 Initial Operational Capability, we would have some other critical, early decisions to make: site selection, authorization for site preparation for the Shemya X-band radar, commencement of design work for that site, and begin construction of the radar site infrastructure. There are a few early long-lead parts that we might want to order at this point. None of this work will be contracted for until a Presidential decision is made to proceed.

The second key point in the acquisition decision process is next year, when, again to make the 2005 schedule, we would have to start the actual building of the radars and associated communications systems at his point we would also want to authorize some selected long-lead parts for the interceptors. These become the second-tier of long-lead time system elements.

The third major acquisition decision is the point at which we would actually commit to buying the interceptors. In terms of the typical program, this is when we say, "We are going to build our weapons." This is a decision that would get made in 2003.

The final decision, the determination that the system is ready, is the easiest one to make. That is the one in which we say, "We have 20 interceptors. This system has been shown to be effective. We're ready to go." It is the prior three that are the major acquisition decision points in the development process.

So, first, we decide whether to commit to construction of the radar construction site at Shemya (the X-band Radar). Second, we decide whether to commit to the other radar upgrades and the communication systems and the building of the X-band radar. Third, we decide whether to commit to the actual interceptor builds. Finally, we get to the IOC.

There are a series of flight tests that are planned all the way through this development program. First, we had the two initial fly-bys to characterize seeker performance against multiple objects. Then we tested the ability of the kill vehicle, which resulted in a successful hit. The fourth flight test demonstrated the integration of the system, but did not result in a successful final intercept. Now we have our fifth test coming up July 7th. Together, these tests will give us a measure of the system's technological feasibility for this summer's DRR.

We have planned a series of additional flights. Flight test #6 is scheduled for later this year. Flight test #8 is critical because it is the first test of the next-generation interceptor booster, the booster planned for production. This decision would be made by the Defense Acquisition Board (DAB) on what recommendation to provide to the Secretary of Defense at that time.

The third milestone point is when we would make the decision to commit to the interceptors. At this point we want to be using the production interceptor. Functionally, the final production interceptor is the same as for the ones we have used in this early round of flight-testing. But when we move from engineering to production, there are many necessary quality and process changes. So, it is important that the production kill vehicle be the final proven design. And this third milestone is scheduled to determine that. Again, this decision would be made in the DAB as to what to recommend to the Secretary.

Throughout the testing process, not only are we testing equipment that becomes progressively more mature, we are presenting new challenges to the system so that each test increases in complexity and sophistication. They also include increasing the sophistication of decoys and penetration aids to ensure the system can handle the threat we project for that time.

There is also a series of test flights (not shown on this schedule) that are not intercept-flights, but which, nonetheless, are crucial. These involve putting up additional target decoys to check out the radars and much of the rest of the system. These are "risk-reduction" flights. There is a whole series of these flights, and they have been going on and will continue. In one test we had 22 different objects in space to test the radar's discrimination capabilities. These tests improve our ability to discriminate and test out various elements of the system.

Independent Reviews of the Program

Next, let me highlight the independent reviews of this program that have taken place. Secretary Cohen recently asked retired General Larry Welch and his team of noted scientists and experts from a wide spectrum of viewpoints to conduct a third review of the program—and he will discuss this with the Committee later this morning. I might note that some of these earlier reports were quite critical of the way we were going about the NMD program.

In his earlier reports, General Welch's team highlighted three basic criticisms. One of them, the so-called "rush to failure" criticism, was the judgment that we were being too schedule-driven as opposed to event-driven in the development of the system. In response, we modified the overall program. You may remember that we had a "three-plus-three" program aimed at fielding a system as early as 2003. As a result of that report, we modified our schedule by extending the IOC two years, to provide for possible deployment by 2005 rather than the original 2003. It gave us more time.

Additionally, we made a major philosophical change, namely to be event-driven rather than schedule-driven. Our major milestone decisions are now scheduled to occur after the major events identified on Chart 6. The events are driving the decisions to commit to further action, not the schedule.

The second point made by General Welch's team in their earlier reports was that we were trying too hard to do too much too soon. He recommended that we adopt a more evolutionary approach. We should start out with simpler decoys and evolve the system over time. That is exactly what we are now doing.

And third, in his earlier reports, General Welch believed

that we did not have as many tests scheduled as we should have had. We have since added a significant amount of testing and testing resources to lower the risk in the program.

Chart 7 shows the four very important and unanimous findings and recommendations from the independent review team. The first one is that the technical capability is available to develop and field the limited system to meet the defined C-1 threat. This is a relatively limited threat, but the technical capability to meet it is available.

Second, the team finds that the NMD program is still on a high-risk schedule. We agree, and this is something we have been saying for a number of years now. Importantly, the report concludes that there is "no technical reason to change the schedule at present." So we are continuing with the schedule that we have now, based on both his assessment and our own, that we have the ability to meet the 2005 date, if things go according to plan.

Third, General Welch's team said that there are inherent restrictions in our flight testing that will be very limiting for the program. That's true. For example, we don't want objects falling onto fisherman in the South Pacific, so we have range safety limitations. We also have limitations on debris in space, and we have limitations on impact area. Our intent is to try to come up with some ways in which we can overcome these limitations.

The team's last point dealt with discrimination. It concluded that while "design discrimination capabilities are adequate to meet the defined C-1 threat ... more advanced decoy suites are likely to escalate the discrimination challenge." Clearly our capability has to evolve with the system and the threat. What was really encouraging about his findings is the fact that he and his team believed we have the inherent capability in our design, should we choose to add the additional sophistication, to be able to handle those sophisticated decoys.

In their most recent report, the Welch team attempts to provide a quantitative illustration of the program's schedule risk. In it, Welch team members highlight the risks associated with the three major decision points mentioned earlier. These are, first, risks associated with the flight that we have coming up, and the decision scheduled in the fall. Then there is the risk regarding the flight with the new booster. Finally, there are the risks associated with the demonstration of the production kill vehicle and the decision on its production release. These are the gating items in the schedule, and these are the events we will use to drive the decision points. General Welch labeled these three major decisions, first, a "feasibility assessment," second, a "decision to purchase," and third, a "decision to deploy."

Shemya Construction Site is the Long-Lead Item

Chart 8 provides a perspective of Shemya Island. It is not a place that one would normally choose for a vacation. It is a very small island, way down at the end of the Aleutian chain. By looking at the size of the airport runway, you can get some idea of the scale.

Shemya is a terrible place in terms of weather. It happens to be a perfect place in terms of geography, because from this vantage point, we can see everything coming up towards the United States from the direction of North Korea. We will need to put a power plant and a radar on the island, and preparing the site for these represents a significant challenge in meeting the schedule for NMD system deployment by 2005. In fact, it is the longest lead item.

Chart 9 gives an idea of average of days per month with wind conditions under 30 miles per hour in Shemya. Shemya's normal weather conditions are not those under which we would like to land a barge loaded with heavy or sensitive equipment. The wind can reach above 100 miles an hour on some days. There are only a limited number of days throughout the year, and not even many during the more favorable summer months, in which the winds average less than 30 miles an hour. There are even far fewer days with winds less than the 10 miles an hour, needed for some delicate crane operations. So Shemya is not an attractive place in terms of high seas, of bringing in equipment on barges, and of construction. Any building has to be done in the summer, and even then the weather may not be very accommodating.

Chart 10 looks at why, if we are to make the 2005 date, we must start site construction in the summer of 2001. For construction preparations to begin, we need to let a contract, probably in this calendar year. That means we need to get a request for a proposal (RFP) out very shortly, in order to have the contract award and be in a position to begin construction. Contract award for the radar construction, of course, will depend on the President's decision regarding deployment. (In making this decision, the President will consider four criteria: status of the threat, the maturity of the technology, affordability, and overall national security, including arms control.) Let me reiterate: the construction—digging the ground, pouring the concrete, putting up the base for the radar—is the long-lead item in deploying this system for the year 2005. Between then and now, of course, we have another 17 integrated Right tests, so there are a lot of parallel actions we must undertake to move this system forward.

Our System Acquisition Approach—And Some Misconceptions

Now let me turn to some other issues, specifically our general acquisition approach, which will shed further light on our programmatic decisions.

Two major stresses on this program have emerged. The first stems from the pace at which the threat has grown, and which in turn has placed a premium on developing such a complex system in a much shorter time frame than might otherwise be the case. The second concerns the technical challenges of mid-course discrimination and hit-to-kill, which we are resolving through modeling, simulation, and both ground and missile testing.

The nearness of the 2005 deadline will not allow business as usual. Certainly the way we must acquire some of our systems in order to meet more rapidly evolving threats is markedly different from the way we did it during most of the Cold War.

The development of the Atlas ICBM in the late 1950s under the leadership of Air Force General Bernie Schriever was accomplished under a similar urgency. He pioneered some of the concurrency in development we use today, an approach that entails risks, yet can yield great payoffs in the long run. The difference between then and now is that some of those acquisition techniques and procedures are now being used for simultaneously acquiring many interrelated systems—essentially, a "system of systems," not just one crash program.

In many respects the Ballistic Missile Defense program, because of its importance, complexity, and unique joint requirements, is paving new ground in the weapons' acquisition world. The standard—or traditional—approach to weapon-system acquisition is risk-averse, and does not allow us to develop new concepts and systems rapidly. As you know, we in Defense have not been able to keep pace with rapid developments in the commercial sector. This inadequacy in our approach to acquisition is magnified when the threat drives the urgency for development. Nonetheless, the program, in spite of the schedule urgency, must be event-driven, (not held to calendar dates even if performance has not yet been satisfactorily demonstrated). This is our approach.

The second major stress on the NMD program involves coping with technological complexity. The hit-to-kill approach we are following allows little room for error—not more than a few inches at very high speeds. There is a premium on accuracy, but that accuracy is meaningless unless the right object is identified correctly (discriminated) and struck. It also puts a premium on our testing program and on our modeling and simulation capability because we cannot do live testing for every eventuality or reality that we might expect to encounter. A single fully integrated intercept flight test, for example, with far-flung equipment ranging across and above the globe, can cost upwards of $100 million and require several months of preparation.

I mentioned earlier that we have been accused of dumbing down our tests and even falsifying results. The charges betray a misunderstanding of the NMD testing program, its objectives and its approach. Any well conceived test program—and the NMD testing regime has survived a number of exhaustive reviews over the past several years, not just by General Welch—involves a series of events, each building on the success or failure of prior events. Yet each test, whether it is a ground test or a flight test, is designed to be sufficiently unique in and of itself so as to isolate variables. Too much attempted in a single test event will not allow program managers to identify problems, causes, and solutions. Yet, if there is too little attempted, the testers waste valuable resources and unrecoverable time.

When we progressed from the first two (non-intercept) flight tests, involving 11 objects each, to the next two intercept flights, involving three objects each, we were not making the targets simpler in order to gain a shallow success. We were examining very different and discrete capabilities of the elements being tested. The target information gathered, especially on the first two (non-intercept) tests, is being used to enhance the development of both the hardware and the software of this very complex system. Future intercept tests will build on this data, so that by the time these intercept tests are completed—along with other non-intercept "risk reduction" target flights—we will have a comprehensive picture of the capabilities of the NMD system to cope with the threat projected for that time. Some seem to expect that the first tests will demonstrate the full capability of the mature system, and they criticize us for not immediately testing to the ultimate capability we project.

Real world constraints—not only range safety limitations I described earlier, but resources as well—preclude us from doing all the ground- and flight-testing we would like, and this means we must do as much modeling and simulation as we can, both for system elements and the whole integrated system. We also know that what works on the test range may not work in a real-world crisis, and we try to second guess those differences using as broad a range of data and experience as we can.

Is it a perfect system? No, but it beats little or no testing at all, which is the problem generally faced by those states that are being given credit by some of our critics for developing unsophisticated countermeasures that are believed by them to be capable of overcoming our planned system.

The ability of the planned system to "work," i.e., handle the countermeasures threats has been questioned rather extensively in the open press. I do not share the assessment that what we are attempting to accomplish with our system is in any way impossible. Neither did General Welch and his team of experts with access to far more data than the critics. Difficult and challenging, yes. Impossible or infeasible, no. Those who charge that the system cannot be technologically feasible simply do not have all the information they need to make such a conclusion. They are not taking into account the inherent capability of the NMD design to adapt to the evolving threat. I believe the tests planned over the course of the next five years will continue to build our confidence in our ability to discriminate, to identify target warheads in spite of anticipated countermeasures, and to destroy any incoming warheads using advanced hit-to-kill technology.

I would like to close by addressing charges that the NMD tests are "rigged," and that we are "falsifying data" and "lying" about the success of the technology that we need to make the system work. I testify here before you today that I would not tolerate, nor would those above me or below me in the Defense Department tolerate, such activity. Ethical or competency problems in any part of my organization would be detrimental to the Department as a whole, and, more fundamentally, betray the trust the American people have placed in us. Many people have worked diligently on this program and remain dedicated to developing this country's first operational national missile defense system.

The very scrutiny that the NMD program has received, still receives, and will continue to receive, may be its surest and most effective defense against allegations of incompetence and for falsifying data. Daily attention from the American people, the Executive and Legislative branches of government, U.S. industry, and independent analysts, together with the sheer numbers of people inside the program representing various and independent public and private entities, help ensure the integrity of the information we use to affirm our system engineering approach.

Chart 11 shows a flow chart to depict the NMD analysis process. Data integrity from NMD Integrated Flight Tests is assured through the use of configuration-controlled data from a variety of independent sources and organizations, which is then assimilated into an Integrated Data Package by an independent contractor outside the influence of the NMD Lead System Integrator. Once developed, all analysts, including the Lead System Integrator, or LSI, use the Integrated Data Package as the benchmark of truth.

The IFT-5 Data Management Plan identifies in excess of 200 data products that are obtained from national test ranges, including Kwajalein Missile Range, Vandenberg Air Force Base, Kauia Test Facility, and the Joint National Test Facility using multiple sensors (optical, infrared, photonic hit indicator, telemetric, and radar). Data is collected by more than 25 providers representing multiple agencies, many providing data independently of the NMD contract and test objectives. These raw data products, under configuration control, are delivered to members of a government team who serve as couriers to transport the data to the data manager for subsequent distribution. Data products then are distributed to over 50 organizations for analysis, a procedure that provides a broad range of independent perspectives. At all levels of data collection and processing, data is controlled and archived.

Data analysis is performed by the LSI and by multiple diverse government organizations, for the Operational Test Agencies and the NMD Joint Program Office. Within the LSI, element-level subcontractors and subject matter experts perform critical analysis using different perspectives, tools and resources. Analysis results are presented by various organizations at a series of comprehensive Post-Test Analysis Briefings.

We also must not ignore the fact that many of the discrimination technologies and techniques the system relies on cannot be discussed in an open forum. There are legitimate national security concerns about divulging information on our discrimination capabilities. Some material has been made public, but there is a great deal more that has not been divulged, and properly so. We withhold this information not to "cover up" what we have been doing, but to prevent access to information by potential adversaries concerning the design specifications of our counter-countermeasures systems. Consistent with the national security of this country, we will continue to be forthright and open with respect to this important defense program.

Public opinion in these matters is of utmost importance, which is one of the reasons we must make every effort to correct the record and defend the integrity of the NMD program. Over the coming months and years, I believe program results can speak for themselves in responding to the criticism that the NMD system cannot operate as designed against the projected countermeasure threat that a state of concern might pose. We believe the established testing program will continue to affirm our assessments thus far. In the meantime, it is vitally important to continue the public discussion and try to resolve any legitimate disagreements.

Mr Chairman, I again thank you and the Committee for this opportunity to discuss our National Missile Defense system.

28

Cohen on National Missile Defense before Senate Armed Services

The intelligence community estimates that "over the next 15 years the United States most likely will face ICBM (intercontinental ballistic missile) threats from North Korea, probably Iran, and possibly Iraq in addition to long-standing missile capabilities of Russia and China," Defense Secretary William Cohen said July 25.

Testifying on the proposed National Missile Defense system (NMD) before the Senate Armed Services Committee, Cohen said the earliest target deployment date of NMD is 2005, but that "deployment decisions will be made in a sequential process, geared to successful accomplishment of successive stages in the development process."

The projected time for a decision as to whether to deploy the NMD interceptors is 2003. Late this summer President Clinton is expected to decide whether to begin construction of the groundworks for NMD in Alaska.

Despite recent developments of a North-South summit and other actions deemed "positive signs" by Armed Services Committee Chairman John Warner (Republican, Virginia), Cohen said that North Korea "could break its current moratorium and begin flight testing the intercontinental range Taepo-Dong II missile at any time and begin deploying it in the next few years."

Iraq, he said, "if freed from international sanctions... would almost certainly restart its own long-range missile development program. Libya has chemical weapons capabilities and has sought longer-range missiles for years." Cohen also noted Iran's test of the Shahab-3, a medium-range ballistic missile, saying that it is "essentially a derivative of the North Korean NoDong missile."

Senator Carl Levin (Democrat, Michigan,) noted in an opening statement that since "key events and major milestones" in the NMD test program are experiencing delays, "the time has arrived. . . to live up to the repeated assurance that the NMD development program would be event-driven and not calendar driven," and that the "2005 deployment goal is no longer realistic and should be adjusted."

If the 2005 deployment target is no longer realistic, Levin continued, "that date should no longer drive the President's decision this year." His advice to President Clinton, he said, would be to "defer any decision to deploy an NMD system, or any possible decision to withdraw from the ABM (Anti-ballistic Missile) Treaty, to the next president."

Following is the text of Secretary Cohen's testimony, as prepared for delivery:

Statement of the Honorable William S. Cohen
Secretary of Defense
Before the Senate Armed Services Committee
Hearing on National Missile Defense
July 25, 2000

Introduction

Chairman Warner, Senator Levin, members of the Committee, I am pleased to have the opportunity to discuss with you the U.S. National Missile Defense (NMD) program. I cannot think of a more important issue to address than protecting the American people from the threat posed by states such as North Korea, Iran and Iraq who are seeking to acquire nuclear, chemical and biological weapons and the long-range missiles to deliver them.

As you and the members of this Committee know, the Department of Defense is developing a national missile defense system, capable of defending all 50 states from limited ballistic missile attack. The President has not made a decision to deploy and I have not made a recommendation. In making that decision, he will consider the threat, affordability, the state of the technology, and the impact on international security, including arms control.

My testimony covers each of those subjects, and addresses the following five areas on which you have asked me to focus:

(1) the status of the ballistic missile threat to the United States and its global interests;
(2) the NMD development effort, including the flight test program and the deployment readiness review;
(3) the Administration's discussions with Russia and our NATO allies regarding the deployment of a limited NMD system;
(4) the status of the Department's analysis of the alternatives of sea-based or boost-phase elements to support the NMD system; and
(5) the Department's efforts to insure that the NMD system is being adequately developed and tested to counter realistic countermeasures.

I. The Threat

For the United States and our allies, the threat posed by long-range ballistic missile is growing. North Korea and Iran have active missile development programs, the latter case fueled by foreign assistance, and are developing new capabilities. Short and medium-range ballistic missiles, particularly when armed with WMD, already pose a significant threat overseas to U.S. military forces and allies. Despite our determined nonproliferation efforts, the worldwide spread of missile technology continues.

In North Korea, through diplomacy, this Administration has won a commitment for a moratorium on further flight tests, during the continuation of efforts to improve relations. However, test launches are only one part of missile development. Other missile development activities—such as ground testing—continue in North Korea. North Korea could break its current moratorium and begin flight testing the intercontinental range Taepo-Dong II missile at anytime and begin deploying it in the next few years.

It should also be noted that North Korea's missile work potentially contributes to threats from other nations, because of North Korea's willingness to export missile equipment and technology. In the case of the shorter-range NoDong missile, North Korea began exporting it after only one flight test and it is possible that such a pattern could be repeated with the Taepo Dong 2, currently being developed.

Iran's program is also an active one. Just two weeks ago, Iran conducted a test of the Shahab-3, a medium-range ballistic missile. The Shahab-3 is essentially a derivative of the North Korean NoDong missile.

If freed from international sanctions, Iraq would almost certainly restart its own long-range missile development program.

Libya has chemical weapons capabilities and has sought longer-range missiles for years.

The Intelligence Community estimates that over the next 15 years the United States most likely will face ICBM threats from North Korea, probably Iran, and possibly Iraq in addition to long-standing missile capabilities of Russia and China.

The arsenals these states are developing will be much smaller, less accurate and less reliable than those of the Russians and Chinese, but they will still pose a significant threat to the United States in the hands of the leaders of those countries. From my perspective, the utility of considering active defenses against missiles from states like North Korea, Iran and Iraq does not depend on a judgment that their leaders are utterly indifferent to the prospect of retaliation. Rather it is based on a recognition that leaders of these isolated states might be prepared to use WMD attacks—and risk retaliation—in circumstances where more traditional, or at least more cautious, leaders would not. Leaders such as Saddam Hussein and Kim Jong-il have established records of indifference to the suffering of their own populations and they value regime survival above all else.

The most troubling scenario would be a miscalculation by states that acquire a missile capable of reaching the United States taking action to start a regional conflict, in the mistaken belief that by threatening strikes at the U.S., their missiles would prevent us from meeting our commitments.

Any nation using weapons of mass destruction against the United States, its forces, or its allies, would face a prompt and overwhelming response. This is a powerful deterrent—and one we will maintain, whatever we do about other defenses. However, far from undermining deterrence, missile defenses complement overall deterrence by enhancing the United States' ability to fulfill its global security commitments to allies and friends. They present a potential aggressor with the prospect that an attack will not only be fatal—because of retaliation—but also futile—because it will be blocked from striking its target.

II. The Technology

A. The NMD Development Effort

On the basis of a recognition of this potential threat, the Congress and the Administration have for five years now funded an ambitious program to devise a national defense against a limited missile attack.

The program has been based on an objective of doing sufficient development work that a decision on deployment could be made as early as 2000. This is an ambitious program, but it is not excessively so. When I became Secretary of Defense, my hope was to give the President the option to field a missile defense by 2003. In 1998, after carefully reviewing the program it became clear to me that that target was unrealistic. Rather than rush to failure, I extended the target deployment date by two years, to 2005. That was identified by BMDO as the soonest it would be ready to deploy. We have always said that even this date is ambitious, but the threat is continuing to develop, and so there is a premium on being able to deploy a defense rapidly.

Accordingly, in designing the system, the engineers were given guidelines to develop a system that could be deployed quickly, and that implied using mature technology. The elements of the system therefore include an X-band radar at Shemya, upgrades to the five existing Early Warning Radars, the existing DSP launch detection system to be supplemented by SBIRS-High, and an interception system incorporating a hit-to-kill EKV—all linked by a command and control system. The key technological advance in this system is the exoatmospheric kill vehicle (EKV). This is the component that destroys the enemy missile in space by a direct collision.

B. The Test Results to Date

The program provides for an extensive and graduated set of tests, of increasing complexity, to help provide the basis for decisions on successive stages of development.

Last October, in the first test of the EKV, it successfully discerned the target from a decoy, positioned itself and obliterated the target warhead with a direct hit.

A second test in January failed because of a problem with the cooling system that prevented the EKV's sensor from working properly in the final seconds of the test. Other elements of the system, including the integrated operation of sensors with the interceptor functioned as designed.

As you know, the third test conducted on July 7, also did not succeed in testing the interceptor system, because the EKV did not separate from its final rocket booster stage. As the committee is well aware, booster failures are a fact of life when you are dealing with missiles; we know how to correct these problems and our R&D program, though ambitious, can accommodate such disappointments.

The 7 July test, while not successful, was not without benefit—and does not show, as some have claimed, that the system is not technologically feasible. It demonstrated that the sensors and battle management systems could and did work together as an integrated system. Satellite sensors and upgraded early warning radars worked as specified, the X-band radar prototype worked better than anticipated, and the command and control system performed well.

The last point is important because no interceptor could locate and destroy an enemy missile without a sound foundation of effective detection and tracking sensors, battle management, and reliable communications to cue and control system elements in an integrated manner. This was just the third intercept test in a series of 19 before a possible 2005 deployment date. Nevertheless, so far in our overall testing process, we have successfully demonstrated the bulk of the system's critical engagement functions.

C. The Stages of Decisions to Deployment

Because of the high risk of the program's compressed schedule, we have phased the major decisions over several years to help spread that risk. Some decisions are schedule-driven so that the initial NMD deployment can be completed by 2005. For example, if we are to have the X-band radar at Shemya in place and operational in time to support a 2005 IOC, a decision will have to be made by late this year to move forward with construction contracts for preparatory work beginning in the late spring of 2001. The timing on that is driven by the weather conditions on Shemya and the short construction season there.

Further important decisions points on the road to a 2005 IOC would be made in subsequent years, as more milestones are passed. In particular, our current plan calls for making a decision on the final configuration of the ground-based interceptor in 2003, after it has been successfully tested with its new booster and has undergone further flight tests that, among other objectives, will increasingly challenge its ability to discriminate among countermeasures.

In sum, deployment decisions will be made in a sequential process, geared to successful accomplishment of successive stages in the development process and on the basis of adequate data and technological assessment of the test program to determine the feasibility of the system.

At the moment, we are reviewing the recent and earlier test results in detail, and I expect a report will be provided to me within the next several weeks on the feasibility of the NMD system design and the maturity of its engineering. This will be an important input for the Department's Deployment Readiness Review (DRR) in early August, and to me as I prepare my recommendation to the President.

D. The Deployment Readiness Review (DRR)

The DRR is an important step in a lengthy, staged set of decisions leading to ultimate deployment. This year's DRR will be the culmination of an ongoing multi-tiered process of evaluation of progress so far, as well as the first of at least three major acquisition decision milestones that will take place over the next five years to determine the system's technological status and operational readiness to move forward toward deployment. Other intermediate decision milestones include a decision in 2001 by the Defense Acquisition Board on initiation of the early warning radar upgrade, building the X-band radar, and integration of the battle management command and control into the Cheyenne Mountain complex. As noted above, another DAB review scheduled for 2003, will make a decision on the final configuration of the interceptor and on proceeding to series production of the interceptors.

Each acquisition decision made will be based on an assessment of the program's progress at that time. The establishment of performance gates for program elements means that the acquisition process as a whole is event-driven based on progress through successive stages on extensive test and development programs.

The DRR event will take place in August at the Defense Acquisition Executive level with full participation from all Department of Defense stakeholders (to include DIA, VCJS, USD(P) and USD (AT&L)). The review will result in a series of findings concerning the NMD system's technological readiness and cost, which then will be forwarded to me for review and evaluation. I will produce my own assessment regarding the technological feasibility and affordability of the NMD system and develop a recommendation to be forwarded to the President through the National Security Council (NSC). The NSC will review my findings and supporting assessments and weigh these factors along with assessments of the threat and implications of NMD deployment for national security policy. The NSC then will recommend to the President how to proceed with the NMD program.

E. Alternate NMD Architectures

Turning to alternative NMD architectures, the NMD system that we are planning was chosen based on the assessment of our best technical experts. The technical experts who designed the system were asked to devise a system that could be deployed rapidly, in time to meet the expected threat, which naturally focused the effort on mature technology.

Other systems were considered, including boost-phase interceptors and sea-based systems, but the technological challenges of those alternatives were judged to be greater than those posed by the system we have designed, making timely deployment impossible. In particular, the sea-based theater missile defense systems currently under development are not capable against intercontinental range missiles and would require fundamental—and time consuming—redesign to be effective against long-range threats.

Similarly, the United States remains interested in exploring the boost-phase intercept concept, but it too, like sea-based systems, cannot substitute for the limited NMD now under development, at least if we are to have the option of having an operational system on anything comparable to the 2005 timeline we have established. There are major technical, geographical and political challenges associated with the effort to intercept a very long-range ballistic missile in the boost phase. No U.S. defense system currently under development has been designed to perform this task. Development of a boost-phase intercept system capable of defeating intercontinental strategic ballistic missiles, therefore, would take many years—well beyond the date by which we expect a strategic ballistic missile threat from North Korea and possibly from Iran will have emerged.

We continue, despite these problems, to study other systems, including sea-based and boost-phase. In response to Congressional guidance, (1) BMDO and the Navy have been conducting an in-depth examination of how naval systems could potentially supplement or complement the land-based NMD system currently in development.

They are completing work on a report that discusses various approaches that employ ship-based radar sensors and interceptor missiles that could contribute to the NMD mission, as well as notional concepts for carrying out these operations and first order costs of these systems. The report is focused heavily on ship-based concepts that—like the land-based system under development—intercept strategic missile RVs during the mid-course portion of their flight path. These sea-based adjuncts are largely dependent on the space-based and ground-based sensors and command and control systems that would be deployed with the ground-based limited NMD currently under development. The report will also briefly discuss the potential for boost-phase intercept of an adversary long-range missile from Navy ships.

There are both significant potential advantages and disadvantages to a sea-based system. A ship-based radar sensor, if deployed forward, near the missile launch site, would provide earlier detection, tracking, discrimination and, importantly, longer time for decisions against certain threats. Certainly, additional sea-based interceptors would provide the potential for layered intercepts at different closing angles and speeds, and increase our ability to handle larger attacks, thereby making it an attractive complement to a land-based NMD system.

Some of the disadvantages of a sea-based system include limitations on operational range in some scenarios, and the current lack of any high performance interceptors and interceptor platforms that could be deployed to meet the near-term threat. This would require a significant R&D program. Additionally, any sea-based, mid-course intercept system would require full land-based sensor architecture to work effectively. As made clear in the 1998 report to the Congress, the Navy Theater Wide (NTW) Block 11 system—a theater missile defense system—alone would have no useful capability against ICBMs or SLBMs.

We have also examined concepts for boost-phase intercept NMD systems. An effective boost-phase intercept system would have the advantage of destroying an enemy missile before it could release multiple warheads or countermeasures. This feature makes it a very attractive concept. However, there are several significant challenges associated with this approach. It requires very quick reaction. Long-range missiles are in the boost-phase for only a few minutes. This would put significant stress on an NMD system because it would require rapid detection and response. The flight path and speed of a missile during the boost-phase are erratic, thus requiring continuous tracking of the missile and relaying that data to the interceptor in flight. In addition, this short time window would also require a highly maneuverable interceptor that could accelerate rapidly to high speed and carry sophisticated sensors able to home in on the missile rather than the hot exhaust plume. This would also require the interceptor to be deployed down-range from and within a few hundred kilometers from the launch site to reach intercept it in time. Such geographic limitations may make it difficult to find third countries willing to host these interceptors.

The most practical role for a sea-based and/or boost phase NMD systems would be as an adjunct to a land-based system, not as a replacement for it. Additionally, sea-based and boost-phase NMD systems would also require amending the ABM Treaty.

F. Countermeasures

A number of critics have charged that our current NMD system design, by focusing on the mid-course intercept, when a missile is in space, leaves itself open to defeat by countermeasures. We understand the serious challenge posed by countermeasures. (Countermeasures are not, of course, a problem unique to land-based, mid-course systems: They can be developed for boost-phase systems as well.)

Having the ability to discriminate between reentry vehicles and various types of countermeasures, simple and complex, has been among the highest priority design considerations and tested aspects of the program. Each flight test has had, and will continue to have, decoys present, and their sophistication will be increasing as we test the ability of the evolving system to counter them. In developing the technology, we will walk before we run.

It is important to point out that the US has been working on countermeasure technology for decades, and it is far more difficult to make effective countermeasures than some critics seem willing to acknowledge, particularly if one takes into account the inherent capacity of the system to be adapted and upgraded against an evolving countermeasure challenge. Our own work also underscores the point that, unless a potential aggressor state tests its countermeasures—and we have seen nothing of that from states of concern so far—those countermeasures may well not work. Without adequate testing, potential aggressors cannot be confident that their missiles or countermeasures would be effective against our advanced discrimination and kill technologies. Nevertheless, having the ability to overcome an adversary's countermeasures must be taken very seriously, and I would make the following points. First, our steadily improving computing power and sensor capabilities will assist us greatly in dealing with countermeasures. Furthermore, the NMD system that we are developing will be far more robust than many suggest. It will not rely solely on the kill vehicle's infrared and optical sensors. In addition to the EKV's organic sensors, the system will employ an integrated set of multi-spectral sensors, space-based and land-based to track incoming RVs and distinguish them from countermeasures. This allows the sensor complex to view the "threat clusters" speeding through space from different angles over the much longer period of time that mid-course intercept affords, and provides the opportunity to reliably discriminate between RVs and various types of penetration aids. Additionally, multiple shot opportunities built into our limited NMD concept dramatically increase confidence of successful intercepts.

Moreover, our NMD system is not designed to be static, but to incorporate increasingly advanced technologies over time to ensure we are able to deal effectively with more sophisticated threats. We will be adding new, capable software tools and technologies to the system, including the infrared sensor suite on the SBIRS-Low satellites, which will be used to help identify and discriminate between RVs and accompanying countermeasures.

III. Costs

My recommendation to the President will also include a current estimate of the cost of the system. Ballistic missile defense is not inexpensive, and we need to be sure every defense dollar is efficiently spent, but the cost of a limited national missile defense is not disproportionate in the context of the overall defense budget over the relevant period. Since 1991, we have spent some $5.7 billion on national missile defense. The current estimate for the full cost of developing and deploying the initial phase of a limited defense is approximately $20.3 billion. Funds sufficient to support the currently estimated cost of phase one are included in our five-year budget plan. The CBO estimate is slightly higher because they estimate higher construction costs, a need for more test/spare interceptors, and more expensive interceptor production. (Higher estimates based on CBO publications are for the second phase, with additional radars and interceptors, and include the SBIRS-Low satellite sensor system.)

These are obviously large amounts of money, and there are always uncertainties about cost estimates at this stage of a program. As a part of my recommendation, I will advise the President on the impact of proceeding with NMD on our overall defense budget priorities, i.e., on the affordability of the program in the context of our total defense needs.

IV. Impact on International Security, Including Arms Control

Commitment to Arms Control

Our work on this subject is not simply a matter of

technological development; it takes into account the broader political and strategic context. As I noted earlier, the basic reason for our consideration of this system is strategic—to supplement diplomacy and deterrence as instruments for preventing potential aggressors from mounting an attack.

However, we recognize that our decisions on an NMD system have potential impacts on other aspects of international security—our relations with our allies and with Russia and China, and on arms control. We do not want in the course of dealing with these limited, but serious, threats from countries like North Korea or Iran, to create new problems with Russia and other nations that we can reasonably avoid. We also place very high priority on preserving, and indeed strengthening, arms control limits, as a means both of fostering strategic stability and of resisting proliferation of dangerous military capabilities. For this reason, President Clinton and this Administration are committed both to protecting the American people from limited ballistic missile threats and to maintaining the ABM Treaty as a cornerstone of strategic stability and a key element in our relationship with Russia. Assessment of the impact of our NMD program on these broader national security interests will be a factor in my own recommendations to the President—and of course of his other key national security advisers.

There is no reason we—and the world—should be faced with a choice between defending our population against the emerging threat of attack by limited missile capabilities of rogue states, on the one hand, and preserving arms control on the other. The ABM Treaty expressly provides for revisions to take account of changes in the strategic situation. The purpose of the ABM Treaty is not to ban defenses altogether. It does not do that—In fact, an ABM system is already deployed to defend Moscow. Rather, the purpose of the Treaty is to ensure that each party's strategic deterrent is not threatened by the missile defenses of the other party. The limited NMD system we are developing would not threaten Russia's strategic deterrent, even at START III warhead levels—or indeed even well below those levels.

V. Discussions with Russia

Over the last year, U.S., Russian and NATO officials have

held intensive discussions on ballistic missile defense. We have stressed that the system we are considering would not threaten the Russian deterrent and is consistent with the purpose of the ABM Treaty. We have proposed modifications to the ABM Treaty that would permit the deployment of the initial system I have described. We have also indicated that, to meet the emerging threat we expect from the Middle East, we would need to deploy a larger system, and would expect to begin negotiations on modifications of the Treaty needed to permit such a system early in the next Administration. We have also emphasized that we are prepared to cooperate with Russia on insuring the transparency of our program—so they will be confident it is no threat to their strategic capabilities.

President Clinton met with President Putin last month and again last week and has had discussions with his counterparts from many of our NATO allies. I covered this topic in considerable detail at the NATO Defense Ministerial in early June and in my Moscow meetings with President Putin and Minister of Defense Marshal Sergeyev.

We seek Russia's agreement to those changes to the ABM Treaty required to permit us to meet our initial goal and defend against these limited threats. An important element of our proposal includes measures of cooperation and transparency that would give Russia confidence that the system was not being expanded beyond its limited scale. We have already made progress on this effort. We have also proposed ways to move ahead to reduce further offensive nuclear weapons under START III.

In June, Presidents Clinton and Putin agreed to establish a joint warning center in Moscow, where Russian and U.S. personnel will monitor global ballistic missile launches. This will reduce the possibility that either side would misinterpret an event as a hostile act.

In Okinawa, the Presidents agreed to move forward with the joint warning center within the year; they also agreed on other concrete measures to cooperate on reducing proliferation threats.

One topic of discussion has been President Putin's recent proposal for cooperation between NATO and Russia in non-strategic (theater) missile defense and indications of Russian interest in the development of missile defense systems that intercept adversary missiles during their initial boost-phase of flight. In my discussions with President Putin and Marshal Sergeyev, I repeatedly stressed that the United States is interested in exploring—first with our NATO Allies and then with Russia—possibilities for cooperation between NATO and Russia on defenses against non-strategic ballistic missiles (missiles with a range less than 3,500 km). I also made clear that defenses against non-strategic ballistic missiles cannot substitute for defenses against the emerging threat of strategic ballistic missiles that could strike the United States.

The NATO-Russia Permanent Joint Council held its first discussion of possible NATO-Russia TMD cooperation in late June, but it will take some time for Russia and NATO to develop specific proposals in this area.

President Putin, Marshal Sergeyev and I also discussed at some length the possibility for boost-phase intercept of ballistic missiles during my visit to Moscow in mid-June. We agreed that U.S. and Russian experts would consider the concept at the U.S.-Russian Defense Consultative Group meetings in late June. At that meeting U.S. experts laid out the various technical and political challenges associated with boost-phase intercepts of long-range missiles. The Russian side asked a few questions but indicated that it was not yet ready to discuss these matters in any detail.

We will continue to explore this idea further in future meetings with the Russians. I would note, in this general context that, any system capable of defending against strategic ballistic missiles at any point in their flight would, by definition, be a strategic ballistic missile defense system falling within the limits of the ABM Treaty. Thus, development and deployment of boost-phase intercept systems for national missile defense would not obviate the need to amend the ABM Treaty.

VI. Discussions with China

We have had extensive discussions of NMD with the government of China. Indeed, NMD was one of the chief topics of my recent meetings with the Chinese leadership in Beijing. The whole issue of missile defense, in all its aspects, is an issue between the US and China. The Chinese, as you know, oppose our NMD program, as they do our R&D cooperation on TMD with Japan. They are also strongly opposed to any sale of TMD capability to Taiwan. We have explained the reasons for our consideration of NMD, and made the point that neither the NMD system we have under consideration nor our TMD cooperation with Japan is designed against China, and that, in any event, we do not expect our relations with China to be such that the question of China using its nuclear capability against the US—or indeed Japan or any other US ally—would arise.

The question of the impact of NMD as such on our relations with China needs to be considered in the light of the fact that China has, for some years, been pursuing development of a more modem, more survivable, and more capable long-range missile capability.

VII. Discussion with Allies

We have had extensive discussions about our NMD proposal with NATO allies and we will weigh allied views, and impact on alliance relationships in our decisions. It is important to do this because we want the NATO alliance to continue to be a strong and effective instrument of Atlantic security in the conditions we will face in the coming years, and that requires a high degree allied understanding of our major defense policies. Beyond that, two of the radars in our NMD proposal are located in NATO countries, and so their consent will be needed for us to use them.

Our basic message to our allies has been that the missile threat from states like North Korea and Iran is growing and presents a potentially significant problem. We have explained the strategic rationale for defenses, and why they would re-enforce, not undermine, deterrence. And we have explained that we are committed to seeking to preserve the ABM Treaty as a foundation of strategic stability and why the ABM Treaty can readily be modified to permit defenses against limited ballistic missile attacks while continuing to foster strategic stability.

As to the allied reaction, I think it fair to say that the allies broadly accept our analysis of the threat and the strategic problem it poses. While they increasingly understand our reasons for considering deploying a defense, they are also very concerned about the Russian (and to some degree, the Chinese) reaction, and are eager to see the ABM Treaty preserved.

None of our allies have formally asked to be included in our NMD system, but many recognize that the same missile programs that threaten us would also be a danger to them. Should any of our allies be interested in cooperating with us to build a defense for themselves against long-range missiles, the President has said we are open to working with them. We have informed the Russians that such measures of cooperation would have to be addressed in the context of further modifications of the Treaty to permit deployments beyond the initial phase.

Conclusion

In summary, the mission of our NMD program is clear: to develop and test in a timely manner a missile defense system that will be able to protect our nation from either the threat or limited use of ICBMs, and be able to deploy that system following a decision by the President. The technical challenges and technology development tasks involved in this mission are daunting. We are, however, in the process of meeting those challenges, and working hard—and carefully—to achieve the incremental success needed to produce a strong and effective NMD system.

Thank you Mr Chairman, for the opportunity to discuss this important issue and for the support that you have provided to me and the Department over the past four years.

29

Fact Sheet: White House on National Missile Defense Decision

The following fact sheet on President Clinton's decision regarding a National Missile Defense system was issued by the White House on September 1. **(In the following fact sheet one billion refers to a thousand million).**

The White House
Office of the Press Secretary
September 1, 2000
Fact Sheet: National Missile Defense

The Clinton Administration is committed to the development of a limited National Missile Defense (NMD) system designed to protect all 50 states from the emerging ballistic missile threat from nations that threaten international peace and security. In the event of an attack, American satellites would detect the launch of missiles; radar would track the enemy warheads; and highly accurate, high-speed ground-based interceptors would destroy missiles before they reach targets in the United States.

National Missile Defense Decision

President Clinton announced today that the NMD program is sufficiently promising and affordable to justify continued development and testing, but that there is not sufficient information about the technical and operational effectiveness of the entire NMD system to move forward with deployment.

In making this decision, the President considered the threat, the cost, technical feasibility and the impact overall on our national security of proceeding with NMD. He considered a thorough technical review by the Department of Defense as well as the advice of his top national security advisors.

The Pentagon has made progress on developing a system that can address the emerging missile threat. But we do not have sufficient information to conclude that it can work reliably under realistic conditions. Critical elements of the program, such as the booster rocket for the missile interceptor, have not been tested; and there are questions to be resolved about the ability of the system to deal with countermeasures. The President made clear we should not move forward until we have further confidence that the system will work and until we have made every reasonable diplomatic effort to minimize the costs.

The Pentagon will continue the development and testing of the NMD system. That effort is still at an early stage: three of the 19 planned intercept tests have been held so far. Additional ground tests and simulations will also take place.

The development of our NMD is part of the Administration's comprehensive national security strategy to prevent potential adversaries from threatening the United States with such weapons and acquiring the weapons in the first place.

Arms control agreements with Russia are an important part of this strategy because they ensure stability and predictability between the United States and Russia, promote the dismantling of nuclear weapons, and help complete the transition from confrontation to cooperation with Russia. The Anti-Ballistic Missile (ABM) Treaty of 1972 limits anti-missile defenses according to a simple principle: neither side should deploy defenses that would undermine the other's nuclear deterrent, and thus tempt the other to strike first in a crisis or take countermeasures that would make both our countries less secure.

This announcement will provide additional time to pursue with Russia the goal of adapting the ABM Treaty to permit the deployment of a limited NMD that would not undermine strategic stability. The United States will also continue to consult with Allies and continue the dialogue with China and other states.

An NMD Program That Meets the Projected Threat

Last August, the President decided that the initial NMD architecture would include: 100 ground-based interceptors deployed in Alaska, one ABM radar in Alaska, and five upgraded early warning radars.

This approach is the fastest, most affordable, and most technologically mature approach to fielding an effective NMD against the projected threat. It would protect all 50 states against emerging threats from both North Korea and the Middle East and is optimized against the most immediate and certain threat, North Korea.

On July 23, 1999, President Clinton signed into law H.R. 4, the "National Missile Defense Act of 1999," stating that it is the policy of the United States to deploy as soon as technologically possible an effective NMD system. The legislation includes two amendments supported by the Administration: the first making clear that any NMD deployment must be subject to the authorization and appropriations process, and thus that no decision on deployment has been made; the second stating it is the policy of the United States to seek continued negotiated reductions in Russian nuclear forces, putting Congress on record as continuing to support negotiated reductions in strategic nuclear arms, reaffirming the Administration's position that missile defense policy must take into account important arms control and nuclear nonproliferation objectives.

NMD Budget

The Clinton Administration has spent approximately \$5.7 billion on NMD, and budgeted an additional \$10.4 billion in FY 2001–2005 to support possible deployment of the initial NMD architecture. Our current estimate for developing, procuring and deploying our initial system—100 interceptors, an ABM radar, upgrades to 5 early warning radars, and command and control—is around \$25 billion (Fiscal Years 91-09). But to put that in perspective, it represents less than 1 percent of the defense budget over the coming six years.

Joint Statement of Principles on Strategic Stability

At the June 4 Moscow Summit, Presidents Clinton and Putin signed a Joint Statement of Principles on Strategic Stability. The Principles state that the international community faces a dangerous and growing threat of proliferation of weapons of mass destruction and their means of delivery, including missiles and missile technologies, and that there is a need to address these threats, including through consideration of changes to the

ABM Treaty. The Principles also record agreement to intensify discussions on both ABM issues and START (Strategic Arms Reduction Treaty) III.

Joint Statement on Cooperation on Strategic Stability

The United States has made clear to Russia that we are prepared to engage in serious cooperation to address the emerging ballistic missile threat and have identified a number of specific ideas for discussion. At the June 4 Moscow Summit, Presidents Clinton and Putin signed an agreement to establish a Joint Center for exchanging early warning data on missile launches; they also agreed to explore more far-reaching cooperation to address missile threats.

On July 21 in Okinawa, Presidents Clinton and Putin issued a Joint Statement on Cooperation on Strategic Stability, which identifies specific areas and projects for cooperation to control the spread of missiles, missile technology and weapons of mass destruction.

30

Clinton Defers Missile Defense Decision to Next President

President Clinton announced September 1 his decision to leave to his successor the critical decision on whether to deploy a National Missile Defense (NMD) system to defend all 50 American states against a limited ballistic missile attack.

In a speech at Georgetown University, his alma mater, Clinton told the audience that the proposed NMD system "as a whole is not yet proven." Several more flight tests are still needed to help decide "whether NMD can work reliably under realistic conditions," the President said. "We need more tests against more challenging targets, and more simulations before we can responsibly commit our nation's resources to deployment," he added.

In the meantime, Clinton has asked the Defense Department to continue pursuing a robust research and development program, saying that the extra time will allow additional technological progress as well as more time to narrow differences about the program with the Russians.

In discussing NMD's impact on U.S.-Russian relations, Clinton explained that pursuing a limited NMD would require the United States to either amend or withdraw from the bilateral 1972 Anti-Ballistic Missile (ABM) Treaty. While Russia has agreed that there is an emerging missile threat that may require amending the ABM Treaty, the President said there will now be more time to discuss how to pursue effective defenses while still maintaining strategic stability with Russia.

In announcing his decision not to authorize NMD "at this time," Clinton also made reference to the views of NATO allies, who have all "made clear that they hope the United States will pursue strategic defense in a way that preserves the ABM Treaty." Allied support is critical if the U.S. decides to proceed with NMD deployment, he said, because "key components of NMD would be based on their territory." By postponing the NMD decision to the next administration, he said, the United States will have "time to answer allied questions and consult further on the path ahead."

Besides allied input, Clinton also addressed NMD and the security situation in Asia. "As the next President makes a deployment decision, he will need to avoid stimulating an already dangerous regional nuclear capability from China to South Asia," he said.

"No nation can have a veto over American security," Clinton stated. At the same time, he also noted that reactions of others around the globe do have a bearing on U.S. national security, and for that reason, he said, "it would be far better to move forward (on the future NMD program) in the context of the ABM Treaty and allied support."

The President announced his decision after determining that it would not have "a significant impact on the date the overall system could be deployed if the next administration decides to go forward." The NMD system could still be ready for operation in the 2006 or 2007 time frame, he said, if the next President decides to move ahead with the system in 2001.

Following is the White House transcript of Clinton's remarks as delivered **(in the speech a billion refers to a thousand million):**

The White House
Office of the Press Secretary
September 1, 2000
Remarks by the President on National Missile Defense
Gaston Hall Gecrgetown University
Washington, D.C.
11:23 A.M. EDT

The President. Thank you very much. When you gave us such a warm welcome, and then you applauded some of Dean

Gallucci's early lines, I thought to myself, I'm glad he can get this sort of reception, because I gave him a lot of thankless jobs to do in our administration where no one ever applauded—and he did them brilliantly. I'm delighted to see him here succeeding so well as the Dean. And Provost Brown, thank you for welcoming me here.

I told them when I came in I was sort of glad Father O'Donovan wasn't here today, because I come so often—I know that at some point if I keep doing this he will tell me that he's going to send a bill to the U.S. Treasury for the Georgetown endowment. I was thinking when we came out here and Bob talked about the beginning of the school year that it was 35 years ago when, as a sophomore, I was in charge of the freshman orientation. So I thought I should come and help this year's orientation of freshmen get off to a good start.

I also was thinking, I confess, after your rousing welcome, that if I were still a candidate for public office I might get up and say hello and sit down, and quit while I'm ahead.

I came today to talk about a subject that is not fraught with applause lines, but one that is very, very important to your future: the defense of our nation. At this moment of unprecedented peace and prosperity, with no immediate threat to our security or our existence, with our democratic values ascendant and our alliances strong, with the great forces of our time, globalization and the revolution in information technology so clearly beneficial to a society like ours, with our diversity and our openness, and our entrepreneurial spirit.

At a time like this it is tempting, but wrong, to believe there are no serious long-term challenges to our security. The rapid spread of technology across increasingly porous borders, raises the specter that more and more states, terrorists and criminal syndicates could gain access to chemical, biological or even nuclear weapons, and to the means of delivering them—whether in small units deployed by terrorists within our midst, or ballistic missiles capable of hurtling those weapons halfway around the world.

Today I want to discuss these threats with you, because you will live with them a lot longer than I will. Especially, I want to talk about the ballistic missile threat. It is real and growing, and has given new urgency to the debate about national missile defenses, known in the popular jargon as NMD.

When I became President, I put our effort to stop the proliferation of weapons of mass destruction at the very top of our national security agenda. Since then, we have carried out a comprehensive strategy to reduce and secure nuclear arsenals, to strengthen the international regime against biological and chemical weapons and nuclear testing, and to stop the flow of dangerous technology to nations that might wish us harm.

At the same time, we have pursued new technologies that could strengthen our defenses against a possible attack, including a terrorist attack here at home.

None of these elements of our national security strategy can be pursued in isolation. Each is important, and we have made progress in each area. For example, Russia and the United States already have destroyed about 25,000 nuclear weapons in the last decade. And we have agreed that in a START III treaty, we will go 80 per cent below the level of a decade ago. In 1994, we persuaded Ukraine, Kazakhstan and Belarus, three of the former Soviet Republics, to give up their nuclear weapons entirely. We have worked with Russia and its neighbors to dispose of hundreds of tons of dangerous nuclear materials, to strengthen controls on a list of exports, and to keep weapon scientists from selling their services to the highest bidder.

We extended the Nuclear Non-Proliferation Treaty indefinitely. We were the very first nation to sign the Comprehensive Test Ban Treaty, an idea first embraced by Presidents Kennedy and Eisenhower. Sixty nations now have ratified the Test Ban Treaty. I believe the United States Senate made a serious error in failing to ratify it last year, and I hope it will do so next year.

We also negotiated and ratified the international convention to ban chemical weapons, and strengthened the convention against biological weapons. We've used our export controls to deny terrorists and potential adversaries access to materials and equipment needed to build these kinds of weapons.

We've imposed sanctions on those who contribute to foreign chemical and biological weapons programs, we've invested in new equipment and medical countermeasures to protect people from exposure. And we're working with state and local medical units all over our country to strengthen our preparedness in case of a chemical or biological terrorist attack, which many people believe is the most likely new security threat of the 21st century.

We have also acted to reduce the threat posed by states that have sought weapons of mass destruction and ballistic missiles, while pursuing activities that are clearly hostile to our long-term interests. For almost a decade we have diverted about 90 per cent of Iraq's oil revenues from the production of weapons to the purchase of food and medicine.

This is an important statistic for those who believe that our sanctions are only a negative for the people, and particularly the children, of Iraq. In 1989, Iraq earned $15 billion from oil exports, and spent $13 billion of that money on its military. This year, Iraq is projected to earn $19 billion from its legal oil-for-food exports that can spend none of those revenues on the military.

We worked to counter Iran's efforts to develop nuclear weapons and missile technology, convincing China to provide no new assistance to Iran's nuclear program, and pressing Russia to strengthen its controls on the export of sensitive technologies.

In 1994, six years after the United States first learned that North Korea had a nuclear weapons program, we negotiated the agreement that verifiably has frozen its production of plutonium for nuclear weapons. Now, in the context of the United States negotiations with the North, the diplomatic efforts by former Defense Secretary Bill Perry and, most lately, the summit between the leaders of North and South Korea, North Korea has refrained from flight testing a new missile that could pose a threat to America.

We should be clear: North Korea's capability remains a serious issue and its intentions remain unclear. But its missile testing moratorium is a good development worth pursuing.

These diplomatic efforts to meet the threat of proliferation are backed by the strong and global reach of our armed forces. Today, the United States enjoys overwhelming military superiority over any potential adversary. For example, in 1985, we spent about as much on defense as Russia, China and North Korea combined. Today, we spend nearly three times as much, nearly $300 billion a year. And our military technology clearly is well ahead of the rest of the world.

The principle of deterrence served us very well in the Cold War, and deterrence remains imperative. The threat of overwhelming retaliation deterred Saddam Hussein from using weapons of mass destruction during the Gulf War. Our forces in South Korea have deterred North Korea in aggression for 47 years.

The question is, can deterrence protect us against all those who might wish us harm in the future? Can we make America even more secure? The effort to answer these questions is the impetus behind the search for NMD. The issue is whether we can do more, not to meet today's threat, but to meet tomorrow's threat to our security.

For example, there is the possibility that a hostile state with nuclear weapons and long-range missiles may simply disintegrate, with command over missiles falling into unstable hands; or that in a moment of desperation, such a country might miscalculate, believing it could use nuclear weapons to intimidate us from defending our vital interests, or from coming to the aid of our allies, or others who are defenseless and clearly in need.

In the future, we cannot rule out that terrorist groups could gain the capability to strike us with nuclear weapons if they seized even temporary control of a state with an existing nuclear weapons establishment.

Now, no one suggests that NMD would ever substitute for diplomacy or for deterrence. But such a system, if it worked properly, could give us an extra dimension of insurance in a world where proliferation has complicated the task of preserving the peace. Therefore, I believe we have an obligation to determine the feasibility, the effectiveness, and the impact of a national missile defense on the overall security of the United States.

The system now under development is designed to work as follows. In the event of an attack, American satellites would protect the launch of missiles. Our radar would track the enemy warhead and highly accurate, high-speed, ground-based interceptors would destroy them before they could reach their target in the United States.

We have made substantial progress on a system that would be based in Alaska and that, when operational, could protect all 50 states from the near-term missile threats we face, those emanating from North Korea and the Middle East. The system could be deployed sooner than any of the proposed alternatives. Since last fall, we've been conducting flight tests to see if this NMD system actually can reliably intercept a ballistic missile. We've begun to show that the different parts of this system can work together.

Our Defense Department has overcome daunting technical obstacles in a remarkably short period of time, and I'm proud of the work that Secretary (William) Cohen, General (Henry) Shelton and their teams have done.

One test proved that it is, in fact, possible to hit a bullet with a bullet. Still, though the technology for NMD is promising, the system as a whole is not yet proven. After the initial test succeeded, our two most recent tests failed, for different reasons, to achieve an intercept. Several more tests are planned. They will tell us whether NMD can work reliably under realistic conditions. Critical elements of the program, such as the booster rocket for the missile interceptor, have yet to be tested.

There are also questions to be resolved about the ability of the system to deal with countermeasures. In other words, measures by those firing the missiles to confuse the missile defense into thinking it is hitting a target when it is not.

There is a reasonable chance that all these challenges can be met in time. But I simply cannot conclude with the information I have today that we have enough confidence in the technology, and the operational effectiveness of the entire NMD system, to move forward to deployment.

Therefore, I have decided not to authorize deployment of a national missile defense at this time. Instead, I have asked Secretary Cohen to continue a robust program of development and testing. That effort still is at an early stage. Only three of the 19 planned intercept tests have been held so far. We need more tests against more challenging targets, and more simulations before we can responsibly commit our nation's resources to deployment.

We should use this time to ensure that NMD, if deployed, would actually enhance our overall national security. And I want to talk about that in a few moments.

I want you to know that I have reached this decision about not deploying the NMD after careful deliberation. My decision will not have a significant impact on the date the overall system could be deployed in the next administration, if the next President decides to go forward.

The best judgment of the experts who have examined this question is that if we were to commit today to construct the system, it most likely would be operational about 2006 or 2007. If the next President decides to move forward next year, the system still could be ready in the same time frame.

In the meantime, we will continue to work with our allies and with Russia to strengthen their understanding and support for our efforts to meet the emerging ballistic missile threat, and to explore creative ways that we can cooperate to enhance their security against this threat, as well.

An effective NMD could play an important part of our national security strategy, but it could not be the sum total of that strategy. It can never be the sum total of that strategy for dealing with nuclear and missile threats.

Moreover, ballistic missiles, armed with nuclear weapons, as I said earlier, do not represent the sum total of the threats we face. Those include chemical and biological weapons, and a range of deadly technologies for deploying them. So it would be folly to base the defense of our nation solely on a strategy of waiting until missiles are in the air, and then trying to shoot them down.

We must work with our allies, and with Russia, to prevent potential adversaries from ever threatening us with nuclear, chemical and biological weapons of mass destruction in the first place, and to make sure they know the devastating consequences of doing so.

The elements of our strategy cannot be allowed to undermine one another. They must reinforce one another, and contribute to our national defense in all its dimensions. That includes the profoundly important dimension of arms control.

Over the past 30 years, Republican and Democratic Presidents alike have negotiated an array of arms control treaties with Russia. We and our allies have relied on these treaties to ensure strategic stability and predictability with Russia, to get on with the job of dismantling the legacy of the Cold War, and to further the transition from confrontation to cooperation with our former adversary in the most important arena, nuclear weapons.

A key part of the international security structure we have built with Russia and, therefore, a key part of our national security, is the Anti-Ballistic Missile Treaty signed by President Nixon in 1972. The ABM Treaty limits anti-missile defenses according to a simple principle: neither side should deploy defenses that would undermine the other side's nuclear deterrent, and thus tempt the other side to strike first in a crisis or to take countermeasures that would make both our countries less secure.

Strategic stability, based on mutual deterrence, is still important, despite the end of the Cold War. Why? Because the United States and Russia still have nuclear arsenals that can devastate each other. And this is still a period of transition in our relationship.

We have worked together in many ways. Signed an agreement of cooperation between Russia and NATO. Served with Russian troops in Bosnia and Kosovo. But while we are no longer adversaries, we are not yet real allies. Therefore, for them as well as for us, maintaining strategic stability increases trust and confidence on both sides. It reduces the risk of confrontation. It makes it possible to build an even better partnership and an even safer world.

Now, here's the issue: NMD, if deployed, would require us either to adjust the treaty or to withdraw from it—not because NMD poses a challenge to the strategic stability I just discussed, but because by its very words, ABM prohibits any national missile defense.

What we should want is to both explore the most effective defenses possible, not only for ourselves, but for all other law-abiding states, and to maintain our strategic stability with Russia. Thus far, Russia has been reluctant to agree, fearing I think, frankly, that in some sense, this system or some future incarnation of it could threaten the reliability of its deterrence and, therefore, strategic stability.

Nevertheless, at our summit in Moscow in June, President Putin and I did agree that the world has changed since the ABM Treaty was signed 28 years ago, and that the proliferation of missile technology has resulted in new threats that may require amending that treaty. And again, I say, these threats are not threats to the United States alone.

Russia agrees that there is an emerging missile threat. In fact, given its place on the map, it is particularly vulnerable to this emerging threat. In time, I hope the United States can narrow our differences with Russia on this issue. The course I have chosen today gives the United States more time to pursue that, and we will use it.

President Putin and I have agreed to intensify our work on strategic defense, while pursuing, in parallel, deeper arms reductions in START (Strategic Arms Reduction Treaty) III. He and I have instructed our experts to develop further cooperative initiatives in areas such as theater missile defense, early warning and missile threat discussions for our meeting just next week in New York.

Apart from the Russians, another critical diplomatic consideration in the NMD decision is the view of our NATO allies. They have all made clear that they hope the United States will pursue strategic defense in a way that preserves, not abrogates, the ABM Treaty. If we decide to proceed with NMD deployment we must have their support, because key components of NMD would be based on their territories.

The decision I have made also gives the United States time to answer our allies' questions and consult further on the path ahead.

Finally, we must consider the impact of a decision to deploy on security in Asia. As the next President makes a deployment decision, he will need to avoid stimulating an already dangerous regional nuclear capability from China to South Asia. Now, let me be clear: no nation can ever have a veto over American security, even if the United States and Russia cannot reach agreement; even if we cannot secure the support of our allies at first; even if we conclude that the Chinese will respond to NMD by increasing their arsenal of nuclear weapons substantially with a corollary, inevitable impact in India and then in Pakistan.

The next President may nevertheless decide that our interest in security in 21st century dictates that we go forward with deployment of NMD. But we can never afford to overlook the fact that the actions and reactions of others in this increasingly interdependent world do bear on our security. Clearly, therefore, it would be far better to move forward in the context of the ABM Treaty and allied support. Our efforts to make that possible have not been completed. For me, the bottom line on this decision is this: because the emerging missile threat is real, we have an obligation to pursue a missile defense system that could enhance our security.

We have made progress, but we should not move forward until we have absolute confidence that the system will work, and until we have made every reasonable diplomatic effort to minimize the cost of deployment, and maximize the benefit, as I said, not only to America's security, but to the security of law abiding nations everywhere subject to the same threat.

I am convinced that America and the world will be better off if we explore the frontiers of strategic defenses, while continuing to pursue arms control, to stand with our allies and to work with Russia and others to stop the spread of deadly weapons.

I strongly believe this is the best course for the United States, and therefore the decision I have reached today, is in the best security interest of the United States. In short, we need to move forward with realism, with steadiness, and with prudence, not dismissing the threat we face, or assuming we can meet it, while ignoring our overall strategic environment, including the interests and concerns of our allies, friends and other nations. A National Missile Defense, if deployed, should be part of a larger strategy to preserve and enhance the peace, strength and security we now enjoy, and to build an even safer world.

I have tried to maximize the ability of the next President to pursue that strategy. In so doing, I have tried to maximize the chance that all you young students will live in a safer, more humane, more positively interdependent world. I hope I have done so. I believe I have.

Thank you very much.

31

Bohlen: Clinton NMD Decision Allows More Time to Consult

A State Department official told members of Congress September 8 that an effective missile defense system will enhance the ability of the United States "to fulfill its NATO and global security commitments, rather than lead to 'decoupling' " of the United States from Europe as some critics of a National Missile Defense (NMD) have suggested.

Assistant Secretary of State for Arms Control Avis Bohlen told the House Subcommittee on National Security that U.S. allies have "uniformly welcomed" President Clinton's September 1 decision to defer NMD deployment to provide additional time to discuss the emerging ballistic missile threat and the corresponding role of missile defenses in addressing that threat.

In a hearing scheduled to explore the theme of "NMD Test Failures and Technology Development," the official said Clinton's action to defer an NMD deployment decision to his successor "has given us more time to work toward narrowing our differences with Russia" and to involve U.S. allies "in shaping a coordinated response to the emerging ballistic missile threat."

Following is the text of Bohlen's remarks as prepared for delivery:

Statement of Avis T. Bohlen Assistant Secretary of State for Arms Control Before the House Committee on Government Reform Subcommittee on National Security, Veterans Affairs, and International Relations.

Friday, September 8, 2000

Good morning, Mr Chairman and Members of the

Committee. I am pleased to appear before you today to discuss our National Missile Defense (NMD) program and how it relates to the Anti-Ballistic Missile (ABM) Treaty.

It is this administration's position that we should not move forward with deployment until we have full confidence that the system will work, and until we have made every reasonable diplomatic effort to minimize the cost of deployment, and maximize the benefit. And, if a future President should decide that deployment is in the national interest, this administration believes we should move forward in the context of the ABM Treaty and allied support.

I am obviously not in a position to speak to the technical or programmatic issues related to this system. I defer on such questions to Lieutenant General Ronald Kadish and Mr Philip Coyle, who can authoritatively address those aspects of the program. Instead, Mr Chairman, I will focus my brief remarks on the diplomatic and political context in which we have pursued the development of an NMD system, and the diplomatic and foreign policy ramifications of deploying such a system.

When the President decided last summer for planning purposes on an initial NMD architecture, he stated that he would make a decision on whether to deploy this system based on four criteria: our assessment of the threat, technological feasibility, cost, and the overall impact on national security.

A week ago today, as you know, the President announced that the NMD program is sufficiently promising and affordable to justify continued development and testing, but that there is not sufficient information about the technical and operational effectiveness of the entire NMD system to move forward with deployment at this time. In making this decision, the President took into account the four criteria I just mentioned, and, he made clear that we will continue to work with our allies and with Russia, and with China, to strengthen their understanding of and support for our efforts to meet the emerging ballistic missile threat and to explore creative ways we can cooperate to enhance their security against this threat as well.

Let me say a few words about the diplomatic and foreign policy context of NMD. At the end of the day, as the President has repeatedly stated, no country can exercise a veto over a decision that he or a future President might conclude is in the best interests of the United States.

At the same time, we cannot ignore the diplomatic and foreign policy implications, or fail to take the views and security requirements of our friends and allies into account as we move forward on this program.

We have an obligation to do what is necessary to achieve consensus within the NATO and Pacific alliances, which are essential to our own security and to reassure others of the steadfast commitment of the United States to preserving the international arms control regimes that they have come to rely on for their own security. Our nation's unique leadership status and international responsibilities require that we take these implications seriously.

As the President stated in his Georgetown University speech last week, "Over the past 30 years, Republican and Democratic Presidents have negotiated an array of arms control treaties with Russia. We and our allies have relied on these treaties to ensure strategic stability and predictability with Russia, to get on with the job of dismantling the legacy of the Cold War, and to further the transition from confrontation to cooperation with our former adversary in the most important arena—nuclear weapons." We continue to believe that the ABM Treaty is, as the President stated, "a key part of the international security structure we've built with Russia—and therefore a key part of our national security." For that reason we have sought to strengthen and preserve the Treaty even as we pursue our efforts to develop a national missile defense. We continue to believe that strategic stability based on mutual deterrence is still important in the post-cold war period because we and the Russians still have large nuclear arsenals and because it guarantees stability in what is still a transitional relationship. As the President said, we are no longer adversaries, but not yet allies. The ABM Treaty provides a framework for ensuring strategic stability between our two countries, reducing the risk of confrontation and providing a basis for further strategic reductions.

NMD and the ABM Treaty

Deployment of the NMD system we are developing would require changes to the ABM Treaty. The deployment of an ABM radar at Shemya, Alaska, of 100 ground-based interceptors, and five upgraded early-warning radars—for the defense of all 50 states—would violate the obligation contained in Article I of the Treaty not to deploy an ABM system to defend national territory. Such activities would also be inconsistent with the locational restrictions of Article III. We of course do not believe that the proposed system would violate the core purposes of the Treaty, and in fact believe that updating the Treaty to permit a limited NMD would strengthen it. Accordingly, we have engaged in extensive discussions with Russia with the objective of reaching agreement on modifications in the ABM Treaty which would allow us to move forward with the limited NMD system proposed by this administration. U.S. officials at the highest levels have, since last summer, engaged in an intensive dialogue with the Russians on our proposed changes to the ABM Treaty.

We have provided to Russia a draft Protocol to the Treaty that would open the way to deployment of our initial NMD system while retaining those provisions of the Treaty that underpin U.S.-Russian strategic stability.

Among U.S. allies, support for NMD is strongly conditioned on first securing Russia's agreement to cooperatively amend the ABM Treaty. Support for U.S. non-proliferation objectives, and other foreign policy priorities, is also often linked to preservation of the ABM Treaty in the eyes of much of the rest of the world. Other nations regard the ABM Treaty as a necessary basis for further progress on nuclear disarmament. The health of the Treaty regime continues to be a valid interest of the international community. The degree to which other nations perceive having a stake in preserving the ABM Treaty was clear during the 2000 NPT Review conference, and has been evident in recent consultations with allied and other governments regarding U.S. proposals to amend the Treaty. For these countries, the ABM Treaty, as a touchstone of U.S.-Russian strategic stability, is clearly perceived as an important foundation of the whole structure of international strategic security and as a necessary basis for continued reductions in nuclear arms.

What We are Doing to Convince Russia and Others of the Necessity of Changing the ABM Treaty

Under secretary (John) Holum's consultations are continuing

to address three broad areas designed to meet Russia's concerns. First, we have made clear to Moscow that in deploying a limited NMD system, we are responding to a new threat from long-range ballistic missiles in the hands of states that threaten international peace and stability, and not seeking to change the core foundation of strategic stability with Russia. We have told our Russian interlocutors that we believe the ABM Treaty should be preserved and strengthened by adapting it to changing international realities and a new, strategic environment that did not exist in 1972, using the amendment procedures established by the terms of the Treaty itself. We have proposed only those Treaty changes that we believe are necessary to allow the United States to address those threats we expect will emerge in the near-term, while establishing the basis for further adaptations of the Treaty in the future, should the emerging threat warrant.

Second, we have sought to demonstrate to the Russians that a limited NMD system will not threaten their strategic deterrent. In fact, in our discussions, criticism by Russian officials of NMD has not focused on the impact of our proposed NMD system on their deterrent, but rather, on their concern that such deployments would establish an infrastructure allowing future breakout.

Finally, in part to address this Russian concern with breakout we have proposed a series of confidence-building and transparency measures. To date the Russians have not agreed to amend the ABM Treaty, but we have come considerably closer to agreement on some key aspects of the problem—for example on the nature and reality of the threat. This progress is reflected in the Joint Statement on a Strategic Stability Cooperation Initiative signed by Presidents Clinton and Putin in New York on Wednesday (September 6). We have also been pursuing close consultations with our NATO and Pacific allies, who have all made clear that they hope the United States will pursue strategic defense in a way that preserves the ABM Treaty.

Their support is important to us for a number of reasons. Our European and Asian allies are crucial to our efforts to counter the proliferation of weapons of mass destruction, including ballistic missiles and missile technology, efforts which continue to be a strong line of defense against the threat of missile proliferation. Moreover, an effective NMD requires the consent of two allies to upgrade the radars that are situated on their territory. Our allies have uniformly welcomed the President's decision to defer a decision on deployment as providing more time for discussion of the emerging ballistic missile threat and the role of ballistic missile defense in responding to that threat. We have kept our allies fully informed of our dialogue with Russia on these matters, and have worked hard to strengthen our allies' understanding and support for our NMD program and our initiatives to preserve, strengthen, and modernize the ABM Treaty. We believe that effective missile defenses would, if anything, enhance the United States' ability to fulfill its NATO and global security commitments, rather than lead to "decoupling." We believe that traditional deterrence would be bolstered if we are able to convince a would-be attacker that his attack would fail before it is carried out in the first place. We will continue this dialogue with our allies in the months ahead. We have also made clear to China that our national missile defense efforts are not directed at them.

Conclusion

In sum, Mr Chairman, the President's decision has given us more time to work toward narrowing our differences with Russia and to involving our allies in shaping a coordinated response to the emerging ballistic missile threat. President Clinton and President Putin have agreed that we should intensify our work on strategic defense while pursuing, in parallel, deeper arms reductions in START (Strategic Arms Reduction Treaty) III. Our two Presidents have also instructed their respective experts to develop further cooperative initiatives, in areas such as theater missile defense and early warning and ballistic missile threat assessment.

We continue to believe that an effective NMD system can be developed and deployed within the context of resolving the concerns of our allies and the objections of Russia.

Let me conclude by reiterating a point the President made in his speech last Friday. The President said that "No nation can have a veto over American security. Even if the United States and Russia cannot reach agreement, even if we cannot secure the support of our allies at first, the next President may nonetheless decide that it is in America's national interests to go forward with deployment of NMD. But by the same token, since the actions—and reactions—of others in the world bear on our security, clearly it would be far better to move forward in the context of the ABM Treaty and allied support." As the President said, "America and the world will be better off if we explore the frontiers of strategic defenses while continuing to pursue arms control, to stand with our allies, and to work with Russia and others to stop the spread of deadly weapons."

32

Time to Get Serious about Missile Defense

The Democratic Party opposes change in the status quo—from school choice to private Social Security accounts—lest it disturb either a core liberal constituency (such as teachers) or a past liberal achievement (such as Social Security). This has been correctly called "reactionary liberalism." And nowhere has this refusal to leave the warm and cozy past been more starkly demonstrated than in the Democrats' knee-jerk response to President George W. Bush's proposal on **missile defense.**

"The president," said House Democratic Leader Richard Gephardt, "is jeopardizing an arms control framework that has served this nation and the world well for decades." Decades? The 1970s and 1980s, the heyday of arms control, were a time of hair-trigger nuclear tension. We went to DEFCON III in October 1973, just a year after the signing of SALT I and the **ABM** Treaty, the alleged cornerstones of strategic stability.

In the 1990s, conversely, the nuclear terror dissipated. Not because of any change in the arms control regimen—arms control was an utter irrelevancy—but because of a fundamental change in leadership and ideology in Moscow.

Some liberals, like my colleague Michael Kinsley, are too bright to oppose **missile defense,** like Gephardt, out of reverence for parchment treaties. It is not treaties, they argue, but the simple existential reality born of nuclear weapons-mutually assured destruction, or MAD—that makes **missile defense** a bad idea. We shouldn't built one, they say, because Russia will then fear that it will lose the ability to retaliate against an American first strike—thus Russia would be more likely to initiate a nuclear war under the theory of "use 'em or lose 'em."

Let's get this straight: they argue that we should not build a **missile defense...** because it risks an out-of-the-blue Russian first strike on the United States. It would be the most massive, genocidal and unprovoked act of war in the history of the human race.

If this seems wacky to you, it is. Even when this first-strike MAD logic was in currency 20 years ago, it was not entirely plausible. It was, however, minimally plausible. The Soviet Union defined itself as our mortal enemy in an existential death struggle with the West, and it had massive armies and navies confronting ourselves throughout the world. We had flash points of conflict in important places—Cuba, Berlin, Korea—where a crisis could conceivably precipitate Armageddon.

Yet even then—with the tension so great, the hair-trigger so tight, the stakes so high—the notion of a first strike was still almost inconceivable. But today? The Russians are neither a superpower nor an existential enemy.

What are the stakes today? The Caspian pipeline? An insufficiency of American loans?

Our worst dispute in the last 10 years was over the Pristina airport. Armageddon over that? After so implausibly deploying **ABM** and MAD, opponents of **missile defense** have one last resort: the nuclear suitcase. What's the point of a **missile defense,** they say, if the bad guys can always slip in a nuke in the hands of a terrorist? By that logic, we should dismantle our continental anti-aircraft defenses because an enemy can always put a bomb in a suitcase rather than on a plane. By that logic, the Navy should strip the fleet of anti-aircraft and anti-**missile defenses** because the enemy—as demonstrated in Yemen against the USS Cole—can always sneak in with a little tugboat and blow you up anyway.

The argument is that if you can't stop 10 percent of threats, then you might as well leave yourself 100 percent defenseless. What nonsense.

Yes, an enemy might slip in a suitcase. But it's not easy. It requires a conspiracy. It requires coordination, timing. It requires many people acting in concert over a long period of time. It risks penetration and error and disruption and defection.

Compare that to a dictator sitting by a console in his capital with a button that will reliably, immediately (within 30 minutes) and incontestably incinerate half a dozen American cities. There is a huge order of magnitude difference between that threat and the smuggled suitcase.

The left has not had a new idea on nuclear weapons in 20 years. And that idea, the "freeze," was the worst idea of a generation. Why, even the European leaders of today, Blair in Britain and Schroeder in Germany, admit that their parties' opposition to the European deployment of Pershing and cruise missiles was a mistake.

The Democrats here, so enthusiastic for the freeze back then, are unrepentant. They are back for Round 2-sporting Cold War arguments so comically anachronistic you have to wonder if they'll ever offer a serious argument on nuclear weapons.

33

Rumsfeld: Star Warrior Returns

A hard-Liner Since the Nixon Era, He Populated The 'Rogue State' *Missile* Threat

The surprise selection of Donald Rumsfeld as Defense Secretary provides a clear signal of President-elect George W. Bush's intent to transform radically the military policy of the United States. Of all the candidates considered for this position, Rumsfeld is the most ardent advocate of ballistic-missile defense and a tougher stance toward Russia and China. A longtime Republican activist with markedly conservative views. Rumsfeld is also known for his opposition to all arms-control measures and for favoring the deployment of weapons in space.

Along with other members of Bush's national security team—Vice President Dick Cheney, Secretary of State Colin Powell and National Security Adviser Condoleezza Rice—Rumsfeld can be expected to push hard for the establishment or a full-scale National Missile Defense system. In 1998, he authored a report on ballistic missile threats that ignited the Republican's current drive for a national missile shield. Now, as Defense Secretary, he will be in a strong position to lead the charge for NMD.

But while NMD deployment will be Rumsfeld's top priority, it is by no means his only major objective. With the blessing of President-elect Bush, Rumsfeld will campaign for a wide range of policy shifts. These will include a greater emphasis on warfare in space, the accelerated procurement of high-tech weapons and a diminished commitment to UN peacekeeping operations. It all looks depressingly like the cold war era, when "national security" meant distrust of all other states and the pursuit of ever more potent weapons.

Rumsfeld's service to Republican Presidents (and

presidential hopefuls) goes back to the Nixon Administration, when he became director of the Office of Economic Opportunity after several terms in Congress. While at the OEO, Rumsfeld impressed the White House staff with his managerial skills, and in 1970 he was made counselor to the President. (It was at this time that Rumsfeld developed close ties with Cheney, who had served as his special assistant at the OEO.)

Fortunately for Rumsfeld, Nixon appointed him ambassador to NATO in 1972, thus sparing him from possible association with the Watergate scandal. When Nixon was forced to abandon the presidency, Rumsfeld was brought back to Washington by the new President, Gerald Ford, to serve first as White House Chief of Staff and later as Defense Secretary. Although not remembered for any major innovations during his fourteen months at the Pentagon (late 1975 to early 1977), Rumsfeld shielded the military from any major penalties following its defeat in Vietnam and laid the groundwork for procurement of a wide range of new weapons systems, including the B-1 bomber and M-X missile.

Following the election of Jimmy Carter, Rumsfeld left Washington for the private sector. From 1977 to 1985 he served as chief executive officer and then president of G.D. Searle, a major pharmaceutical corporation later acquired by Monsanto. Several years later, he took control of another large company, the General Instrument Corporation. As at Searle, he slashed costs (mainly by eliminating staff) and boosted profits, giving him a reputation as a skilled, tough-minded corporate manager.

During his years in the private sector, Rumsfeld retained his links to the military establishment (serving for a time as chairman of the RAND Corporation, a prominent military think tank) while developing new ties with conservative figures in the corporate world. Among his close confidants is Theodore Forstmann, a corporate buyout specialist who owned Gulfstream Aerospace (in 1999 he sold it to General Dynamics for $4.8 billion) and managed the buyout of General Instrument, giving Rumsfeld a paper profit of $11 million. Fortsmann is also the major figure behind Empower America, a political advocacy outfit boasting many prominent Republicans (Rumsfeld among them) on its board of directors. Described by the *New York Times* as "a home for Washington's conservative elite," Empower America has campaigned for big tax cuts, space defenses and school vouchers.

Urged no doubt by his conservative buddies, Rumsfeld agreed in September 1996 to take over management of Bob Dole's failing presidential compaign. Although he was unable to secure victory at the polls, Rumsfeld did breathe some life into the campaign by persuading Dole to promise mammoth tax cuts and to adopt a tougher stance on military policy. Under prodding from Rumsfeld, Dole lashed out against President Clinton on his handling of the Iraq situation and called for the deployment of a national missile shield by the year 2003. In this sense, Rumsfeld laid the foundation for George W. Bush's 2000 campaign against Vice President Al Gore.

After the 1996 election, Rumsfeld returned to the corporate world—he took over Gilead Sciences, a biotechnology firm, and sat on the board of several corporations (including Asea Brown Boveri, a giant European electrical firm, and the Tribune Company)—while continuing his support for fight-wing military causes. Especially significant was his close association with the Center for Security Policy, a think tank established by former Reagan Administration official Frank Gaffney Jr to campaign for the deployment of "Star Wars" Defenses.

Having gained renewed stature among the Republicans in Congress for his hard-line views, Rumsfeld was selected in 1998 to chair the Commission to Assess the Ballistic Missile Threat to the United States. Composed of six Republicans and three Democrats, the Rumsfeld Commission (as it came to be called) examined classified intelligence data on the ballistic missile programs of Iran, Iraq and North Korea in order to calculate their future capacity to attack the United States. By employing worst-case reasoning to the often contradictory data on these countries' military capabilities, the commission concluded that one or another of the "rogue states" could deploy missiles capable of striking the United States in as little as five years—half the time predicted by the CIA.

Although these findings were challenged by Director of Central Intelligence George Tenet and prominent figures in the arms-control community, the Rumsfeld commission's report was seized upon by Republican activists as incontrovertible evidence that the United States must proceed rapidly with the development of a full-scale missile defense system. This is the "most important warning about our national security system since the end of the cold war," House Speaker Newt Gingrich asserted at the time.

Fearful of being portrayed by Congressional Republicans as ignoring a major threat to US security, President Clinton agreed in early 1999 to proceed with development of a limited NMD system—one aimed at protecting the Western United States against a hypothetical North Korean missile attack—while putting off a decision on actual deployment. But this did little to satisfy the hawks on Capitol Hill, who sought to develop a much more robust system covering the entire nation. At Rumsfeld's urging, moreover, Bush made this a central theme of his campaign.

While a candidate, Governor Bush articulated other themes originally crafted by Rumsfeld during the Dole campaign of 1996. These include a promise to get tougher on Saddam Hussein and other "rogue state" leaders, to pursue the development of new high-tech weaponry and to abjure involvement in UN-sponsored peacekeeping missions. Together, these themes came to represent the skeleton of a new approach to national security—one that favors protection of the United States and its overseas assets rather than, say, the construction of a stable world order or the enforcement of international law.

Throughout the campaign, Bush declared his intention to undertake a sweeping transformation of US military policy. At the very least, this would entail the development and procurement of new high-tech weapons and a greater emphasis on war in space. But more than this, it would involve a shift in the very orientation of US strategy. "Our military requires more than good treatment." he declared at the Citadel in September 1999. "It needs the rallying point of a defining mission."

Although unclear on the details, Bush sketched out the broad outlines of this new mission. In place of the "vague, aimless and endless deployments" of the Clinton era (read: Bosnia, Haiti, Somalia, Kosovo), US military power would henceforth be reserved for more pressing objectives—to protect US national interests around the world and to defeat any power that might be so foolhardy as to threaten these key interests. More emphasis will also be placed on "homeland defense," meaning the protection of the United States from missile attackx and other hypothetical threats for rogue states and terrorists.

In announcing Rumsfeld's selection as Defense secretary, Bush made it clear that he expects his top military official to carry out this strategic transformation. "We must work to change our military to meet the threats of a new century," Bush declared on December 28. "And so one of Secretary Rumsfeld's first tasks will be to challenge the status quo within the Pentagon, to develop a strategy necessary to have a force equipped for warfare of the twenty-first century."

In his response to Bush, Rumsfeld indicated that he has every intention of conducting a major overhaul of military policy. "It is clearly not a time at a Pentagon for presiding or calibrating modestly. Rather, we are in a new national security environment. We do need to be arranged to deal with the new threats, not the old ones."

It is still too early, of course, to calculate all the consequences of this shift in outlook. Many of the initiatives favoured by Bush—the development of high-tech weapons, the acceleration of research on ballistic missile defense—have already been undertaken by the Clinton Administration. But there is no doubt that Bush and Rumsfeld will push much harder for deployment or a national missile shield and for the deployment of weapons in space. They are also likely to abandon the ABM treaty, which prohibits missile defenses of the sort they favor.

In pursuing these policies, the new administration will inevitably inflame US relations with Russia and China, thereby precluding any further progress on arms control. It is very likely, in fact, that Russia and China will respond to US initiatives by expanding their own nuclear arsenals and by forging a closer military relationship. Relations with China will become particularly tense, especially if—as is expected—Bush approves the delivery of new warships and antimissile weapons to Taiwan. The result will be a more unstable and polarized environment, producing exactly the sort of world in which the Republican's instinctive preference of Cold War-like policies will find a natural outlet.

The pursuit of missile defense and the abrogation of the ABM treaty will also alienate many US allies, most of whom oppose NMD. One likely result is the further development of an autonomous European military posture, with all that this entails. And, of course, we can expect diminished US support for the UN. Where all this leads is anybody's guess, but it is hard to believe that the final outcome will be a more peaceful world.

By Michael T. Klare

Michael T. Klare, a professor of peace and world security studies at Hampshire College in Amherst, Massachusetts, is the **defense** *correspondent of The Nation.*

Index